"If you've ever felt like you ought to be smart about wine, this is the book. Aldo makes wine approachable and never dumbed down."

—Madeline Puckette, cofounder of *Wine Folly*

"A meal at Le Bernardin is always an incredible experience, especially with Aldo's expert knowledge and effortless charm! It can be intimidating to choose wine, but with *Wine Simple*, we can all feel like world-class sommeliers."

—Chrissy Teigen

"I always feel at ease drinking wine with Aldo. While he is a renowned sommelier, he helps me learn and listen to the wine, and this book will make you fall in love with wine again."

—José Andrés, chef/owner of ThinkFoodGroup

"Whoever thinks wine is all about snobbery and intricate complexity should read this book! In less than three hundred pages, Aldo Sohm manages to open the doors of this universe with wit, fun, and great pedagogy. A perfect, personal beginner's guide by a legend in our industry, *Wine Simple* will surely be the bedside book for a new generation of wine lovers."

—Pascaline Lepeltier, Master Sommelier and managing partner, Racines NY

"This is undoubtedly the best introduction to wine that I've ever encountered. I wish I'd had access to a book like this when I was beginning my journey as a wine lover. Aldo Sohm makes oenophilia fun without making it dumb, proving yet again that he is one of the world's greatest sommeliers—which is to say, a great teacher."

—Jay McInerney

Wine
Simple

A Totally Approachable Guide

Wine Simple

from a World-Class Sommelier

Aldo Sohm

with Christine Muhlke

CLARKSON POTTER / PUBLISHERS

New York

Copyright © 2019 by Aldo Sohm, Inc.
Illustrations copyright © 2019 by Matt Blease

All rights reserved.
Published in the United States by Clarkson Potter/
Publishers, an imprint of Random House, a division of
Penguin Random House LLC, New York.
clarksonpotter.com

CLARKSON POTTER is a trademark and POTTER with
colophon is a registered trademark of Penguin Random
House LLC.

Library of Congress Cataloging-in-Publication Data
Names: Sohm, Aldo, author. | Muhlke, Christine,
   author.
Title: Wine simple : a totally approachable guide
   from a world-class sommelier / Aldo Sohm with
   Christine Muhlke.
Description: First edition. | New York : Clarkson Potter/
   Publishers, [2019]
Identifiers: LCCN 2018060755 | ISBN
   9781984824257 (hardcover) | ISBN
   9781984824264 (ebook)
Subjects: LCSH: Wine and wine making—Amateurs'
   manuals. | Wine tasting—Amateurs' manuals.
Classification: LCC TP548.2 .S64 2019 | DDC
   641.2/2—dc23
LC record available at https://lccn.loc
   .gov/2018060755

ISBN 978-1-9848-2425-7
Ebook ISBN 978-1-9848-2426-4

Printed in China

Illustrations by Matt Blease
Book and cover design by Alaina Sullivan

10 9 8

First Edition

To the curious wine drinker

contents

8

Introduction

Glossary

intro

▶ Every lunch and dinner, five days a week, you'll find me ping-ponging between Le Bernardin and Aldo Sohm Wine Bar. It takes me just forty steps to get from one to the other, but there's a world of difference between them: At Le Bernardin, a four-star restaurant in New York City, diners order from a 40-page, 900-bottle wine list, with prices that stretch into the five figures. At the wine bar, where people hang out on stools and couches, they're selecting from a much tighter list, with glasses starting at $11. Well, maybe they're not that different after all—I'm asked many of the same questions at each: What should I order with my food? What should I try if I usually drink X? Can I find a good value in my price range? There are wine novices and connoisseurs at both places. It's my job to help them find the perfect glass. But I can't do it without them.

While young customers who have saved up for a meal at Le Bernardin might feel a little nervous about showing a guy with a weird-looking silver cup around his neck how little they know about wine, they open up at the wine bar, letting the questions flow. I love this curiosity—it's what wine is all about. And to be honest, without those questions, I can't help a customer find that perfect glass. I wanted to write a book that not only teaches people the basics of wine but also gives them the tools they need to get to know their palates—what they like and don't like— and the vocabulary to help them describe it so they can go into a restaurant, wine bar, or store and dial in the bottle or glass that will delight them.

True, wine has lots of snobby associations and tons of words and details to memorize. But it doesn't have to be intimidating. You really just need to know a handful of words and a smidgen of geography to be on your way. If it makes you feel any better, I'll never know everything there is to know about wine. Luckily, I believe that the only way to learn—besides researching like crazy—is by making mistakes. So let's start drinking!

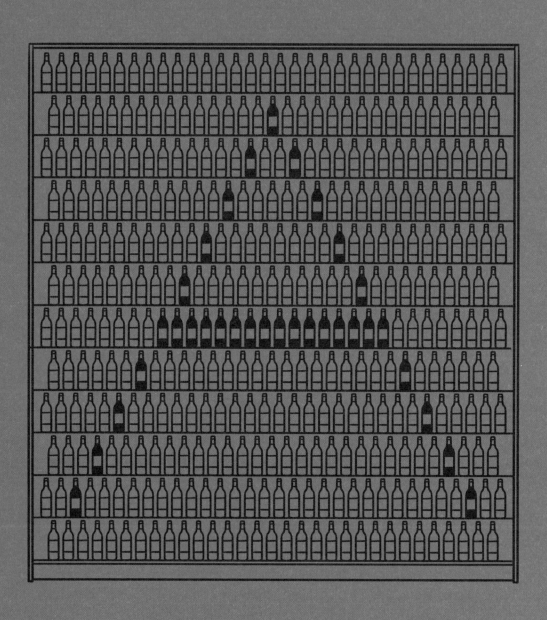

About Aldo

(Or, How an Austrian Kid Who Hated Wine
Ended Up the Wine Director of a
Three-Michelin-Star Restaurant in New York City)

➤ How I ended up the wine director at Le Bernardin is still a mystery to me (and my parents). But as I've learned over the years, life takes amazing turns when you're open to challenge and adventure—and, of course, lots of hard work. And luckily for me, wine is one of those things that guarantee a nonstop journey of knowledge and pleasure: I'll always be happy to keep learning, sip by magical sip.

When I was a teenager in Innsbruck, Austria, I wanted to be a chef: My friend's dad cooked on a cruise ship, and I admired that free spirit. I went to a tourism college to study with a world-champion chef, but all that screaming in the kitchen was too much for me. The last two weeks of my summer internship at a restaurant, they were short-staffed, so they made me wait tables. I was in heaven. Even the chef said, "Oh my God. If we'd known that, we'd all have been better off!"

My first front-of-house job, at the age of nineteen, was at a hotel in the remote valley of Ötztal, Austria. I was happy to be earning my own money and to have time to mountain bike on my days off. It wasn't until my third job—at a high-end resort where I worked breakfast, lunch, and dinner—that the idea of a career in wine really clicked for me. There was a Swiss couple who were so enthusiastic about food and wine, they would talk about what they would eat for dinner while still at the breakfast table. I'd never seen anything like it! One day, they asked me what they should drink with their meal. I had no idea! So I bought some books on wine and read as much as I could between services. I could have bullshitted them, but I was curious about what sparked their passion.

It turns out it sparked a passion in me, too. I couldn't believe how much there was to know about wine. The regions and kinds of grapes seemed infinite. There was an artistry behind winemaking, and so much history, too. All my colleagues wanted to hang out during break, but I was like, No, no, no. I've got to finish this book before dinner! Around this time, my dad, who would have a glass of wine or two from Austria or Italy on the weekends, took me with him to buy wine. I researched like crazy and used the money I'd saved to buy a bottle of 1983 Darmagi by Angelo Gaja. It was a hell of a lot of money—about $400 in today's dollars—but that was all I wanted in the world. I was under the spell of great wine.

By the time I ended up at a five-star resort in 1992, I was special-ordering books and cross-referencing them. Although guests were ordering bottles for $20 to $50, I started reading more about classic benchmark wines. Soon, during tastings, I began looking for tannins, looking for alcohol, looking for fruit from every sip. Then I began going to tastings after work with people I befriended from other restaurants. Sometimes we'd drive an hour to the Riedel glass factory to do their glassware tastings, marveling at how the shape of their Burgundy wineglass amplified the fruit of that variety. I saved and bought multiple sets from the second-quality shelf.

When I was twenty, I worked hard to get a job at Hotel Arlberg Hospiz, which had a legendary wine program. They were known for having one of the biggest cellars for large-format wines, especially Bordeaux—eighteen-liter bottles of Château Margaux, six-liter bottles of 1924 Château Palmer, that kind of thing. There, I worked with my mentor, Adi Werner, and also befriended the cellar master, Helmut Jörg. I asked to join the tastings he did for clients. He let me, as long as I set them up and broke them down. I didn't miss a single one. We tasted not just in Austria and nearby Northern Italy but deep into France, America— all over the world. (I've always found foreign things more interesting.) My friends couldn't believe I was spending all my free time doing this and wasn't even getting paid. But the deeper I got, the more fascinated I was.

My father sent me to Florence for a summer

to learn Italian, the idea being that sommeliers should speak at least one foreign language. I also assigned myself the task of drinking wines from every village in Chianti. For the first time, I was able to taste the differences in *terroir*—the actual soil in which the grapes had been planted—and by August, I could tell you blindfolded which village the wine came from.

Five years after that summer in Italy, I started studying for my sommelier's diploma, a rigorous two-year process. The second year, a new professor named Norbert Waldnig came in and shook things up. It turns out he was the Austrian candidate for the Best Sommelier in the World competition, and when he asked for volunteers to be tour guides during the event in Vienna, my hand shot up. There, I was electrified by the atmosphere, the tension, the pure intimidation as each candidate was grilled for an hour or two in front of a huge audience, TV cameras and all. After I'd finished my certificate a year later, in 1999, the professor said he wanted me to be the Austrian candidate for the next year's national championship. No way! But his team trained me, giving me questionnaires, running me through blind tastings on wines and liquors in black glasses that concealed their color, timing my decanting skills, quizzing me on wine descriptions, and more. They even worked on my body language. I came in second but was bumped up when the winner was disqualified. I'd gotten a taste, and I was hungry to go to the European championship.

It took me many more years of training and competing, not even going out to a movie or dinner with my friends, but finally I won the Austrian championship in 2002—and again in 2003, '04, and '06. I realized that all the top sommeliers competed in English, so I wanted to go to America to learn. I did what every Austrian sommelier did and wrote Wolfgang Puck. I never got a response. I can't blame him: Today, I field daily requests from Austrian sommeliers who think New York is all *Sex and the City*. In 2004, my trainer said he knew of an Austrian chef in New York who was looking for a sommelier.

When I first met Kurt Gutenbrunner at his restaurant, Wallsé, he told me I was nuts. I was at the top of my game in Austria, with total job security. (I had a tenured job teaching at the tourism college and was also training students there for competitions, including the Best Young Sommelier in Austria winner—the highest form of winning to me.) Why would I leave? I told him that nothing in life is safe. I was bored at thirty-three; I couldn't imagine being bored until I was sixty. He hired me on the spot.

I landed in New York on July 4, 2004. I'd never seen a rat before, let alone a cockroach. I took the first apartment I looked at in Williamsburg, Brooklyn. The kitchen was so filthy, I hired a guy from the restaurant to help clean. It took us a week!

With the help of great trainers, I won the Best Sommelier in America competition in 2007. A couple of weeks later, I got a call from Le Bernardin, one of the best restaurants in New York. I was thrilled to be able to work with a brilliant chef like Eric Ripert and be challenged by his complex, culture-spanning sauces, and to be able to learn from Maguy Le Coze, who has run the restaurant since it opened in 1986. I always joke that Michelin created its standards for three-star restaurants based on her life!

The US competition qualified me for the Best Sommelier in the World competition in 2008, but I didn't sign up to compete for personal reasons. Eight weeks before the event, the first runner-up backed out. Andrew Bell, the US president of the association, asked me if I wanted to do it again. I said yes and happily won. It was worth the grueling training.

Eric and Maguy came to me with the idea for the Aldo Sohm Wine Bar in 2013. I had never thought of opening my own place. First of all, I consider ego a sign of weakness. Why would I put my name on something, especially when Le Bernardin's name is so well known? Next, New Yorkers go to a restaurant for the food,

not because it has a great wine list. But then I thought about it: Most wine bars are opened by sommeliers who partner with a sous-chef from their last job and open a carbon copy. But I wouldn't have to do that: I'd have the real thing! Plus, I'd have the best of both worlds: access to the incredible wines and connoisseur clientele of Le Bernardin, plus the ability to make a home for all the smaller winemakers from emerging regions. I could sell a vintage Burgundy while, nearby, someone was sipping an $11 glass from the Canary Islands. We opened in 2014.

It's been an incredible experience, and the questions I've fielded while working the floor at the wine bar were the inspiration for this book. I wanted to write something as fun and approachable as what we've created there. Sommeliers can be intimidating and, well, sometimes kind of snooty. This is not that book!

To bring it to life, I worked with coauthor Christine Muhlke. In the decade-plus that we've known each other through Le Bernardin, for which she wrote *On the Line* with Eric Ripert, I've known her to be knowledgeable about food and really curious and open about wine—especially about how much she still has to learn. (Though we may disagree about the natural wines that she loves, we're working to find a middle ground and enjoy teasing each other about it at every opportunity.) I wanted to work with her because she is, in many ways, who this book is for: people who love food and want to go deeper on wine, but who are intimidated by much of the somm-speak that's out there—or at least put off by what Christine calls the "bro-y 'sommsplaining'"—and don't have the time to take a wine course. And, as a fellow die-hard city cyclist, I know she's brave/crazy enough to take on a project like this.

I never did learn the name of that Swiss couple who set me on this path all those years ago, but I would sure like to thank them. I hope that my book sparks a passion for wine in you, too.

Why Do We Need Another Book on Wine?

(And why from a sommelier?)

→ **Because so many of the books out there—and you'll find some of my favorites on page 242—are by professionals, for professionals.** The language can be intimidating to someone who's just starting to learn. But I'm not writing for my peers or for seasoned collectors. I'm writing for those of you who would love to know what (or where) Burgundy is. I want to teach you how to form your own strong opinion about wines. By the time you've finished this book, you'll be able to look at a wine list with your eyes wide from the excitement of possibility, not from fear.

Unlike many of the great wine writers I admire, I'm not at a desk all day, typing between tastings. Every working day for the last twenty-five years, I've been on the restaurant floor, helping diners decide what they should drink with their meals. I've opened thousands of bottles and listened to many more questions about the hundreds of bottles on my lists. I'm constantly being told what intimidates and frustrates people about wine as I try to coax out what guests have liked in the past so I can guide them to the best bottle for their food. It's these hands-on experiences that have given me a unique perspective. My dedication to service and hospitality is what this book is all about: making sure you end up with a glass of wine you're happy with, whether it's from a restaurant or the dodgy-looking liquor store you stopped at on the way to your friend's house for dinner.

The world of wine is constantly expanding, and it's important to me to stay ahead of the curve—especially when it comes to finding hidden (affordable) gems. I'm constantly searching for new bottles to add to my lists. Based on the economy and the global price of wine at that moment, that often means that I'm diving into regions like Portugal and Greece, where I can find a beautiful bottle for $20. I'm here to help you look for undervalued alternatives to the classics.

I make wine, too. I realized that I could no longer criticize wine without knowing how hard it is to make it. So I partnered with Gerhard Kracher, a renowned winemaker in Austria, to create our own label. This incredibly humbling project has given me new respect for every bottle I pour, as well as a better understanding of how it's made, which I hope to communicate in these pages.

I want to help people build a base of knowledge that guides them in restaurants and wine shops. More important, I want to open their minds. I'm lucky that I get to work with millennials. Every day, I witness not only how good they are at quickly researching whatever questions they have about wine on their phones. (I have to admit, my inner twenty-five-year-old, who had to mail-order books, is a little jealous.) I also get to experience their rawness and curiosity around wine. They're not easily starstruck, and they're really open. They're looking for coolness and craftsmanship, for wine that has a story behind it. They want the producer with dirt under her fingernails, not the expensive bottle that's associated with the fancy château. When I looked around, I didn't see many books that really spoke to them. Because while Google can instantly answer a wide range of questions about wine, it can't teach you how to develop a palate.

Wine is constantly changing, with regions and grapes becoming popular that even I had never heard of. While wines from the Jura might have seemed edgy a few years ago, today we're seeing amazing offerings from the Canary Islands in Spain and Douro, Portugal, and the Auvergne region of France, just to name a few. There are new wines popping up all over. This book will cut through the boring, wonky stuff to give you the essentials you need to know to be able to form an opinion about wine, I hope; but more important, it will also instill the curiosity to keep learning.

And finally, there are so many myths that can make wine feel stuffy and intimidating. My aim is to demystify it for you. Because what is wine really about? Enjoyment.

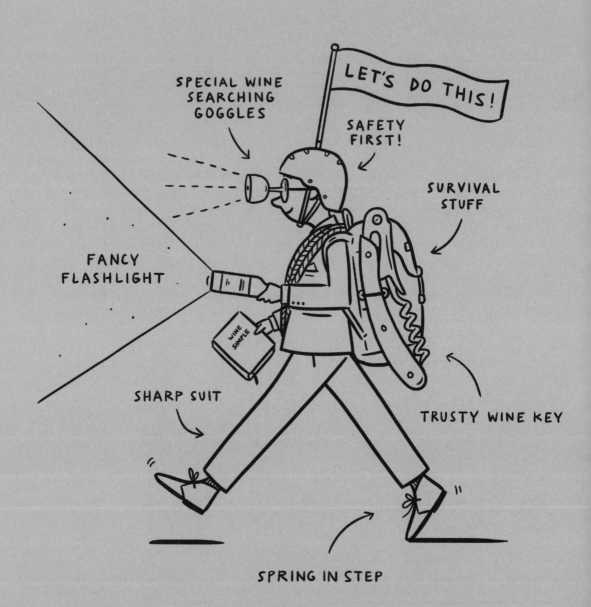

How This Book Works

→ Rather than write a textbook, I've put together easy-to-absorb hits of information—though you should still read it from start to finish! Use it to learn the basics, then go back and thumb through it after you've tasted your way around a bit to see where you can learn more. Maybe once you know that you like light, aromatic whites—rather than fruity and full-bodied ones, as you originally thought—you can discover new varietals to try. Then, after you've figured out that Grüner Veltliner is your thing (I'm Austrian—I can dream), you can flip to Wine & Food (page 245) to figure out what to serve it with at home. Later on, use it as a reference resource for when, say, you're ready to splurge on a birthday wine (page 167), or now that you've gotten into Champagnes (page 40), you want to see what's beyond the extra-brut style.

Wait, how will you know that Grüner is your favorite? By drinking a bunch of different wines; some you'll love, some you won't be able to stand. Books are great, but experience is the true teacher. So let this be your guide to getting out there to buy, taste, and learn with confidence.

You'll come across a lot of technical terms on these pages. The first time a word is introduced, you'll find the definition at the bottom of the page, as well as in the glossary on page 262.

Most important, have fun, don't get intimidated, and keep an open mind. That's key! Never lose your excitement, and remember that nobody knows it all. I once asked Jancis Robinson MW, the world's foremost expert on wine, a question about a grape variety, and she said, "Wait a moment. I have to look." I was so surprised, and yet it was an excellent lesson: There's no shame in researching; the shame is in *not* asking questions.

■ **MW**
Abbreviation for Master of Wine; a highly regarded qualification given by the British Institute of Masters of Wine.

Aldo's Wine Rules

Taste. Taste. Taste. It's the only way to learn!

There's a lot to be learned from a great bottle of wine. But there's even more to be learned from one that you didn't like.

Be open, be curious, and let your enthusiasm show. If the people selling you wine are still snobby, they're in the wrong business.

Always ask the person who's helping you what he or she is most excited about. You get the best recommendations this way.

Just because a wine is expensive doesn't mean it's good. Many of the wines I drink on the weekend cost less than $25.

If you don't like the bottle you've opened at first, taste it again every thirty minutes or so to see how it's evolved. Or even try again the next day.

Don't wait for a special occasion to open a special bottle.

A great winemaker is more important than a great vintage.

Wine's number one job is to bring us together.

In the end, there are no rules when it comes to wine.

I

What Is Wine, Anyway?

It's cultural. It's historical. It's a lifestyle product. It brings us together across countries and generations.

► And yet wine is simply fermented grape juice. (Or, to be a little more technical, it's the juice from crushed grapes in which the sugars are fermented—with the help of ambient or inoculated yeast—into alcohol and carbon dioxide.) Depending on the grape varietal and its color, wine can be fermented in wooden casks, stainless steel or concrete tanks, plastic containers, or clay amphorae buried in the ground. Some wines are bottled immediately and sold young, while other wines spend time in their fermentation vessels before making their way into bottles, or are aged further in bottles prior to release. The differences in flavor, color, and even texture are infinite.

Grapes become sweeter and less acidic as they ripen, making more sugars available for fermentation and resulting in more powerful wines. Hotter climates and seasons naturally produce sweeter grapes and therefore more powerful wines with a potentially higher alcohol level. Nowadays, winemakers are moving into cooler regions, whether through higher elevation or along foggy coasts, so that their wines have a freshness and acidity—not to mention a more moderate alcohol level—that their warmer counterparts lack.

■ amphorae
Used since ancient times, these large clay vessels, buried in the ground, are filled with crushed grapes with the skins on and sealed for aging.

How Wine Is Made

➤ Wine is fermented grape juice. Sure. But so many factors—when and how the grapes are picked (manually or mechanically?) and pressed, whether commercial or wild yeast is added to kick off the fermentation, and how long and in what vessel the wine is aged before bottling—affect what ends up in the glass. All those decisions—and many more—are made by the winemaker, whose job it is to transform something elemental into something monumental. Winemakers are like chefs: They might start with similar raw ingredients, but what kind of dish they create is entirely in their hands. (And, okay, nature's.)

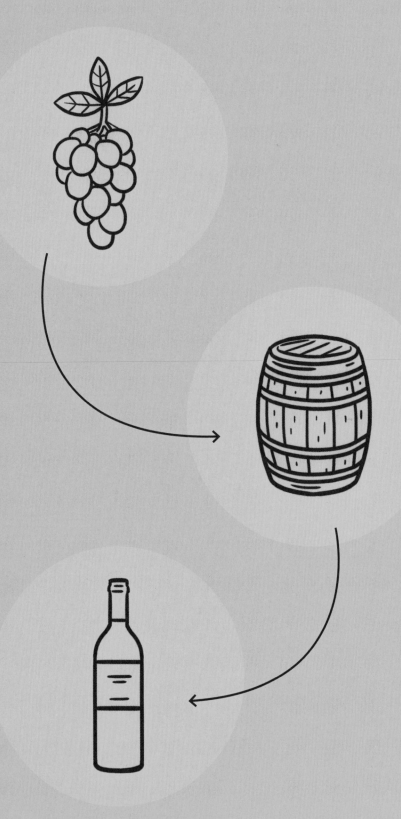

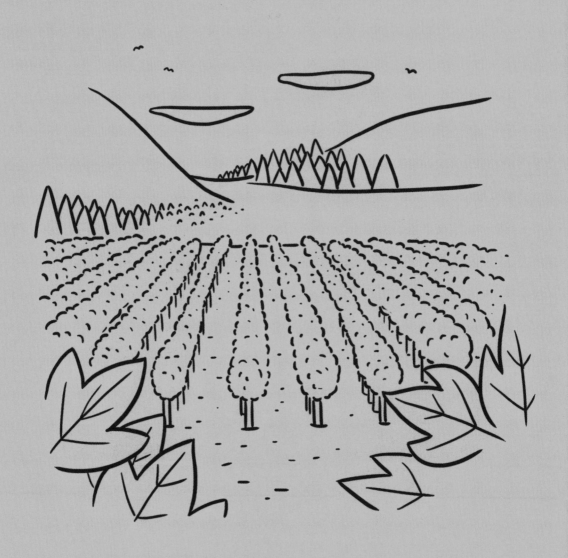

Nature's Part

There's so much that goes into making good wine. Here are the key factors from the farming side.

⚪ Climate

Grapevines are like humans: They like warm days and cool nights, bright sun—but not too much!—and water at the right moments. Grapes from hot climates are much more powerful. Heat means riper, more sugary grapes. The more sugar, the higher the alcohol level. Grapes from cooler climates are fresher and the resulting wines more moderate in alcohol.

◼ Weather

Vineyards need rain, but the timing has to be just right. Winter and early summer are key moments in the growing cycle. Harvesttime rainfall can result in soggy grapes. And drought? Just ask a Californian what a nightmare it is. Summer hailstorms can also wipe out a crop and damage vines.

Of course, climate change is having a huge impact on the wine world. While hotter summers wouldn't be such a big deal in cooler regions, those warmer winters mean that the vine-eating bugs aren't killed by cold, and the plants' essential "bud break" can start early. The danger of fatal spring frosts has increased. (Many European regions suffered huge frost damages in 2017, with some losing 90 to 100 percent of their crop. Imagine that you only have one chance each year to make your wine, i.e., your money!)

▼ Leaf Work

How many leaves the winemaker keeps on the plant throughout the growing season can affect its health. If they trim away too many, the grapes can get sunburned. If you've ever tasted wine that was like bitter chocolate, it was due to sunburn. If they leave too many leaves on and it's a rainy summer, they might have to deal with fungus and rot.

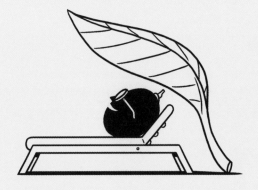

People think sun is the most important factor for happy grapes, but really it's the balance among sun, rain, and cool nights.

The Winemaker's Part

There are many decisions in the winemaking process that impact the end result. Here are some of the most essential.

△ Chaptalization

Depending on the country's winemaking laws, some winemakers might chaptalize the <u>grape must</u>, meaning enrich it with a restricted amount of sugar. Sounds bad, but it's not. In cooler regions, where grapes have lower sugar levels, this process raises the wine's alcohol level and gives it more backbone.

● Fermentation Temperature

Yeast is very temperature-sensitive. The cooler the temperature, the slower the yeast works. As a result, the fermentation time is stretched, allowing the grapes to impart more of their characteristics. You can especially taste this with New Zealand sauvignon blancs, as they often have a Swedish Fish flavor that results from cold fermentation. Too-warm fermentation isn't good, either, as such a rapid process leads to muted flavors.

☐ Cold Soaking

Often done in warmer climates. After harvest, the grapes are cooled down, crushed, and left to sit on the skins in a refrigerated or cooled-down room so the yeast can't begin fermentation. This helps extract color, <u>phenolics</u>, and flavor compounds from the skins. The resulting wines are a touch fresher and also darker.

● Whole-Cluster Fermentation

This is what it sounds like: wine left to ferment in bunches instead of the grapes being removed individually from the stems. Used mostly for red wines, it's often done partially, meaning, say, 25 percent of the crop is left in bunches. The

---

■ <u>grape must</u>
Just-pressed grape juice.

■ <u>phenolics</u>
Several hundred chemical compounds found in wine that affect everything from the color to the taste to the texture you feel in your mouth.

result is that the wine's tannins are a bit firmer, the acid is zippier, and there is a touch of noticeable carbon dioxide, as well as a slightly vegetal aroma. The tannins come from the stems—it's key that they're mature, not green and the tannins give the wine a little more structure, which helps it in the long run for aging. This technique is often found in wine production in Burgundy, Rhône, Beaujolais, California, and Australia.

Malolactic Fermentation

Technically, this isn't a fermentation but a process in which temperature-sensitive bacteria transform harsh malic acid (the type of acid found in green apples) into softer lactic acid (the kind found in yogurt). This is done by controlling the temperature as much as possible—not easy. Sometimes, after fermentation, the tank will be cooled down to stop the process. Or the barrel can be warmed up. This is common with chardonnays and most reds. It's easier to taste in white wines: They have this slightly creamy, milky flavor and are rounder on the tongue because of the lactic acid.

▼ Longer Lees Contact

After the wine has fermented, it will be placed in racks and separated from the gross lees. Letting the wine "sit" on the dead yeast cells, or lees, even a few months longer before bottling can make a huge difference in the wine's texture and complexity. The young and dynamic Austrian winemaker Johannes Hirsch used to do April and September bottlings of his wine. Even though it was the same wine, I always found the September bottling, which had more contact with the lees, much better.

Aging Vessel

Whether one chooses to age wine in oak or stainless steel makes a big difference. Oak-aged wines are rounder in flavor. Wines aged in stainless seem crisper and sometimes have a tiny touch of CO_2, giving them a slight effervescence. They are often on the reductive side, since CO_2 can't escape the steel.

Fining

The addition of bentonite (a type of clay), egg white, or even fish bladder strips the wine of some of the naturally occurring protein to make sure the wine is stable and not cloudy. This method is controversial among natural winemakers because, like antibiotics, it can also strip away some of the "good" proteins.

☐ Filtering

What it sounds like: Wine is passed through a filter. If wine is unfiltered, it might look hazy or cloudy, or might have sediment floating in it. This appearance is one of the first things natural wine fans look for in the glass. Don't think unfiltered wine is lazy: It can have more flavor.

Resting

After a wine is bottled, the flavor closes up. I call it "bottling shock." Winemakers can decide how long to let the wine rest in the bottle at the winery so it can recover before going to market.

THE WINEMAKER'S PART

■ **lees**
A sediment of dead yeast cells that have sunk to the bottom of the fermentation vessel or bottle.

■ **reductive**
To simplify a complex topic, this is a style resulting from a winemaking technique in which the reduction of oxygen evaporation during fermentation creates an aroma of shaved white cabbage/ sauerkraut, even matchstick or sulfur. Particularly popular with sommeliers.

Wine Vessels

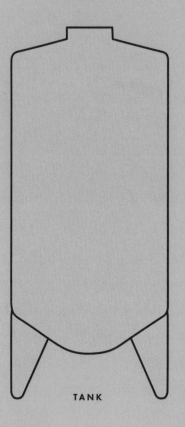

TANK

Tank

A stainless steel fermentation container; can also be plastic. Does not add or change flavor.

Amphora

An ancient fermentation and aging vessel made from lined clay that is sealed and sometimes buried in the ground. Amphorae give wine a textural difference and can have a kombucha-like profile, as well as a certain salinity, or saltiness. In the Republic of Georgia, for thousands of years they've used qvevri, which are made from terra-cotta, and, unlike amphorae, are always buried in the ground.

Cask

A traditional aging container; typically wood or stainless steel, which affects the flavor as described in "Aging Vessel," on page 29. Can be anywhere between 100 and 10,000 liters in capacity.

Barrel

This traditional aging container is typically made of oak, which adds not only richer fruit and vanilla flavors but also a slightly broader texture, since the wine is able to breathe. Wines aged in stainless steel tend to be a little tighter, since the oxygen can't escape.

Egg

This currently trendy fermentation and aging container is made from concrete. The wines become texturally different, with finer tannins, and therefore feel a little fuller in the mouth. Winemakers believe that concrete can soften a wine's texture the way a barrel does—minute amounts of oxygen may penetrate the concrete, thereby making for a unique (and, these days, desirable) texture.

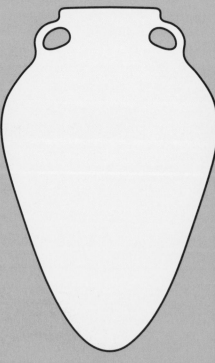

AMPHORA

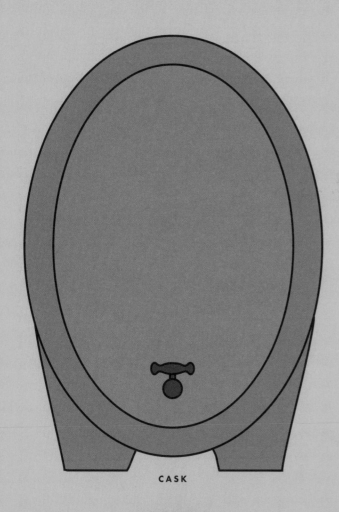

CASK

ALL ABOUT OAK...

→ In the (very) old days, oak barrels were used simply for transport. They didn't become a thing until winemakers in Bordeaux and elsewhere decided that, hey, wine tastes better after it's spent time in new barrels! (Each time the barrel is used, it gives off less flavor.) After key critics began favoring oaky wines, well, I'm surprised there are still any oak trees left. Oak does indeed give wine a vanilla flavor, depending on the wood's country of origin and how many times the barrel has been used. Taste a Spanish Rioja or a California chardonnay and you'll know what I mean. Too much is, of course, never a great thing. Large-scale winemakers began using cheaper oak chips, even sawdust. And the terms *creamy*, *oaky*, or *buttery* used before "chardonnay" became an insult. California winemakers have recently moved away from making vanilla bombs.

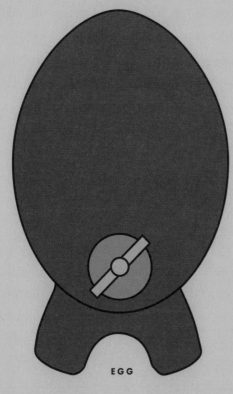

EGG

BARREL

31

Key Winemaking Styles

White

→ This one's easy! In general, white wine grapes produce white wine, with or without skin contact—i.e., after the grapes have been crushed, they're sometimes left in the tank to macerate for an hour or two so that the flavorful phenolic compounds in the skins can infuse the juice before it's pressed and filtered. This skin contact makes the wines more expressive and complex.

WHITE WINE FROM RED GRAPES

But like anything else in life, there are exceptions. In some cases, such as with *blanc de noir* (literally "white from black") wines, red grapes are used to make white wine, not to mention Champagne, which often blends pinot noir and pinot meunier. When used to make white wines, red grapes are pressed immediately and without maceration (see page 35) to avoid extracting any color.

▪ skin contact
When grape must is left in contact with the grape skins during maceration or fermentation, adding color and flavor.

How to Make White Wine

Grapes are destemmed or the clusters are left whole, then crushed.

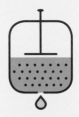

Grapes are pressed to remove skins and seeds.

Juice ferments into wine.

Wine is kept briefly in storage tanks or aged longer in barrels.

Wine is filtered, bottled, and released soon thereafter.

WHITE WINE

Red

→ If you press a red grape, you'll get white juice. The color comes from the skins, which are extracted during maceration, as are their gentle <u>tannins</u>. The thicker the skins, the longer the <u>maceration</u> time. Red grapes may be thick-skinned (such as cabernet sauvignon, merlot, malbec) or thin-skinned (pinot noir, gamay, nebbiolo, grenache), the former, of course, resulting in darker wines.

Don't be fooled when you see a translucent red wine, though: It's not necessarily lighter in terms of flavor and body, and a lighter red wine isn't inferior to a darker one. This effect is solely the result of the thickness of the grape's skin and the maceration time. In fact, if you see a really dark-looking pinot noir, you can be certain that another varietal was blended in to get that color.

■ <u>tannins</u>
Chemical compounds present in grape skins and seeds. Tannins give red wine more backbone and ageability, and they soften with time. They're also what can dry out your mouth, just like when you've sipped too-strong tea.

How to Make Red Wine

After crushing, juice macerates with the grape skins to extract color, flavor, and tannins.

Juice ferments into wine.

Wine is gently pressed to remove skins, stems, and seeds.

Wine is aged in barrels (time varies).

Wine is filtered, bottled, and either released or aged longer in the bottles.

Rosé

→ Rosé comes from red grapes that have been macerated for just a few hours or so to extract a little bit of color from the skins. Rosé is often a blend of different varietals, such as mourvèdre, pinot noir, and grenache, to which a little bit of white wine is sometimes added.

Rosé has seen an incredible spike in popularity in the US: In 2017, it was the number one fastest-growing beverage category, with a 25 percent annual sales increase. The demand for rosé from Provence—a French region once looked down upon for its simple wines—has outstripped the grape supply. Now you should also try rosé made outside Provence, such as Ode to Lulu from California, Domaine Vacheron from Sancerre, Stein from Germany, and Gobelsburg Cistercien from Austria.

Orange

→ Orange wines, which originated in Slovenia and northeast Italy based on the ancient Georgian technique, are super popular right now with natural wine drinkers. They're made like red wines but using white grapes: The juice is macerated with the skins for up to several months to extract more flavor, which means they also have body and tannins similar to those of a red wine. That orange hue comes from the flavonoids on the skin of the grapes. Orange wines can often be cloudy and have reductive flavors.

RED / ROSÉ / ORANGE

■ maceration
Soaking grape must on the skins to extract color, aroma, and tannins.

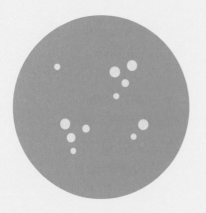

Sparkling

→ Champagne might be seen as the go-to for a celebratory first glass, but at Le Bernardin, I've occasionally been known to pair every course in a long tasting menu with Champagne to show its versatility beyond an apéritif. In fact, I'd argue that sparkling wines are the best food-pairing wines you can find.

Champagne is easy to drink, but technically, it's very demanding to make, since there are not one but two fermentations that need to be managed. It's exactly this dual process that makes its flavor so complex—and its price tag so (justifiably) high.

Before I start digging too deep—and yes, I'm going to nerd out here, but only to show you just how worthy of respect this type of wine is—let me explain the differences in production among sparkling wines. The simplest style, labeled "sparkling wine," is achieved by carbonation—that is, simply injecting carbon dioxide into white or rosé wine. Those big, round bubbles are the giveaway that it was made using this cheaper method. If a sparkling wine costs $3.99, you can bet they didn't bother with riddling and _dosage_ (doh-sahj).

The Tank Method

EXAMPLES Lambrusco, Prosecco

Also called _charmat,_ it is what it sounds like: fermentation that's done in a tank rather than in bottles, a cost-effective approach that results in low-price sparkling wines. With this method, the second fermentation takes place in large pressurized tanks. Then it's filtered, a _dosage_ is added, and it goes right to market. Forget aging! The result is a straightforward wine without a lot of complexity. (Sorry, Prosecco.)

The Ancestral Method

EXAMPLES _Pét-nat_

Also known as the _méthode rurale_ or _méthode ancestrale,_ it is an increasingly common technique that experts believe predates the _méthode champenoise,_ or traditional method. Just like any other wine, sparkling wine is first fermented in a barrel (or a stainless steel or concrete tank). Then, before all the residual sugar has been converted into alcohol and CO_2, the wine is chilled, riddled (the bottle is agitated and turned), and disgorged before it's bottled. After fermenting in the bottle for at least two months, the wine is ready. The result is delicately sparkling, refreshing, and often super easy to drink. One of my favorites is Bugey-Cerdon La Cueille from Patrick Bottex. You'll find this method increasingly used for fizzy and fashionable _pétillant naturel_ wine, better known as _pét-nat_.

The Tank Method

1 – First fermentation in tank.

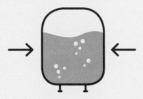

2 – Second fermentation in large, pressurized tank.

3 – Filtered and *dosage* added.

4 – Bottled and sold.

The Ancestral Method

1 – First fermentation in barrel (or tank).

2 – Wine is bottled with residual sugar.

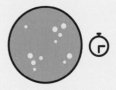

3 – Ferments in bottles for at least 2 months.

4 – Ready to drink!

■ *dosage*
A mixture of wine and sugar syrup or rectified (reduced) grape must.

■ *pétillant naturel (or pét-nat)*
A natural winemaking technique that results in lightly effervescent wines.

The Traditional Method

1 – First fermentation in barrel (or tank).

2 – *Tirage* is added and wine is bottled.

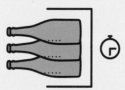

3 – Wine is crown-capped and stored horizontally for second fermentation. After fermentation, it is aged on the lees.

4 – *Rémuage*, or riddling, gradually move the lees down into the neck.

5 – Disgorging process removes the lees from the bottle in a process that involves freezing the bottle's neck.

6 – *Dosage* is added to adjust sugar level.

7 – Wine is corked and secured with metal cage.

■ secondary fermentation
Literally the second time a wine is fermented.

■ *cuvée*
A batch or blend of wine.

■ crown cap
The type of ridged bottle cap you see on beer and soda bottles.

The Traditional Method

EXAMPLES Champagne, Cava, Crémant

Also known as the *méthode champenoise* in France, *metodo classico* in Italy, and *méthode cap classique* in South Africa, this method is the most complex. In Champagne, it starts with the blending of the base still wines, called the *vin clair*, typically a blend of pinot noir, pinot meunier, and chardonnay. The cellar master continually tastes the mixture until he or she achieves the perfect balance, sometimes adding reserve wines (aged base wines set aside from previous vintages) before putting the finished base mixture into oak barrels or large wooden casks—though concrete eggs and stainless steel tanks are sometimes used.

I've tasted these base wines, and it's amazing how challenging they are: very citrusy and mouth-dryingly tart. It's proof of how much the wine evolves with the second, or secondary fermentation.

After this *cuvée* is finished, the *tirage* (tee-rajh), a mixture of wine, sugar, and yeast, is added. The wines are then bottled and closed with a crown cap before being stored horizontally in the cellar for the secondary fermentation, which lasts four to six weeks.

The now-sparkling wine is then aged on the lees (dead yeast cells from the *tirage* that have floated to the bottom of the bottle). This stage has a significant effect on the quality. In Spain, Cava must be aged on the lees for a minimum of nine months (thirty months for vintage). Vintage Champagne must be aged on the lees for a minimum of thirty-six months—that's three years! In short, aging on the lees is where the quality of the Champagne is defined and the bubbles become really fine and elegant.

If the sparkling wine is destined for half bottles, the process stops here. It would be too costly and labor-intensive to complete the process for half the volume. (If you were to taste a full bottle and a half bottle from the same vineyard side by side, you'd notice the difference in complexity. And, I hate to say it, but a magnum of Champagne tastes better than a regular-size 750 mL bottle, too.)

For full-size bottles, next comes the *rémuage* (reh-moo-ahj), or riddling: Over the course of several weeks, the bottle is gradually riddled and moved from a horizontal to an almost upside-down position in order to collect the lees in the bottle's neck. If you just stood the bottle upright, the lees would stick to the sides of the bottle and never make their way into the cap. This is slow, labor-intensive manual work—though some of the commercial Cava houses riddle mechanically in just days.

Finally, the disgorging process. The bottle's neck is frozen using a chemical solution. When the crown cap is removed, the frozen lees deposit pops right out. In order to compensate for the loss of liquid, the bottles are topped off with a mixture of wine (for *brut nature* style; to learn more, see the next page) and, depending on the style (extra brut, brut, *demi-sec*, *sec*), sugar syrup (aka *dosage*). The *dosage* is added to adjust the sugar level for a final bit of seasoning—not unlike adding a dash of salt to food before serving to focus and elevate the flavor.

The bottles are now stoppered with a proper Champagne cork and secured with a metal cage to keep the cork from popping out from the pressure, which is equivalent to almost double that inside a car tire.

How Sweet Is It?

Only wines made in the Champagne region of France can be labeled "Champagne."

The *dosage* level defines the sweetness level of the Champagne or sparkling wine. Terms like "extra brut" and "brut" that you see on labels refer to the number of grams of residual sugar (RS) added per liter before bottling. Here are the most common. Oh, and *brut* is pronounced "broot."

BRUT NATURE (0 TO 3 g/L)

If you're just getting into Champagne, don't start here! Brut nature Champagne is really tart and austere. However, with a little age (about ten years), these are the most memorable bottles. I still think about the 2002 Prévost I had last year . . .
→ **Try:** Champagne La Closerie Les Béguines from Jérôme Prévost; Champagne Vouette & Sorbée

EXTRA BRUT (0 TO 6 g/L)

Focused, citrusy, with a touch of tartness.
→ **Try:** Chartogne-Taillet Chemin de Reims; Agrapart & Fils Minéral

BRUT (0 TO 12 g/L)

The extra sugar gives a little richness and softness.
→ **Try:** If you don't have too much Champagne experience, start here for the most pleasant beginning. If you like it on the sweeter side, try a Veuve Clicquot or a Moët & Chandon Brut Impérial as a reference point for the higher side, while Louis Roederer and Billecart-Salmon are much more dry.

A WORD ON SUGAR AND SPARKLING WINE

→ <u>Added sugar, or a dosage, is like makeup: It conceals flaws.</u> While it makes most people look better, add too much and you won't recognize who's underneath. However, going without sugar isn't the answer, either. I did a *dosage* tasting with Alexandre Chartogne of the excellent Chartogne-Taillet. We tasted Champagnes with different *dosage* levels in ascending order of sweetness, and it was truly fascinating: The zero dosage was too austere and tart—it felt like chewing on a rock. With each gram of added sugar, the flavors blossomed . . . until the sugar took over and concealed the wine's flavors. Think of adding sugar to lemonade to make it less tart and drinkable—until it becomes cloying. Same with Champagne!

In recent years, the levels of added sugar in Champagne have gone down significantly, partly because the grapes are much riper (hello, climate change). In addition, smaller, single-vineyard growers have focused on farming to yield better grapes. The result is richer, more complex base wines that need less added sugar. (Large Champagne houses often have to purchase grapes from vineyards all over the region to meet demand, giving up craftsmanship as a result. While some manage better than others, the fix is often higher sugar levels in the *dosage*.)

A Bubbles Cheat Sheet

CAVA

From: Spain
Flavor profile:
Fruity, acidic
Method: Traditional
Aging: 9 months (standard),
15 months (riserva),
30 months (gran riserva)
Price: $10–$25

PROSECCO

From: Italy
Flavor profile:
Fruity, acidic
Method: Tank
Aging: None
Price: $10–$15

LAMBRUSCO

From: Italy
Flavor profile:
Dark fruit, floral, acidic
(made using red grapes)
Method: Tank (commercial),
Ancestral
Aging: None
Price: $15–$25

SPARKLING WINE

From: Anywhere!
Flavor profile:
Fruity, acidic
Method: Traditional, Tank,
Carbonation
Aging: Varies
Price: $10–$30

PÉT-NAT

From: Anywhere, but
mostly France
Flavor profile:
Kombucha-y, acidic
Method: Ancestral
Aging: None
Price: $15–$30

CHAMPAGNE

From: France
Flavor profile: Fruity,
toasty, acidic
Method: Traditional
Aging: 15 months
(nonvintage),
36 months (vintage)
Price: $30+

What Does "Natural Winemaking" Really Mean?

➡️ There is a huge political debate going on between supporters of "conventional" winemakers, who might spray pesticides on their grapes and use a variety of chemicals to create the wine they want, and "natural" winemakers, who believe that the grapes should be organic or biodynamic, and the juice should go into the bottle, without any added sugar, sulfur, or acidifiers—unfiltered and unfined. I find that natural wines often have a cloudiness, funkiness, and volatility (meaning the flavors change quickly). Here are some of the terms and certifications used for these alt-wines.

Natural wine

is farmed organically or biodynamically, without the use of pesticides during the growing process. Nothing is added to the juice to affect flavor, and intervention during the fermentation process in the cellar, such as yeast additions or acidity adjustments via chemicals, is kept to a minimum. As a result, natural wines are not filtered (hence the signature cloudiness), and a minimal amount of sulfites—if any—is added during bottling to assist in preservation. Not all natural wines are certified organic and, more confusing still, not all organic and biodynamic wines are natural. Keep reading!

In the US, the USDA controls the use of the term *organic*, whereas Demeter has trademarked Biodynamic. As a result, there are two types of organic listings on domestic wine bottles. Those labeled "USDA Organic" are made from organically grown grapes, and all additives—such as fining agents and yeast—must be organic. These wines are made without the addition of sulfur, though naturally occurring sulfites will still be present. Obviously this sounds great, but the reality is that sulfur dioxide (SO_2) is the best natural preservative for wine. That's why you'll find very few wines with this label on the market.

"Made with certified organically grown grapes"

on the label means that the wine has the same allowed additives as the "USDA Organic" wines, but the bottle is permitted to contain up to 100 parts per million (ppm) of total SO_2 for red wines and 150 ppm for whites and rosés.

The European Union certifies wines made with both organic grapes and organic additives as "EU Organic." GMOs are not allowed. Sulfur regulations are the same as those for "Made with certified organically grown grapes" wines in the US.

NATURAL WINEMAKING

■ sulfites
Sulfur dioxide (SO_2); also referred to as sulfur. A preservative that is either added to wine during the winemaking process (typically just before bottling) or present on grape skins before fermentation.

■ fining agents
Elements added to wine to remove trace proteins or sediments that might make wine cloudy. Bentonite, egg whites, and casein are used.

And then there's biodynamic

Biodynamic and organic farming are similar in that neither uses chemicals. But biodynamic farming, based on the principles of the early twentieth-century Austrian philosopher Rudolf Steiner, is a holistic approach that sees the vineyard as an interlinked ecosystem in which the plants, fields, forests, animals, soil, compost, people, and "spirit" of the place work together in harmony as part of a cycle, feeding one another. The farmer also follows the lunar cycle to determine when to fertilize, plant, and harvest. The health of the soil is treated homeopathically. (The farmers even bury cow horns packed with the manure of a lactating female cow in the soil during the winter to create spring compost . . .)

If a wine is labeled "biodynamic," that means the grapes were farmed biodynamically, and the winemaker didn't use any common manipulations such as yeast additions. A wine that is labeled "made from biodynamic grapes" means the vintner used biodynamically grown grapes but followed less strict rules in the winemaking process. While this category is certified by organizations like Demeter USA and Biodyvin, the reality is that a growing number of winemakers use biodynamic practices but skip certifications, which can be costly and time-consuming.

I've spoken to many winemakers about why they follow this spiritual practice. Alsatian winemaker Olivier Humbrecht MW said that his switch to biodynamic farming practices, such as leaving more leaves on the vines to shade the grapes, ultimately allowed him to reduce the alcohol levels in his wines. (Contrary to what you might think, too much alcohol is not a good thing; it masks the flavors of the wine and heats up the mouth unpleasantly.) After the French winemaker Alfred Tesseron converted the vineyards at Château Pontet-Canet to biodynamic and began aging his wines in amphorae, his wines skyrocketed up the point scales of major critics thanks to their improved quality. (Learn more about wine ratings on page 187.) Sometimes wineries convert without publicizing it, like the fabled Domaine de la Romanée-Conti, Domaine Leflaive, and parts of the vineyard used to make Cristal, while others are much more vocal about it. As Jancis Robinson wrote in her excellent book *The 24-Hour Wine Expert*, "It sounds completely crazy but results in some pretty exciting wine—and notably healthy-looking vineyards."

Sustainable

This refers to a range of practices that are not only ecologically healthy but also socially responsible. It's based on things like how the winery manages its water and energy use, whether it uses lighter bottles to cut down on its carbon footprint during shipping—even how the winery relates to the surrounding community. Sustainable farmers may farm largely organically or biodynamically but have the flexibility to choose what works best for their individual property and region. Some third-party agencies like EMS (Environmental Management System), Salmon-Safe, and SIP Certified offer sustainability certifications, and many regional industry associations are working on developing clearer standards. In general, sustainability is expensive to implement, but it's a very forward-thinking and green response to climate change.

Key Varietals

→ A varietal is the kind of grape used to make a wine of the same name. Each type has its own distinct personality due to the thickness of its skin, the flavor of its flesh, even the size of its seeds. While each varietal has common characteristics, the soil, climate, and location in which the grape is grown—and, of course, the winemaker—determine the final results in the glass. Even though a sauvignon blanc planted in the warm South African sun will make a wine that's more amped-up than one made from sauvignon blanc grapes planted in the cooler regions of France, they are still siblings on the tongue, even in a blind tasting.

As you read through this section, make note of which grapes sound most delicious to you. Then go a little deeper by learning how they vary from country to country. Even just knowing grape and country can help you the most when buying wine, as they cue the sommelier and wine-store staff in to where that happy spot on your palate lies. But don't get stuck on the key varietals—explore others and keep an open spirit. You can get some really good wines for much less money.

whites

Pinot Grigio

→ *The entry-level white. Uncomplicated, easygoing, and always satisfying, this light wine gets along with everyone. Invite it to your next party.*

This grayish varietal—a mutation of the pinot noir grape—develops a pink skin when fully mature. The leaner versions are the most popular, as they're very refreshing. Sadly, pinot grigio is often terribly overcropped and delivers wine with unspecific flavor. When done right, pinot grigio has a pretty perfume and hints of bitter almond. The best examples are found in Friuli. It can be a great party wine, cheap and crowd-pleasing.

Pinot gris from Alsace smells and tastes very different compared to its Italian counterpart. It's often much richer in flavor and body, with a touch of honey on the palate, often due to the <u>botrytis</u> that is common in the region.

■ botrytis
A naturally occurring fungus that concentrates a grape's sweetness and can impart a honeyed flavor to dry wines. Also called noble rot.

KEY FACTS

FLAVORS
Lemon
Melon
Peach
Almond
Honey
Yellow apple

DESCRIPTORS
Light
Zesty
Fruity

MAJOR GROWING REGIONS
Alsace
Veneto
Friuli
Alto Adige
Willamette Valley
Sonoma

BY ANY OTHER NAME
Pinot gris (France)
Grauburgunder
  (Germany)

LOOK FOR

→ **Cantina Tramin**,
Alto Adige, Italy

→ **Cantina Terlano**,
Alto Adige, Italy

→ **Venica & Venica**,
Friuli, Italy

→ **Neumeister**,
Styria, Austria

→ **Trimbach**,
Alsace, France

→ **Zind-Humbrecht**,
Alsace, France

THE ESSENTIALS

☐ Italian pinot grigios are crisp, refreshing, and easy to drink. Those from Alsace tend to be richer.

☐ Pinot grigio from Friuli and Alto Adige are more aromatic.

☐ Those from the Veneto are more neutral in flavor because they're mass-produced.

☐ Whenever you see a pinot grigio advertised on a billboard, you're paying for the ad campaign, not the product.

☐ You can get some good ones once you're willing to spend over $15.

WHITE ○ PINOT GRIGIO

Sauvignon Blanc

KEY FACTS

FLAVORS
Grass
Grapefruit
Gooseberry
Lime
Black currant leaf
Bell pepper (green, yellow, red)

DESCRIPTORS
Zesty
Herbaceous
Acidic
Powerfully aromatic

MAJOR GROWING REGIONS
Loire
Bordeaux
New Zealand
California
Austria
Italy

BY ANY OTHER NAME
Sancerre
Pouilly-Fumé
Menetou-Salon
Saint-Bris
(these are the essential appellations)

→ *All flavor, all the time, sauvignon blanc is the darling of wine drinkers who've graduated from pinot grigio—and not just for its value-to-flavor ratio.*

It feels like sauvignon blanc took over from pinot grigio on the fashionable scale. This aromatic variety has very distinct flavors, with a vegetal quality and herbaceousness that can sometimes tip into cat-pee territory.

Sauvignon blancs from the Sancerre appellation of France are the most prominent in the States, with price tags that have risen to meet their popularity. I like Sancerres from the village of Chavignol, grown on *terre blanche* (rich limestone containing layers of seashells from the Jurassic period—soil that is also found in the top vineyards of Chablis and southern parts of Champagne). This soil delivers very fine, zesty, and pure Sancerres that age beautifully—I've been lucky to have tasted vintages going all the way back to 1959.

New Zealand landed on the international scene with its Cloudy Bay sauvignon blanc, made in the Marlborough region. These sauvignon blancs have a rich, herbaceous flavor of intense tropical fruit and black currant leaves. They typically come in screwtop bottles, as drinkers in New Zealand and Australia prefer them. (To be honest, New Zealand sauvignon blancs are too much for me: They're so loud, it's like trying to sustain a conversation in a club for two hours.)

Austria's most famous region for sauvignon blanc is Styria, where the wines have a flavor that's somewhere between the intense New Zealand sauvignon blancs and the zesty, mineral Sancerres from the Loire. The entry-level ones to try are light, elegant, crisp wines that have a crunchiness evocative of biting into a Granny Smith apple.

LOOK FOR

→ **From Loire Valley, France:**
Sancerre from **Gérard Boulay**, **Domaine Vacheron**, **Domaine Francois Cotat**, and **Domaine Pascal Cotat**

Pouilly-Fumé from **Jonathan Didier Pabiot**, and **Didier Dagueneau**

→ **From Burgundy, France:**
Saint-Bris from **Domaine Goisot** (the only sauvignon blanc legally allowed in Burgundy)

→ **From Styria, Austria:**
Tement, **Neumeister**, **Gross**, and **Lackner-Tinnacher**

→ **From Marlborough, New Zealand:**
Cloudy Bay, **Craggy Range**, and **Coopers Creek**

Myth! <u>*The more flavor there is, the better the wine.*</u> *Sometimes you can have too much of a good thing.*

THE ESSENTIALS

☐ On a scale of intensity, New Zealand sauvignon blancs are EDM, Aussie SBs are power ballads, and Sancerre is smooth jazz.

☐ Sancerre *is* sauvignon blanc! So is Pouilly-Fumé, for that matter. The French are tricky because they only put the appellation on the bottle, not the varietal. Of course, there is an exception! In Alsace, they list the grape on the bottle first.

☐ When people graduate from pinot grigio, they're often attracted to the step up in aromatic intensity that sauvignon blanc offers. Think of pinot grigio as a lean filet mignon, while sauvignon blanc is a big bone-in rib eye whose fat gives it all that flavor.

☐ There are plenty of affordable sauvignon blancs out there, but don't go below $10 or you'll be sorry.

☐ Serve them as cold as you possibly can, but no colder than 45°F (see page 193).

WHITE ○ SAUVIGNON BLANC

53

Chardonnay

KEY FACTS

FLAVORS
Yellow apple
Green apple
Pineapple
Lemon

DESCRIPTORS
Fruity
Fresh
Buttery
Full-bodied

MAJOR GROWING REGIONS
Burgundy
California
Australia

BY ANY OTHER NAME
Chablis
Montrachet
White Burgundy

■ *terroir* (tare-wah)
A French term referring to how the soil, climate, and terrain of a vineyard are discernible in a wine's flavor.

→ *The grape with many faces (and names), chardonnay can range from fresh and focused to rich and powerful.*

There are so many styles of chardonnay that it's hard to neatly characterize its flavor. It's not a very temperature-sensitive grape to grow, which means you could literally plant it in your own backyard! While chardonnay reflects its *terroir*, more important, it showcases the craftsmanship of the winemaker. Whether it's a lean, minerally Chablis (a French appellation) or an austere *blanc de blancs* Champagne from the village of Le Mesnil; a rich Montrachet from Burgundy—where chardonnay makes up almost all the area's whites—or a creamy, buttery California chardonnay, it's nothing if not versatile. See for yourself: Compare a few bottles of the examples above and you'll be stunned.

California chardonnay is frequently heavily oaked or treated with inexpensive oak chips to cause it to absorb the sweet oak flavor that ultimately makes the wine more flavorful. There are often a few grams of residual sugar, resulting in a more voluptuous wine. The clichés about oaky California chardonnays exist for a reason, but there is a generational shift occurring, as many young winemakers did internships in France between 2004 and 2014 and brought back their knowledge of a style that favors subtler oak. California's most dynamic areas for chardonnay are currently Sta. Rita Hills and Santa Barbara, where the wines remind you more of Burgundy for the freshness, with the sexy Californian lushness of the fruit. Oregon, too, has been bottling more citrusy, linear styles that are quite different from their Californian counterparts.

When customers tell me they don't like chardonnay, but they like Chablis and white Burgundy, I always keep a straight face: Those are chardonnays, too—they just use the name of their appellation, or region, rather than their grape varietal. Champagne? Chardonnay is its base, as you learned on page 39.

Elsewhere in the world, Australian chardonnays are similar to their California cousins with their burst of flavor; they also contain higher residual sugar. New Zealand's chardonnays are on the more aromatic spectrum. Because they're fermented at a lower temperature, they have more of a Swedish Fish aroma. Unlike their Aussie neighbors, these wines have lower residual sugar levels and keep the oak flavors behind the fruit aromatics. South Africa and Argentina are also ascending in quality and production.

THE ESSENTIALS

☐ **Chardonnay cheat sheet:** Chablis is fresh and minerally; white Burgundies are rich and majestic; California and Australian chardonnays are creamy, buttery, and often oaky—the loudest of the bunch. And if Cali chard is too rich and Chablis too acidic, consider South Africa or the new California, especially Santa Barbara, or Oregon.

☐ Compared with its white wine siblings, chardonnay has quite a high acid level and a distinctive green apple character—not to mention a little more body, thanks to the rounder feeling that oak aging gives it.

☐ Because chardonnay is most often made in (or with) oak and oak is expensive, you're going to have to pay a little more for this grape.

WHITE ○ CHARDONNAY

LOOK FOR

→ **Domaine Louis Michel & Fils**, Chablis, France

→ **Domaine Roulot**, Burgundy, France (if you want to splurge)

→ **Bénédicte & Stéphane Tissot**, Jura, France

→ **Sandhi**, Santa Barbara County, California

→ **Lingua Franca**, Willamette Valley, Oregon

→ **Velich**, Burgenland, Austria

→ **Three Oaks**, Geelong, Australia

■ oaked
Wine aged in barrels made from toasted oak. The hard grape tannins interchange with the soft wood tannin, adding a rich vanilla flavor and creamy mouthfeel.

■ linear
A wine that tastes zippy and precise, with all of the flavors seemingly attached in a straight line.

Don't Say You Hate Chardonnay but Love White Burgundy

Because France and Italy label their wines by appellation (region) rather than varietal (grape), it can be hard to remember what's in the bottle. Here's a cheat sheet of double meanings so you don't trip up the next time someone asks you what wines you do and don't like.

APPELLATION (REGION)		VARIETAL (GRAPE)
Barolo	⟷	Nebbiolo
Beaujolais	⟷	Gamay
Bordeaux	⟷	Cabernet-merlot blend
Bourgogne blanc	⟷	Chardonnay
Chablis	⟷	Chardonnay
Pouilly-Fuissé	⟷	Chardonnay
Chianti	⟷	Sangiovese
Chinon	⟷	Cabernet franc
Côtes-du-Rhône	⟷	Grenache
Saint-Joseph	⟷	Syrah
Pouilly-Fumé	⟷	Sauvignon blanc
Sancerre	⟷	Sauvignon blanc
Soave	⟷	Garganega

White Burgundy

Chenin Blanc

KEY FACTS

FLAVORS
Lemon
Lemon curd
Pear
Honey
Quince
Citrus blossom
Damp straw
Wet wool

▷ **DESCRIPTORS**
Citrusy
Fresh
Acidic

◉ **MAJOR GROWING REGIONS**
Loire Valley
South Africa

◌ **BY ANY OTHER NAME**
Chenin

→ *This under-appreciated grape has both versatility and complexity. Why it's not more popular is a bit of a mystery. The upside? It's a terrific value.*

Chenin blanc is something of an underdog, with a growing following thanks to its great quality for the price—especially for those from France's Loire Valley. These dry wines have a pleasing complexity: An oaked chenin blanc could be mistaken for a pricey Burgundy. (Try Château de Brézé and you'll be shocked.) Because of its high acidity, it is often used for sparkling wine production. An inexpensive bottle of sparkling Vouvray, Saumur, or Montlouis will remind you that you don't always have to spring for Champagne.

South Africa is the biggest grower of chenin blanc because of its high, consistent yields—quite the opposite of the Loire Valley. The same goes for California's Central Valley, where it's blended with colombard grapes for high-volume wines.

Dry chenin blancs are really popular among sommeliers and offer a great value (i.e., you can find good ones at restaurants). What makes the grape so interesting is that its acidity is a bit higher than other varietals', which means it's able to produce a wide range of wines: sparkling, dry, off-dry, *and* sweet.

L O O K   F O R

→ **From Loire Valley, France:**

Vouvray from **Domaine Huet** and **Philippe Foreau**

Montlouis from **François Chidaine** and **Domaine la Taille aux Loups**

Anjou from **Thibaud Boudignon** and **Domaine Mousse**

Saumur from **Domaine du Collier** and **Domaine Guiberteau**

Savenière from **Domaine aux Moines**, **Eric Morgat**, and **Coulée de Serrant**

Sandlands, Amador County, California

Sadie, Swartland, South Africa

WHITE ○ CHENIN BLANC

THE ESSENTIALS

☐ Those graduating from chardonnay will appreciate chenin blanc's depth and higher acidity, not to mention its character: The fact that there aren't many large-scale producers means the chances are higher you'll buy from a small farmer.

☐ To be safe, stay in the Loire Valley—wines here are more precise, with a distinct high acid and slightly tighter fruit. When you're ready, venture into South Africa, keeping in mind that they can be hit-or-miss.

The oaked chenin blancs from Château de Brézé (in the Loire Valley) make me think of white Burgundy.

Riesling

KEY FACTS

FLAVORS
Peach
Apricot
Pineapple
Passion fruit
Rose

DESCRIPTORS
Aromatic
Floral
Citrusy

MAJOR GROWING REGIONS
Mosel-Saar-Ruwer
Rheingau
  (Germany)
Alsace (France)
Clare Valley
  (Australia)
Wachau Valley
  (Austria)
Washington State

BY ANY OTHER NAME
Rhein Riesling

→ *Incredibly sophisticated, nuanced, and layered, Riesling is also the most flexible food wine. Even better: It can be really cheap!*

Pronounced REECE-ling, this queen of grapes has a strange standing: While many sommeliers and wine professionals praise it for its excellent value, high quality, and incredible versatility with food—not to mention that its freshness and acidity are exactly what pros are personally looking for after a day of tasting—the general drinker simply finds it too sweet. That's because the cool-climate-loving grape develops high acid levels that need to be tamed through aging with a little residual sugar. As a result, it develops the most seductive aromas as it ages—if you see an old bottle, set aside your preconceptions and taste it. You're in for an unforgettable experience!

Rieslings have a wide spectrum, from bone-dry—an increasing number of them due to market demand; we're seeing more and more warm summers—to off-dry (fruity) to sweet wines. It's also a varietal that really showcases the differences in soil, whether it's sandstone or volcanic; blue, gray, or red slate; and so on.

My go-to is always Mosel-Saar-Ruwer wines from Germany. In this cool northern area, the Rieslings express their *terroir*. Maybe I'm crazy, but I believe that even non-wine people can taste whether Mosel-Saar-Ruwer Riesling comes from, say, slate or limestone. (Really!) More German wineries are producing dry Rieslings: Look for the word *trocken* ("dry") on the label, and check out the alcohol level: If it's 12% or above, your wine will be dry. My partner thinks Riesling is too sweet, but lately I've been using her really good palate as a guinea pig. I've been serving her more and more dry Rieslings from Peter Lauer, Dönnhoff, Leitz, and Franzen. When she says, "This is really good. What is it?" I respond, "Your least favorite varietal." ☺

Austria is always connected with Riesling, though Germany produces far more of it. Plus, it's on the southern edge of getting too warm to grow well. There are some really excellent examples in the Wachau Valley, such as the classics from Emmerich Knoll, Prager, Alzinger, and Franz Hirtzberger. A little farther northeast in the Kamptal region is Schloss Gobelsburg, one of my favorite Austrian producers.

Alsace, in the eastern part of France, has such diverse soil that the wines change from vineyard to vineyard. The issue in Alsace was knowing when the wine had residual sugar, but since 2008 they must be dry by law (the exception: Riesling labeled with a *lieu-dit*). The US produces a good amount, particularly in Washington State and New York's Finger Lakes region.

I can always tell when I'm tasting an Australian Riesling: It tends to have petrol-like flavors.

L O O K   F O R

→ **Peter Lauer**, Saar, Germany

→ **Trimbach**, Alsace, France

→ **Hirsch**, Kamptal, Austria

→ **F.X. Pichler**, Wachau, Austria

→ **Tatomer**, Santa Barbara County, California

→ **Hermann J. Wiemer**, Finger Lakes, New York

→ **Grosset**, Eden Valley, Australia

THE ESSENTIALS

WHITE ○ RIESLING

☐ Riesling is the most delicate, finessed, and challenging white. The higher acidity levels, layered fruit, and palpable *terroir* mean this is a wine you can't just chug: You're more likely to stop and think about what you're tasting. If you're having a great meal and want something to hold up to it, Riesling should definitely be on the table. If you want to have something simple to drink while you chat about work, open a pinot grigio.

☐ Aged Rieslings can be a terrific bargain. A Kabinett or Grosses Gewächs from Germany—their quality is equivalent to, say, a grand cru chardonnay—will cost around $70. Which grand cru can you buy for $70? Exactly none.

☐ **Myth: All Riesling is sweet.** No way! For a general indicator, look at the alcohol percentage on the label: Once you go above 12%, Riesling gets drier. (Below 12% you're looking at sweeter.)

reds

Sauvignon

Cabernet

KEY FACTS

→ *A rich, powerful crowd-pleaser with tons of versatility—and flavor.*

FLAVORS
Black currant
Leather
Tobacco
Cedar

DESCRIPTORS
Intense
Full-bodied
Dark fruit
Tannic

MAJOR GROWING REGIONS
Bordeaux (Left Bank)
Napa Valley
Washington State
Santa Cruz
Chile
Coonawarra

Cabernet sauvignon—commonly referred to as cabernet or cab—is certainly one of the best-known grapes in the wine universe. Its small, thick-skinned berries deliver a very dark style of wine, with a distinctive flavor that calls to mind cigar boxes and black currants. Some of the world's best-known, most powerful wines are cabernet-based: think Château Latour, Château Lafite Rothschild, and Château Haut-Brion—all from the Bordeaux region, where cabernet originated—as well as the high-end Sassicaia in Italy and cult California cabs like Harlan Estate, Screaming Eagle, and Colgin.

Cabernet requires a warm region with a long ripening period to coax out its best characteristics (that pure, ripe, dark cassis flavor, which is very lush yet precise, with distinctive tobacco flavors); otherwise, it will have an herbaceous, green bell pepper aroma. Because of its smaller ratio of juice to skin and seeds, it's higher in tannins, thereby requiring more aging to soften it.

In the US, cabernet is mostly planted in Napa, Sonoma, and the Santa Cruz Mountains in California, as well as in Washington State.

Napa's and Sonoma's warm climates produce cabernets that are richer and more concentrated—depending on the location and *terroir* from which the wines come: Napa's exposure and cooling daily fogs can make the vineyards topographically more similar to Burgundy—versus the cooler elevation of the Santa Cruz Mountains, which creates cabs that are more balanced in their fruit and tannins. Washington's desertlike climate makes for fruit-forward wines with a higher alcohol level.

You'll find a good number of cabernets in South America, thanks to French winemakers who have partnered with local vineyards. Argentine cabernets tend to have a clove-like flavor, while Chilean cabs have a distinct eucalyptus tone.

The small Coonawarra region of Australia produces some of the best cabernets in the country, with smooth tannins and lush fruit.

For fun, get some friends together to try tasting a Left Bank Bordeaux (for more information, see page 89), a Napa cabernet, and an Australian cab to taste the differences.

THE ESSENTIALS

☐ This is your crowd-pleaser red. To me, it rarely disappoints.

☐ The popularity of cabernet means a higher scale of production. You can go down to $10 a bottle and not hate life.

☐ If you're going to splurge on one red wine, a Bordeaux is always a safe bet.

☐ **Myth: The heavier the bottle, the better the wine.** Pure marketing from the cabernet world!

☐ These full-bodied reds benefit from aerating in a glass or decanter. (See page 212.)

RED ● CABERNET SAUVIGNON

LOOK FOR

→ **Domaine Eden**, Santa Cruz Mountains, California

→ **Echo de Lynch Bages**, Bordeaux, France

→ **Gramercy Cellars**, Washington State

→ **Vasse Felix Estate**, Margaret River, Australia

→ **Bodega Catena Zapata**, Mendoza, Argentina

Merlot

KEY FACTS

FLAVORS
Dark cherry
Plum
Blueberries
Dark chocolate
Tobacco
Cedar
Leather

DESCRIPTORS
Bold
Rich
Round
Plummy

MAJOR GROWING REGIONS
Bordeaux
Napa
Chile

→ *If it's fallen out of fashion, then why are some of the world's most expensive wines based on this pleasing, concentrated grape? Because it's delicious.*

A single line in *Sideways*—"If anyone orders merlot, I'm leaving"—made sales plunge. And yet the world's most famous wines are based on this varietal, which originated in the Bordeaux region (think Château Pétrus). The little village of Pomerol, home of Pétrus, produces some of the finest examples, and it's not super difficult to find some great "little" wines from smaller châteaux in appellations just five miles away. Look for Fronsac with Paul Barre, Clos Puy Arnaud, and Castillon Côtes de Bordeaux. The early-ripening fruit has a rich, fruity flavor and softer tannins—not to mention

Merlot brings softness to a blend.

higher alcohol levels. The result is a smooth richness, with a long, seamless finish that really stays with you.

Because it's such an easy and early-maturing grape, it's planted all over the world. You'll find it in Tuscany, blended into Chianti to lend it structure and richness, as well as in high-priced Super Tuscans.

While it fell out of fashion in California, it's still widely planted in Washington State. You'll also find some interesting merlots from New York's Long Island region. And in Chile, it's popular for blending with the local carménère grape.

THE ESSENTIALS

☐ If you don't like tannins, opt for a merlot over a cabernet sauvignon.

☐ **Myth: All Bordeaux is expensive.** Go into the Right Bank of Bordeaux to find far more affordable producers.

☐ That line in *Sideways* was funny, but don't let it be your mantra. You'll miss out.

LOOK FOR

→ **Château Bourgneuf**, Pomerol, France

→ **Domaine de Galouchey**, Bordeaux, France

→ **Miani**, Friuli, Italy

→ **Coléte**, Napa Valley, California

→ **Bodega Chacra**, Patagonia, Argentina

→ **Montes**, Valle del Colchaqua, Chile

RED ● MERLOT

67

Pinot Noir

KEY FACTS

🐑 FLAVORS
Cherry
Strawberry
Cranberry
Violet
Mushroom
Spice

▷ DESCRIPTORS
Fruity
Earthy
Complex

◉ MAJOR GROWING REGIONS
Burgundy
Sonoma
Sta. Rita Hills
New Zealand
South Africa

💬 BY ANY OTHER NAME
Pinot nero
Spätburgunder

→ *Complex and fascinating, sophisticated pinot noir is the most challenging—and rewarding—red.*

Until the movie *Sideways* came out, Americans were more into rich, dark, concentrated, and oaky reds like cabernet and merlot. Now the thin-skinned red grape—which requires cool growing conditions, an expert winemaker, and a seasoned drinker to appreciate its stateliness and subtlety—is the popular one.

Although it's a diva in the vineyard, pinot isn't a powerful varietal. Rather, it's known for its sweet red-berry fruit, and its delicacy, freshness, and elegance. With its seductive finesse and long finish, once you've tasted a fully mature and peaking pinot noir from Burgundy, you'll be hooked for life. (Whether you become one of those people who go deep into learning to understand the region's complicated allocations—something that takes serious collectors years to master—is up to you.)

While the grape originated in Burgundy, it is also grown in Champagne, the Loire Valley, Alsace, and Jura. Germany produces some interesting clones, like Spätburgunder, at really competitive prices. California, Oregon, Chile, and Argentina are also in the game. New Zealand, Australia, and South Africa are producing them, but keep in mind that pinots grown in warm climates taste jammy and are, in my opinion at least, less appealing.

The best pinot noirs are about finesse, delicacy, and vibrancy. The moment you've tasted a perfectly mature pinot, you'll chase this experience for the rest of your life!

LOOK FOR

→ **Domaine Marquis d'Angerville**, Burgundy, France

→ **Domaine Sylvain Pataille**, Burgundy, France

→ **Benedikt Baltes**, Franken, Germany

→ **Rust en Vrede Vineyards**, Stellenbosch, South Africa

→ **Barda**, Patagonia, Argentina

→ **Joseph Swan**, Russian River Valley, California

→ **Bergström**, Willamette Valley, Oregon

→ **J. Hofstätter**, Alto Adige, Italy

THE ESSENTIALS

☐ Pinot noir isn't a blockbuster like cabernet sauvignon. It's much subtler and, to be honest, not as easy to understand.

☐ Because pinot is such a diva, you pay a price for it. Don't go below $20.

☐ **Myth: All pinots are great.** I wish!

☐ Pinots are pale or translucent in color. Really dark ones have been blended with a darker varietal.

RED ● PINOT NOIR

■ jammy
Tasting term for wine with concentrated fruit and a rich mouthfeel.

Syrah

> **→** *This dark, powerful red is rich in flavor and smooth in acid and tannins, with a seductive sweetness and peppery finish, making it a* ==*perfect starting point for discovering wine.*==

KEY FACTS

FLAVORS
Black pepper
Olive
Dark fruit like
blueberries and
blackberries

DESCRIPTORS
Juicy
Lush
Spice-driven

MAJOR GROWING REGIONS
Australia
Northern Rhône

BY ANY OTHER NAME
Shiraz

Australian shiraz (aka syrah) is the gateway red for beginners. One of the finest red varietals, syrah also currently happens to be trendy among sommeliers.

Interestingly, syrahs are really good for the first couple of years, with their black olive/black pepper components. They even have the iron quality of blood. Their high-pitched acids make them appear lighter than they actually are. Then they close up for seven to ten years before they really blossom, showing aromas of truffle,

My favorite steak wine!

porcini, dried leaves, and a seductive red currant flavor. These aren't chugging wines for your next party, as they demand a level of attention from the drinker.

The varietal is practically synonymous with Australian wine, which can range from affordable to the country's most famous, Grange by Penfolds (it fetches consistently high scores from critics). Syrah was once so big and jammy you could have practically spooned it from your glass, but young winemakers are now moving toward a relatively lighter, more French style that's lower in alcohol and has more layered flavors. And it's increasingly popular in Sonoma, where some vineyards are also making wines that are getting close to their French counterparts. But France has been working with syrah for centuries, and has mastered the form. Try starting out light with a Crozes-Hermitage or Saint-Joseph, and work your way up to a fine Côte-Rôtie, a majestic Hermitage, and a fierce Cornas. (The first two might be the least expensive syrah yet from a smaller appellation.)

While Australian shiraz is a great starting wine, their cousins in the Northern Rhône region require a little "drinking experience," as syrah challenges the taster much more owing to its *terroir*, winemaking style, and perfect balance of concentrated fruit, supple tannins, and elevated acidity in its youth. Once you've understood syrah, you'll get your reward!

RED ● SYRAH

LOOK FOR

→ **Piedrasassi**, Santa Barbara County, California

→ **Domaine Jamet**, Rhône, France

→ **Alain Graillot**, Rhône, France

→ **Domaine Jean-Louis Chave**, Rhône, France

→ **Pax**, Sonoma, California

→ **Mullineux**, Swartland, South Africa

→ **Jamsheed**, Yarra Valley, Australia

THE ESSENTIALS

☐ A wine salesperson recently told me, "Cabernet is a no-brainer. Pinot noir? We just have to make sure it gets delivered. But syrah is a hard sell." For me, though, I would buy an average syrah over an average cabernet any day. While cab can be a little commercial or one-dimensional, syrah literally pushes the winemaker to work harder, since the grape is so demanding in the vineyard.

☐ I think of syrah as the Meryl Streep of wines! If you have a great one, it's so elegant and striking, with genuine character, supercharged with a black olive component (the one characteristic Ms. Streep does not share). You won't have conversation about anything other than the glass of wine in front of you.

☐ Australian syrah is undergoing a renaissance, but unfortunately, few of those more finessed bottles are being imported to the US. If you want something more nuanced, look to France and Sonoma in the US.

Nebbiolo

➡️

KEY FACTS

👅 **FLAVORS**
Rose
Violet
Cranberry
Cherry
Licorice
Dried leaves
Tar
Leather

▶ **DESCRIPTORS**
Floral
Fragrant
Fruity
Earthy
Tannic

📍 **MAJOR GROWING REGIONS**
Piemonte
Lombardy

💬 **BY ANY OTHER NAME**
Spanna
Chiavennasca
Picotendro

■ **astringent**
An astrigent wine causes a drying, slightly puckery feeling owing to tannins that bind to proteins on your tongue.

A connoisseur's wine, often at a connoisseur's price. Once you've tasted an aged Barolo or Barbaresco, though, you'll understand why wine people love them so much.

The most fragrant red varietal, nebbiolo is elegant and structured: Its high acid and tannins mean that in blind tastings it is often confused with pinots from Burgundy, especially older bottles. (Those high tannins, however, can sometimes make the wine come across as astringent in its youth; these wines can be sulky, self-involved adolescents until they're about five years old.) The varietal originated close to the town of Alba in the Piemonte region of northwestern Italy, which is famous for its white truffles. When it comes to expensive tastes, it seems that what grows together goes together.

It's believed that nebbiolo got its name from *nebbia*, the Italian word for "fog," which frequently rolls through this Alps-facing region in the fall, thereby allowing the grapes to mature slowly and late. Barolo and Barbaresco are the most famous appellations, but they come at a serious price. These are investment wines that you want to hold on to—you'll thank yourself in twenty, thirty, forty years! In the meantime, it's best to start with a regular nebbiolo d'Alba, which is often just artificially <u>downgraded</u> young-vine Barolos and Barbarescos. Keep an eye out for Perbacco by Vietti, an absolute steal at around $25.

Given that this varietal is so particular to where it's grown, it's seldom found outside of Italy. There are some other nebbiolo clones found farther north, such as lampia, which tends to be a bit lighter, as are the wines from the Ghemme and Gattinara appellations. In the Alpine climate of the Lombardy province, nebbiolo is known as chiavennasca, and is made in a bit more rustic (but no less delicious) style.

LOOK FOR

→ **Vietti**, Piemonte, Italy

→ **G. B. Brulotto**, Piemonte, Italy

→ **Clendenen Family Vineyards**, Santa Maria Valley, California

→ **Antichi Vigneti di Cantalupo**, Piemonte, Italy

→ **Vallana**, Piemonte, Italy

→ **Ar.Pe.Pe.**, Lombardy, Italy

THE ESSENTIALS

☐ **Myth: Nebbiolo is always $$.** Well, go outside of Barolo to look for nebbiolo d'Alba and you'll find some steals. Or go up into the northern regions and look for ones from Ghemme or Gattinara.

☐ Nebbiolo is phenomenal to drink in the fall with rich food.

☐ If you look a little bit, you can buy aged nebbiolos for not too much money. There are real steals!

☐ Looking for a wine that you can hang on to for a while? Nebbiolo is a great bet.

RED ● NEBBIOLO

■ <u>downgraded</u>
Rows of vineyards are downgraded, or declassified, when the winemakers plant new vines.

And a Few More Noteworthy Varietals I'd Like to Mention

Assyrtiko

Citrusy, Smoky, Green Apple

This high-quality white grape, native to the Greek island of Santorini, has spread over the islands and become increasingly popular. I think of it as a Greek interpretation of Chablis, with perhaps a little more lushness in the fruit due to its sunny southern location. It's great matched with seafood. The varietal's higher acidity means that many sommeliers and wine professionals really love it, so you're going to be seeing more of it on wine lists. Another great thing about these wines: They're inexpensive.

My favorites are Gaia Estate Thalassitis, Argyros Estate Atlantis White, and Hatzidakis Santorini Assyrtiko.

Cabernet Franc

Dark Fruit, Spicy, Structured

For those who like a little spice and freshness with their dark fruit. Because it's not that easy-drinking, this Bordelais variety, which hails from Spain, is often used for blending with cabernet sauvignon; on the Right Bank it's used to spice up the unctuous merlot. While cabernet franc from cooler regions and vintages can have a green, vegetal flavor (think bell pepper or jalapeño) that some find off-putting, climate change seems to be taking care of this problem. In the Loire Valley, look for the appellations Chinon, Bourgueil, and the powerful Saumur-Champigny. On the Tuscan coast, cabernet franc delivers rich and juicy examples, while in Friuli Venezia Giulia, they're lighter and more spice-driven.

Gamay
Fruity, Floral, Fun

This is what you're drinking when you drink Beaujolais. Gamay delights with its juiciness, unpretentiousness, and seemingly endless drinkability. (In French natural wine circles, this chuggable quality is referred to as *glou-glou*, the sound it makes when you pour it straight down your throat.) We should add affordability to this list, too, as you can get a great bottle for well under $30. And unlike wines from neighboring areas, gamay wants to be drunk while it's young.

The Beaujolais region suffered a serious setback thanks to all that "Beaujolais Nouveau" business, in which just-corked bottles are unleashed on France every fall, announced by a forced marketing hoopla. But a handful of winemakers are turning the area away from the big *négociants*. Look for organically farmed bottles from Marcel Lapierre, Jean-Louis Dutraive, Julien Sunier and Antoine Sunier, and Jean Foillard, to name a few. In the US, some Californian winemakers, such as Pax Mahle and Arnot-Roberts, are making some really interesting gamays.

Grenache
Fragrant, Red Fruit, Leather

Mostly known for its starring role in the powerful Châteauneuf-du-Pape, you'll also find this fruit-forward variety in Spain, where it's known as garnatxa or garnacha. This grape has the tendency to develop high alcohol levels and always offers a little cherry or strawberry flavor. There's an elegance, but the ABV has to be in check.

Albariño
(See page 107.)

■ *négociants*
Companies that buy grapes from different vineyards and sell them to winemakers.

Listan Blanco (Palomino)
Citrusy, Savory, Fresh

There are some great examples of now-fashionable Canary Island wines made from this white grape, which give me hope for the new Spanish wine market. In the country's Jerez region, home of Sherry, this grape is known as *palomino fino*. There, it's a rather neutral varietal, but the *terroir* of the Canary Islands gives listan blanco quite some character. Look for wines from Envinate and Bodega Juan Francisco Fariña.

Malbec
Dark Fruit, Bold, Spicy

In America, malbec took over as the darling red once California cabernet became too expensive. This grape originated in the Cahors region of southwestern France, though these days it's commonly associated with Argentina, where it's more fruit-forward and really inky in color. Malbec is very straightforward, juicy, lush, and easy enough and can go from rich and concentrated into an almost pinot-ish direction. This is a great steak wine, not to mention always affordable.

In Cahors, try Château Lagrézette and Château de Haute-Serre. From Argentina, I'm a fan of Luca, Mendel, and Esperando a los Bárbaros from Michelini Bros.

Sangiovese
Bright, Earthy, Dark Red Fruit, Peppery

If you travel to central Italy, especially to Tuscany, chances are that your red wine is sangiovese, or at least has some of the grape in it. Its noticeable acidity and high-toned dark fruit (think sour cherry and plum) make it the perfect base for Chianti—both the region and the wine after which it is named. My favorite producers are Montevertine, especially their entry-level Pian del Ciampolo, which is based on sangiovese. Fèlsina and Castello di Ama also make delicious Chiantis. The sangiovese grosso clone, now called Brunello, delivers powerful wines and is among Italy's most famous. Also try its little brother, Rosso di Montalcino. Personally, I love the sangiovese from Corsica (called nielluccio).

Key Wine-making Regions

➤ Where a wine comes from can tell you quite a bit about what you'll taste in the glass—knowledge that will help you navigate wine lists and store shelves. As you'll hopefully experience from the next-level tasting on page 228, a chardonnay grown in France will taste different from one hailing from, say, California or South Africa.

That has as much to do with the soil, elevation, and climate of a particular area—which can vary even between neighboring vineyards—as it does with winemaking styles and traditions, which can also vary from one vineyard to the next. But each country still manages to express itself on the tongue. Take Austrian Grüner Veltliners. Their signatures include the minerality that the country's rocky soils and loess (loamy sediment) impart to the grape and the greener, more sustainable growing practices that have long been the norm in this forward-thinking country. A Grüner grape grown in, say, loamy soil in the dry, sunny hills of Napa just won't taste the same.

There are an endless number of wine regions, and "new" countries enter the game each year. Thanks to wine's growing popularity, you'll now find bottles hailing from China, Sweden, England, and more. For this book, I'll focus on the essentials, with each country followed by its main grapes. See which country's characteristics speak to you, then do a little "traveling" the next time you order a glass.

Influential Factors of Wine Regions

▲

Terroir

→ *Terroir* is one of those intimidating wine terms that get thrown around a lot regarding a wine's flavor. As we defined it earlier, the French word refers to how the soil, climate, and terrain of a vineyard are discernible on the tongue. Not only do the grapes derive a certain quality from the minerals present in the soil, be it sand, clay, limestone, or rich loam, the microclimate and altitude or position specific to that vineyard also have a unique impact. (The idea of the minerals affecting flavor has not been scientifically proved. In fact, in 2013, researchers at UC Davis found that fungi and bacteria might play a bigger part in "geotagging" a wine and affecting its flavor.)

This is very easy to test. Take the French vineyards Bâtard-Montrachet and Bienvenues-Bâtard-Montrachet. They're separated by a six-foot-wide path, but the wines they produce taste very different. That's because Bâtard is situated on a gentle slope above Bienvenues, and the thin soil, situated on a bed of limestone, is deeper and more clayey at the bottom of the slope because of rain runoff. This is an expensive example, of course, but you can find other winemakers who bottle from different sections of their vineyard. Try the same vintage and same producer and compare.

You can taste *terroir* in food, too. A friend of mine in London, who'd always been skeptical about the concept, became obsessed with the arugula on Italy's Amalfi Coast, where the spiky leaves have a much spicier and more intense flavor. His hotel gave him some seeds, which he planted in his London garden. When the arugula finally popped up during the gray, chilly spring, he was disappointed to find that the leaves were not only round, they tasted as bland as the supermarket stuff. I laughed and said to him, "You forgot to factor in the *terroir*! Just because you plant vines from Pétrus in London doesn't mean you're going to make world-class wine."

Warm vs. Cool Climates

→ Whether the vines had a long, hot, dry summer or a short rainy one has a big impact on a wine's sweetness, acidity, body, and even alcohol level. Warm climates tend to produce bigger, rounder flavors and boozier wines, while cooler temperatures result in wines with fresher fruit and crunchier acidity, not to mention lower alcohol.

I wish it were as easy as making a map of the world that neatly divided itself into warm and cool climates, but elevation and proximity to water within a region change that equation. (Think of the sunny Sonoma Valley versus Sonoma's foggy coast . . .) And, getting geekier still, you can have a cool year in a warm climate, or vice versa. Mind blown? Welcome to my job.

DID YOU KNOW...

. . . that grapes can get sunburned? And no, it's not pretty: Those leathery skins and sugary flesh attract wasps, which burrow into the grapes, exposing them to oxygen and increasing volatile acidity and vinegar compounds—and those aren't tastes that everyone loves.

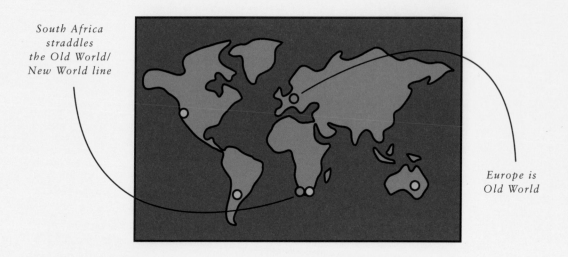

South Africa
straddles
the Old World/
New World line

Europe is
Old World

▲
What's That New World/Old World Thing About?

→ Basically, any wine not made in Europe is considered New World. While wine snobs used to consider Old World wines superior and New World wines cheaper and lower-quality, today even they concede that incredible wines are being made around the globe.

To generalize, we say that New World countries have warm climates—look to Australia, California, Argentina—and the Old World climates are cooler. Of course, there are exceptions in each country. With global warming, all bets are off, and flavor profiles are changing year by year: These days you'll find wines on Bordeaux's Right Bank with a California-like 15 to 16% ABV, thanks to record-breaking hot summers, and some winemakers are harvesting early just to preserve some of the fruit's acid.

It's also assumed that New World wines have lusher fruit and therefore higher alcohol thanks

to their higher sugar content, and that New World winemakers love to add oak. But that's changing, especially in California and parts of Australia. The idea that all New World reds are big and jammy is nonsense! That said, I can taste the ripeness of California grapes even in wines made in a more European (less-oaked) style. And I do believe that New World wines tend to have simpler aromas and show their soil less readily.

It's *not* a generalization to say that the Old World is tied to wine laws. A New World winemaker can decide to put underripe grapes in the mash to balance out a warm year's harvest or "color in" his pinot with darker grapes to make it look higher-quality. In France, he'd be sent to jail.

There is one country that straddles the Old World/New World flavor line perfectly. Among sommeliers, we say that in a blind tasting, if you're not sure if it's from the New World or the Old World, think South Africa! Its wines combine the lushness of a warm climate with the elegance of a cool one—often a killer combination.

ASK ALDO

Are there some regions that are more reliable in quality than others?

☐ <u>Bordeaux</u> is at the top of my list, as much as I hate to say it! (I hope Eric Ripert never reads this page: I've been fighting him on his love of Bordeaux since day one at Le Bernardin!)

☐ <u>Austrian whites</u> are incredibly reliable, no matter how low the price.

☐ The <u>Sonoma Coast</u> is rather consistent, though it depends on the producer.

☐ With <u>Mendoza malbecs</u>, you know what you're getting. Are they the greatest? No, but they're reliable.

☐ The <u>Loire Valley</u> is pretty steady, especially in Sancerre.

☐ <u>Tuscany</u> can be safe—for a steeper price.

☐ <u>New Zealand sauvignon blancs</u> are straightforward. Whether or not you like them is another matter!

All About Appellations

➡️ Once you start learning about the greatest wines in the world, France will be mentioned immediately. It's the first country that created an appellation system, meaning wines are analyzed and researched according to their *terroir* (soil, climate, exposure, and consistency of the wines over a decade). Originally called the AOC (Appellation d'Origine Controlée), this designation was recently changed to AOP (the *P* is for Protégée, or "protected"). This system is strictly confined to villages, varietals, yields, minimal alcohol levels, and typicity of the wine. French winemakers don't have the freedom to plant whatever grapes they want without having their wine downgraded and removed from the designation. However, a growing number of younger natural winemakers take a rebellious pride in producing wines under the catchalls "Vin de Pays" ("wine from the country") or "Vin de France" ("wine from France") label, its lowest designation.

In Italy, a dizzying number of small local varieties are protected by the DOC (Denominazione di Origine Controllata) laws, similar to France's AOP. On top of that, they created another one for more "special" wines: the DOCG (Denominazione di Origine Controllata e Garantita). As governments change in Italy faster than they have a chance to pass a law, this system is leaping behind the trade to support winemakers. When the French grapes cabernet sauvignon, merlot, and syrah came to Tuscany, they were labeled as "Vino da Tavola" ("table wine"), as the varietals weren't anchored by the law. It also meant that both Italy's flagship wines, like its Super Tuscans—blends that include French varietals—and the simple bulk Tetra Pak stuff were in the same category. That's when the IGT (Indicazione Geografica Tipica) was created to separate them. It's an area-/region-specific designation with no further distinction.

When it comes to officially designated wine-growing regions in the US, the closest we have to the European appellation system are AVAs (American Viticultural Areas), the boundaries of which are lightly governed.

Note that none of these designations indicate quality or merit. These labels are more about national pride in unique grapes.

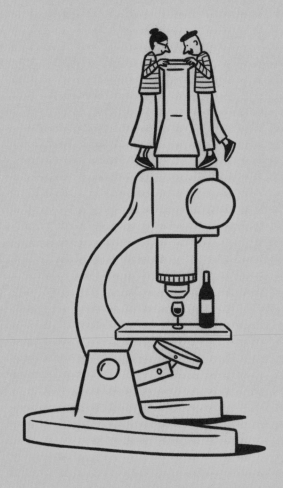

■ **appellation**
A legally defined geographical location that indicates where a wine is grown. In France, the appellation—known as an AOC or AOP— can also dictate the specific style of wine.

■ **typicity**
The character of a wine, typical of its style or region.

■ **downgraded**
Wines are "downgraded" or "declassified" by the vineyard when it has to tear out old vines and plant new ones. It's still grown on, say, a Barolo vineyard, it's just not labeled as such, hence the value. Top producers can make really tasty entry-level wines from these younger vines. So in this instance, it's not necessarily a bad thing.

■ **AVAs**
American Viticultural Areas, or our take on the appellation system. This indicates a federally designated wine-growing region.

France

→ **Wine originated in ancient Georgia. The Greeks and Romans later developed it further, sure, but it is the French who honed their growing and winemaking techniques over centuries—make that millennia. That's why today the French are most associated with the art and craft, not to mention the lifestyle, of wine.**

Around the world today, you'll find winemakers planting pinot noir, cabernet sauvignon, syrah, and chardonnay. All French! You'll find them aging wines in oak barrels. Also French! And building entire luxury conglomerates on the bottles of their labor. Super French.

There are eleven key wine regions in France, each with its own particular soil, climate, and, you could say, approach. From the *grands châteaux* of Bordeaux and Burgundy to the scrappy, farmer-led natural movement in the Auvergne and Jura regions, everyone is dealing with fluctuating weather conditions that require the utmost attention. It's care—and pride—that you can taste.

France is maintaining tradition while evolving. If you ever get the chance to listen to Alexandre Chartogne talk about how long it took him to understand his vineyards, you'll be blown away. These winemakers are committed to their land and want to pass it on to the next generation(s).

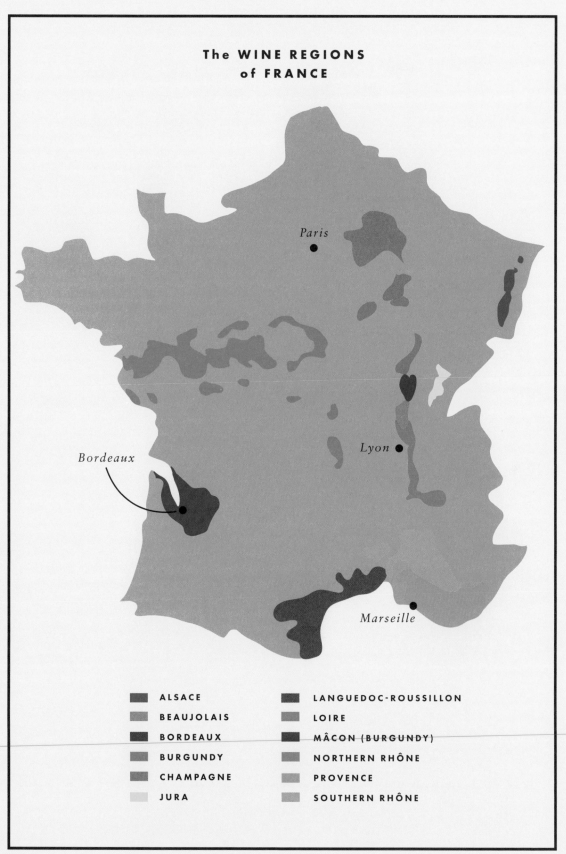

The WINE REGIONS of FRANCE

Paris

Lyon

Bordeaux

Marseille

FRANCE

ALSACE

BEAUJOLAIS

BORDEAUX

BURGUNDY

CHAMPAGNE

JURA

LANGUEDOC-ROUSSILLON

LOIRE

MÂCON (BURGUNDY)

NORTHERN RHÔNE

PROVENCE

SOUTHERN RHÔNE

● Alsace

→ **RED**
Pinot noir

WHITE
Riesling, Gewürztraminer, Silvaner (or sylvaner), pinot gris, pinot blanc, Muscat

A little bit French in their traditions, a little bit German in their comfort with residual sugar, Alsatian wines have a food-friendly richness that's easy to love.

This northeastern region on the border of Germany has a long history of going back and forth between the Germans and the French. One of the (many) consequences is that it's the only region in France that labels wines with their grape varietal rather than their appellation, as is done in Germany. Ninety percent of this region's wines are white. They used to be on the sweeter side, but today's tendency is toward a pure, dryish, aromatic style, often with a honeyed, smoky scent. (In fact, starting in 2008, standard bottles of Riesling *must* be dry.) There are fifty-one grand crus in the region, which will be specified on the label and are far more price-friendly than Burgundy's. This is an accessible region with extremely food-friendly wines. As my Le Bernardin colleague Sarah Thomas says, Alsace is a great entry point for people who won't try Riesling because they don't like sweet.

■ grand crus
Designated areas of quality. Premier cru is the ranking below grand cru.

● Burgundy

→ **RED**
Pinot noir

WHITE
Chardonnay, aligoté

The majestic area, Burgundy delivers the finest wines in the world, whether red or white.

An obsessive quest for quality has been taking place for centuries in Burgundy's picturesque foothills and flatlands. That dedication to winemaking, combined with its history and a relatively cool climate, results in some of the world's best wines. Here it's not about the power. It's about finesse and how much is going on in the glass. Whether it's a peaking red Burgundy, made from the pinot noir grape, with its perfectly integrated tannins, seductively delicate fruit, and trufflelike quality; or a great chardonnay, with its fresh, powerful butterscotch aroma, elegant green fruit, and honeysuckle components, there's a reason these wines are fiendishly expensive and obsessively sought after.

Because of its multiple levels of organization, it really takes time to understand this complex region, located between Dijon and Mâcon. Burgundy (which the French refer to as Bourgogne) counts four regions—five, if you include Beaujolais: Côte-d'Or, Côte Chalonnaise, Côte Mâconnais, and the satellite appellation Auxerrois. Seems simple, right? But then, for example, the east-facing vineyards of the Côte-d'Or are divided into Côte de Nuits (mainly for reds) and Côte de Beaune (reds and whites). Some vineyards at the top of the pyramid are classified as having premier cru and grand cru status. And so on.

Why do people bother to learn? Well, once you've tasted Burgundy's finest—and therefore most expensive—pinot noirs and powerful, oak-aged chardonnays, you'll understand why some people dedicate years to learning how to decipher the region's labyrinthine designations.

All About Crus

➡️ At its most basic, <u>cru</u>, or "growth," means that a panel of wine brokers in the mid-1800s classified the vineyard as superior in its *terroir*—best grapes, soil, exposure—consistently delivering high-quality wines. Bordeaux and Burgundy each uses its own cru classification system, with grand cru ("great growth") ranking highest, followed by premier cru, village appellation, and regional appellation.

Is it worth it to pay significantly more for a bottle from a château that was deemed worthy in 1855? It all depends on the winemaker. Let's put it this way: Kobe is considered the world's best beef, but if the chef overcooks it, it's no better than one from Outback Steakhouse.

Few other countries have such a regimented system. Italy might put "cru" on a label to indicate a single-vineyard wine, but it's not a mark of quality. The closest things are Grosses Gewächs ("GG") from Germany and Erste Lage from Austria. These terms mean other things, too, like the fact that grand cru status is determined by a government division while Grosses Gewächs are appointed by a private club, but that's a whole other story . . .

How do I navigate the Burgundy cru classifications?

My advice? Your best bet is to work slowly up through the ranks until you reach the peak, so you really understand the differences. Start with a bottle designated "Bourgogne blanc" (or "rouge") from unclassified vineyards, often located in the foothills or flatlands. If you're into it, next try a village level, from vineyards from a particular village located closer to the (most desirable) hills. You'll definitely notice more body. The chardonnays, for example, are not as light and citrusy. You can find some great values at this level, especially downgraded wines from big-name producers. Now try a *lieu-dit* (unclassified single vineyard) wine before you go up into the prime real estate of the hills to a premier cru and, finally, a grand cru. The grand crus hail from the middle of the hill, where the sun hits the vines at the perfect angle, and the soil is rich from erosion. They're also the most expensive, as in put a zero (or two . . . or three) behind what you'd pay for a Bourgogne blanc. Now, you decide if it's worth it!

FRANCE

▪ <u>cru</u>
A French vineyard that is recognized for exceptional quality based on a classification system dating from the 1800s.

● Beaujolais

→ **RED**
Gamay

WHITE
Chardonnay

From punch line to poster child for easy, fun, affordable reds.

This area, just south of Burgundy in central France, has undergone quite a change in the last decade. Once associated with cheap wine that was sold practically immediately after bottling, it's home to the now-fashionable gamay grape. The area is super charming to visit, with fantastic people making unpretentious wines that are simply delicious. While there are still a lot of large *négociants* making wine, many small producers are applying considerable passion to their work, and the natural wine movement has taken root here. You'll rarely see a well-crafted wine labeled as "Beaujolais." Instead, look for one of the ten Beaujolais crus, with such labels as Morgon, Fleurie, Régnié, and Moulin-à-Vent.

CÔTE ROANNAISE

→ Beaujolais is no longer anything new. But the Côte Roannaise in the Loire Valley is home to producers of some delicious, easygoing gamays. My favorite is **Domaine Sérol**: These wines have a sexy drinkability. Inexpensive and very tasty! I especially love their Éclat de Granité, which is about $21 a bottle.

● Bordeaux

→ **RED**
Cabernet sauvignon, merlot

WHITE
Sauvignon blanc, sémillon

Big and rich. There's a reason kings have been drinking these powerful wines for centuries.

The legendary wines of this region in the southwest deserve special recognition for their longevity on the palate and how beautifully they perform in the glass. Bordeaux wines are the benchmark for classic great wines, and they consistently age very well. (When you ask critics for their lifetime top ten, I promise you there will be at *least* two Bordeaux in there.) Not only is the *terroir* excellent and the access to the cooling ocean breezes beneficial for the grapes, they've been making wine here since before the 1700s, so they've had time to get it right. The proximity to a harbor also means that they've been selling to the British—who have very fine palates for wine—for centuries. The bar was set very, very high a long time ago, and things are still made in a traditional way to meet classic standards.

The LEFT & RIGHT BANKS of BORDEAUX

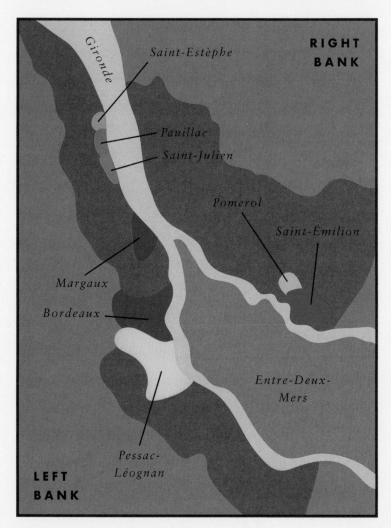

RIGHT BANK

Gironde

Saint-Estèphe

Pauillac

Saint-Julien

Pomerol

Saint-Émilion

Margaux

Bordeaux

Entre-Deux-Mers

Pessac-Léognan

LEFT BANK

SOHM SECRET

How to Find a Bordeaux Bargain
Should you discover that you love Bordeaux and are ready to spend a little more, don't focus on recent vintages, which are snapped up faster than *Hamilton* tickets. Instead, you'll find terrific value in aged Bordeaux, often for far less than newer bottles. And because Bordeaux only gets better with time, you're buying something you could actually drink now. Win-win!

FRANCE

The region is not quite as complex to parse as Burgundy. The Gironde estuary separates Bordeaux into the Left and Right Banks. The **cabernet sauvignon–dominated Left Bank** (the appellations of Saint-Julien, Saint-Estèphe, Pauillac, Margaux, and Pessac-Léognan) is much more on the commercial side, with the most famous of the châteaux absorbed by luxury conglomerates. The **merlot-driven Right Bank** (Pomerol, Saint-Émilion) is home to small, artisanal farmers—much more my speed. I also have to mention the **Entre-Deux-Mers** region: The farmers here deliver inexpensive whites

made with an ethos that's far from the tour-guide châteaux on the other side of the Gironde.

Producers in Bordeaux call their wineries *châteaux*, or "castles," but often it's only just a normal house. The Médoc was classified in 1855 and few changes have been made to it, so don't get stuck on trying only the famous first growths (premiers crus), as the wineries have often long since changed ownership. For instance, Château Pontet-Canet, designated a fifth growth, converted to biodynamic farming and forward-thinking cellar techniques and is currently the shining star of Pauillac.

Cristal is 100 percent biodynamic starting in 2020.

Champagne

→ **RED** Pinot noir, pinot meunier | **WHITE** Chardonnay

My Five Favorite Champagne Houses

Louis Roederer
Deutz
Dom Pérignon
Krug
Billecart-Salmon

My Six Favorite Grower Champagnes

Agrapart & Fils
Chartogne-Taillet
Frédéric Savart
Bérêche & Fils
Pierre Péters
Christophe Mignon (Best value, $50)

Just as Champagne isn't only for birthdays and New Year's Eve, the region isn't only filled with fancy commercial houses. Indie upstarts are revolutionizing the game.

Champagne is a specifically designated area about an hour and a half east of Paris. The zone was the last region the Romans set up for winemaking because it was too cold. Anything bubbly produced outside of this area is simply called sparkling wine (or crémant, if it's from one of eight designated regions outside of Champagne). It's typically a blend of the above three varietals listed above—though four more are allowed within the designation.

The typically commercial region was revolutionized in the mid-'80s, when Anselme Selosse took over his family's grand cru vineyards. He turned away from the high-yield, low-quality grapes that were common at the time. Instead, he focused on the fruit. He embraced organic farming, smaller yields, and naturally occurring yeast for fermentation; he decreased the number of new oak barrels for aging and reduced the amount of added sulfur dioxide (SO_2). Although he was seen as a heretic at the time, in 1994 he was named France's best winemaker in every category, an unheard-of honor. And today, not only will you find more independent spirits like him in Champagne, but the big houses have begun to follow his lead, too, making it an exciting time to enjoy the food-loving wines from this region.

THE (CORPORATE) HOUSE THAT GROWERS LOVE

→ When I was traveling in Champagne for a week, I asked all the growers I met which big house they respected the most. They all came up with one answer—which never happens with farmers! They all said <u>Louis Roederer</u>. Half of their grapes are farmed organically, and they have a forward-thinking philosophy. They talk to their farmers, they do seminars, they pay people fairly. They have tremendous respect for the cellar master. And they're good humans. Champagne is an area dictated by the money, but Roederer is one of the smaller houses—there, quality comes first.

Try a few glasses and you'll understand the French saying, "With Burgundy, you <u>think</u> stupid things. With Bordeaux, you <u>say</u> stupid things. And with Champagne, you <u>do</u> them."

Why I Love Grower Champagne

➤ If you've been to an indie wine store, you probably didn't recognize a lot of the labels on the Champagne shelves. That's because some of the most exciting winemaking going on in that region is taking place at small vineyards, where men and women are crafting Champagnes that have incredible personalities, with fascinating quirks that you'll never find at the big houses. Put simply, a grower Champagne is made by a small farmer who owns his land and produces, sells, and markets his own wine. At first I stayed with the big houses because they're more consistent, but I've evolved to love grower Champagne with a passion.

Think of it this way: Houses like Moët & Chandon, Veuve Clicquot, and others are luxury companies and must produce a consistently excellent product that's worthy of the price tag. They buy grapes from all over the region, combining multiple wines until they get the right blend—one that consumers will immediately recognize as theirs. Let's face it: We live in a world where we expect things to taste the same every time . . . forever!

House Champagnes tend to be a little sweeter. That's because, unlike the single-vineyard fruit harvested by growers, they blend grapes from across the region that aren't necessarily grown to maturity. In order to balance out the harsh acidity of grapes, they add sugar.

I think of grower Champagne, which is often farmed biodynamically, as being like an apple from the farmers' market: It might have a brown spot and not be presented in a polished pyramid, but the flavor is incredible, and I know it wasn't treated with a bunch of chemicals, harvested while green, coated with wax, and shipped here from South America. Just saying!

The quality of grower Champagnes can zigzag based on that year's weather, which can make them a bit of a gamble.

I encourage you to try for yourself. Do a side-by-side tasting with a bottle of, say, entry-level Moët and a bottle of Chartogne-Taillet Sainte Anne Brut. Hopefully you'll agree that small is beautiful.

FRANCE

○ Jura

→ **RED**
Pinot noir, poulsard, trousseau

WHITE
Chardonnay, savignan

If you like natural wines, this is a region you'll want to explore—especially the whites.

Small producers making highly individual wines dominate this Swiss-bordering region east of Burgundy, just an hour's drive from Geneva. As Burgundy wines became more and more expensive, people started to look for alternatives, finding some great, mineral-driven wines in this area.

SAVOIE

→ Jura is already known for its adventurous whites. But the neighboring Savoie, with its local white varieties, is what's really interesting me these days. There, Domaine Belluard focuses on the white grape grignet, bringing out its unique personality. (Try their sparkling Les Perles du Mont Blanc.) Domaine des Ardoisières focuses on local and also rare varietals, such as the red persan grape, planted in small, steep microparcels.

● Languedoc-Roussillon

→ **RED**
Grenache, Syrah, carignan, cinsault

WHITE
Grenache blanc, muscat

Powerful bargains to be found in a sea of so-so wine.

This large region in the southwest always struggled with the reputation of producing bulk wine. But the *terroir* here is great, with many vineyards based on limestone and the sunny French Riviera climate making the wines a bit more powerful. Many interesting projects have popped up in the last decade, producing wines that can be rather inexpensive for what you get in the glass. But you have to taste a fair amount of them to find one that's good. The appellations of Minervois, Faugères, Saint-Chinian, and Corbières are producing really interesting, mostly blended wines with richness and excellent layers. Look for bottles by La Grange des Pères.

● Loire

→ **RED**
Gamay,
cabernet franc,
pinot noir

WHITE
Sauvignon blanc,
chenin blanc, melon de
Bourgogne (muscadet)

Accessible, inexpensive, and delicious discoveries to be made—especially when it comes to natural wine.

The château-dotted area around the Loire River south of Paris is one of France's most picturesque places to visit. It's also where the natural wine movement established its roots. The long region is divided into four very diverse areas.

The Central vineyards (upriver), known for its Sancerre and Pouilly-Fumé, produces some of the world's finest sauvignon blancs, not to mention some pinot noirs that make for light reds and zippy rosés.

If you're looking for a lot of value, taste the sauvignon blancs from the Menetou-Salon area west of there, which tends to be overlooked.

Around the historic city of Tours is the Touraine appellation, which produces wines from many varietals, ranging from dry to sweet. Vouvray and Montlouis, made from chenin blanc, are used for dry (*sec*) to medium-dry (*demi-sec*) to sweet (*moelleux*) wines. These wines are great values and age extremely well thanks to their high acidity.

The villages of Chinon and Bourgueil are known for their reds made from cabernet franc, which often take on the aroma of bell pepper. Anjou and Saumur, where cabernet franc and gamay are common, are also home to arguably the best chenin blancs.

Going down the Loire River to the Muscadet region, the local varietal is melon de Bourgogne (nothing to do with Burgundy). It's a bone-dry, super-fresh, savory wine that pairs brilliantly with seafood. Oddly, it doesn't have much traction, which means there are still great deals!

● Mâcon and Chalonnaise

→ **RED**
Pinot noir

WHITE
Chardonnay,
aligoté

The affordable alternative in Burgundy.

If you don't want to spend $100 but still want a great French chardonnay or pinot, this is where to look. There are no grand cru designations in this area, but that doesn't mean the quality's not there. In the northern part, you'll find some really interesting chardonnays from the AOPs Rully, Mercurey, and Montagny to the Côte Chalonnaise—they're not as complex as what you'll get in the Côte-d'Or, but certainly fun to drink, and at a cost that's easier to swallow.

The traditional kir is made from the citrusy, crisp white aligoté from the Bouzeron—just add a teaspoon or so of crème de cassis to a glass. The village of Givry produces the most interesting reds from this region. Try a bottle from Domaine Joblot.

The Côte Mâconnais region has become a new hot spot for interesting chardonnays made by famed Côte de Beaune producers like Lafon and Leflaive, who are investing in the region.

FRANCE

● Northern Rhône

→ **RED**
Syrah

WHITE
Viognier, marsanne,
roussanne

The wines in this extremely diverse region range from elegant to fierce and include some of the world's most famous syrahs.

The smaller of the two Rhône regions—and, I have to confess, my favorite. Why? For starters, most of these appellations are made up of the area's small wineries. The granite soil on these steep hills results in charismatic, often powerful wines with what I like to call "edges," or qualities that make you stop and think.

The viognier grape produces peach-perfumed, low-acid wines from the Condrieu appellation, while marsanne and roussanne are used to make the majestic Hermitage Blanc. (This is where Domaine Jean-Louis Chave bottles one of my desert-island wines.)

Northern Rhône reds are among my absolute favorites—let's just say they make up at least 50 percent of the reds in my basement cellar at home! I love their rich, concentrated flavors that magically have a high-pitched acidity and simultaneous brightness to their fruit. Nowhere does syrah deliver such distinct wines as in this steep-sloped area. The fragrant and elegant Côte-Rôties are found in one appellation; drive an hour south and you'll get the majestic Hermitages and the fierce Cornas. (Work your way up to bottles from Domaine Jamet, Ogier, Thierry Allemand, and Noël Verset.)

These wines can get expensive, but there are plenty of smart buys around. Stay in the appellation of Saint-Joseph and try the wines from Domaine Monier Perréol, Pierre Gonon, and the *négociant* Domaine Chave. The Collines Rhodaniennes also offers bang for the buck: Producers like Domaine Jamet and Domaine Faury produce lighter, more price-sensitive versions of the *grands vins* ("great wines").

○ Southern Rhône

→ **RED**
Grenache, syrah, cinsault | **WHITE**
Grenache blanc

The home of grenache, from humble to regal.

While wines from the Northern Rhône can be challenging to buy owing to their limited availability, it's quite the opposite down in the south. This large region, influenced by the cold mistral wind from the north that is tempered by the warming sandy soil, produces almost as much wine as Bordeaux—mostly the hearty, firm, inexpensive workhorse wine that is Côtes-du-Rhône.

Châteauneuf-du-Pape is the region's most famous appellation, a grenache-based blend of up to thirteen varieties. The thin-skinned grenache grape is known for its lighter-colored, high-alcohol wines that can creep up toward 16%. Downhill and east of Châteauneuf-du-Pape is Gigondas, known for its powerful reds. Tavel is a rosé appellation with some really rich rosés, made primarily from grenache and cinsault.

○ Provence

→ **RED**
Mourvèdre, syrah | **WHITE**
Marsanne, roussanne, grenache blanc, ugni blanc, vermintino, sémillon clairette

Provence stands for so much more than rosé.

This sunny, drop-dead-gorgeous southern region is best known for its easy-drinking rosés, which means that it's long been overlooked—until now. Sure, there's an ocean of celeb-driven producers in Provence, but there are also some really interesting, noteworthy winemakers who give you a lot of wine for your dollar. Triennes, owned by the highly regarded Burgundy producer Domaine Dujac, sells for $16 to $19. Same for a bottle of Château de Pampelonne. My favorite on the higher end of the rosé spectrum is Domaine Tempier, from the Bandol appellation, which delivers a lot of fruit and complexity in the glass.

Domaine Tempier's red Bandols are even more iconic. Most of Provence's powerful yet lighter reds are influenced by the mourvèdre grape, which lends richness and an almost baconlike smokiness. They taste great young and age really well. They're also delicious with fish when slightly chilled.

If you travel to the western tip of this surprisingly diverse region, toward the picturesque Les Baux-de-Provence in the Rhône delta, you shouldn't miss Domaine de Trévallon. They're not cheap, but won't disappoint. On a budget? Sulauze's Les Amis is a sound natural wine for just over $20.

FRANCE

Italy

→ **Italians know better than anyone how to sell lifestyle and emotions—and it doesn't stop at wine.**

We might think it's all Prosecco, pinot grigio, and Chianti, but this large, extremely diverse country has tons of local varieties that are way off the beaten path. There are over 350 authorized varieties, plus 500 more that have been documented. While the '80s and '90s saw winemakers jump into the global game by ripping out their indigenous grapes and planting more mass-marketable varieties like cabernet sauvignon, some of their children have been attempting to restore order by going back to what's grown best in their area for

centuries. Like Italian food, Italian wines are very region-specific when it comes to style and flavor, which makes for an incredible journey.

There is no country with a wider range of varietals than Italy. It takes real dedication and time to discover them all. They're interwoven into each province and culture and have been since the time of the ancient Romans, who are responsible for spreading winemaking throughout Europe. While Piemonte and Tuscany are the most famous regions, with world-renowned wines such as Barolo, Barbaresco, Brunello di Montalcino, and Super Tuscans, I'm often very happy with the simple house wine I find myself drinking in just about every restaurant there. In Italy, it's key to explore the lesser-known varietals!

The WINE REGIONS of ITALY

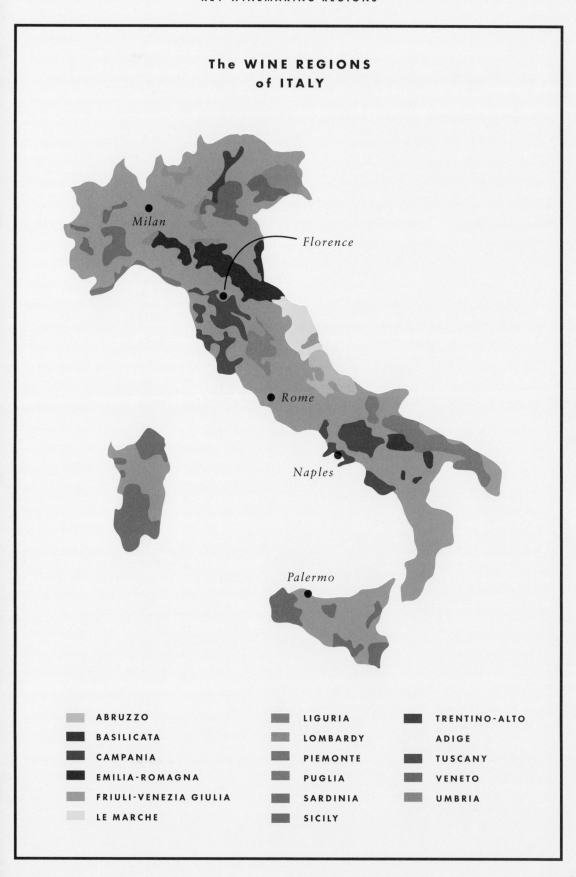

Milan

Florence

Rome

Naples

Palermo

ITALY

ABRUZZO

BASILICATA

CAMPANIA

EMILIA-ROMAGNA

FRIULI-VENEZIA GIULIA

LE MARCHE

LIGURIA

LOMBARDY

PIEMONTE

PUGLIA

SARDINIA

SICILY

TRENTINO-ALTO ADIGE

TUSCANY

VENETO

UMBRIA

● Campania

→ **RED**
Aglianico

WHITE
Greco, fiano

Crisp, fresh whites and rich reds that can age.

You'd think that it would be really hot in this southern region on the shin of the boot, but the elevation in the hills east of Naples produces some really interesting, fresh whites—I love the Fiano di Avellino from Ciro Picariello—and some robust reds. Be sure to try the rich red Taurasi! And aglianico is considered the nebbiolo of the south. I love drinking from this area.

○ Friuli

→ **RED**
Refosco, merlot

WHITE
Ribolla gialla, sauvignon blanc, pinot grigio, friulano

Look here for great whites and natural wines.

While Italy isn't necessarily famous for its white wines beyond pinot grigio, this progressive area north of Venice, bordering Austria and Slovenia, is one of the best areas for whites. The cool evenings and hot days of this maritime climate give the wines character and freshness, and sometimes they have more complexity due to fermentation in oak barrels. Friuli also produces a good amount of natural and skin-contact wines—this dynamic region is partly responsible for the natural wine movement in Italy. Friuli's reds, especially the refosco, are relatively easy and fruit-forward. This is the era when orange wines are really booming. Interesting fact: There has historically been a good exchange between the vineyards of Slovenia and the Italian region of Friuli, as the border runs through the vineyards.

● Lombardy

→ **RED**
Chiavennasca

SPARKLING
Pinot bianco, pinot grigio, chardonnay

Bold reds and big-ticket bubbles.

To me, the most interesting region here is Valtellina, in the steeply sloped Alpine valley in the far north, which is warmed by winds from the south. There they grow a local clone of nebbiolo called schiavenasca, which goes perfectly with the region's cold cuts and cheese-topped risottos. Vineyards like Grumello, Inferno, Sassella, and Valtellina Superiore produce structured, concentrated wines that are quite affordable. Franciacorta, Italy's high-profile sparkling wine area, comes close to Champagne in terms of quality—and, unfortunately, the price tag, too. This sparkler is a blend of chardonnay, pinot noir, and pinot bianco.

● Piemonte

→ **RED**
Nebbiolo, barbera, dolcetto

WHITE
Moscato (muscat), cortese

The fabled land of Barolo, Barbaresco, and white truffles.

Set just outside of Turin in the northwest, Piemonte, or Piedmont, is home to Italy's most famous wines. Up front are the two most majestic, nebbiolo-based wines, Barolo and Barbaresco. They have been scientifically proved to have the most <u>aromatic compounds</u> of any varietal, covering a full spectrum of components from cherries to strawberries, tar, flowers, mushrooms, and soil, and are magic when aged. (In fact, you wouldn't want to taste them too early: When young, all those tannins can be too astringent.) These are wines that make you slow down to think as you taste, and they require a great meal alongside perhaps something with the local white truffles in the fall?

As a result of the excellence of Barolos and Barbarescos, they get pricey pretty quickly. So if you want to explore, go a step down and buy a nebbiolo d'Alba, which is often a younger wine downgraded from the Barolo region.

I often go up to the northern part of Piemonte, northwest of Milan, and buy wines from the Ghemme and Gattinara regions. Made from the local nebbiolo clone spanna, they're a touch lighter and just as fragrant. And, since you're not battling with collectors for them, the prices are much lower. Try Travaglini, with the funny-shaped bottle, as well as wines from Cantalupo, Vallana, and Proprietà Sperino—all of which you can find with some age on them at a decent price.

The Piemontese varietal barbera has also received some attention. I like the dark, fruity, cherry aromatics and weight of these reds, which are sometimes fermented in oak barrels.

The region's wine for daily drinking is dolcetto: Uncomplicated and easy to sip, it's a great glass for after work with some salumi and Parmesan.

And if you're talking about Piemonte, there's no way around the town of Asti, with its simple, fruity, sparking Asti Spumante—my favorite with ripe strawberries—just don't put your berries in the glass! (Save the Champagne for a special occasion . . .)

● Puglia

→ **RED**
Primitivo, negroamaro

Budget-friendly wines with muscle.

In the past, this area produced concentrated grape must, which other regions had to use by law—despite their protest: If you had to enrich your grape must, you had to use it from Puglia, even if you were making a Chianti Classico in Tuscany. In recent decades, this poor southern region has received a lot of EU subsidies, and it's showing some results. (Not only with the wine.) It's a very warm area, which means that the wines have muscle. To me, they're a bit on the commercial side. However, they are very generous for those on a smaller budget.

ITALY

■ **aromatic compounds** Literally what you smell. These chemical compounds are released as alcohol evaporates.

● Sicily

→ **RED**
Frappato, nero d'Avola, nerello mascalese

WHITE
Grillo, catarratto, grecanico, zibibbo

While too diverse to categorize, I will say there are so many affordable gems here.

I like Sicilian wines for their value and ease of pairing with food. This sunny southern island produces a wide range of wines, thanks in no small part to its many microclimates. The wind not only has a cooling effect on the (otherwise sun-baked) grapes in the southern Acate Valley and Marsala, it also helps prevent fungus growth. The cooling altitude of Mount Etna makes grapes grow more slowly, resulting in lower sugar and firm acidity. Add to this the region's volcanic soil, and the result is wines with both power and elegance.

You'll find a wide range of reds and whites, as well as some really interesting wines aged in clay amphorae. The ones from Marco De Bartoli have a clean elegance. (Literally: He's one of the few winemakers who actually washes out his amphorae, which are uniquely above ground!) In addition to his white grillo, he's most famous for his Marsalas. Also try the amphora line Pithos from local great COS. The brave souls at Tenuta delle Terre Nere also make some delicious single-vineyard wines up on Mount Etna, which is still an active volcano (!).

Marsala was created in Sicily in 1773 by the British trader John Woodhouse, who was in search of a less expensive alternative to Sherry.

● Trentino–Alto Adige

→ **RED**
Teroldego, lagrein, schiava, pinot nero

WHITE
Pinot bianco, sauvignon blanc, nosiola

Look to Trentino for great reds, and to Alto Adige for Italy's best whites and pinot noirs.

These northern regions are strongly influenced by the Alps, which means a shorter growing season and cooler nights, the latter of which are key for the grapes' flavor development.

Trentino delivers hearty reds, mainly from the local teroldego grape, as well as the white nosiola. It's also known for the major sparkling wine producer Ferrari Trento. (Unfortunately not related to the carmaker!) The white pinot bianco and red schiava are the workhorses in Trentino: elegant and effortless to drink, and rather versatile with food.

Farther north, Alto Adige is the kind of place where you can try different varietals at seemingly every meal. It is known for some of the best pinot neros, particularly on the eastern side of the Adige River. The local lagrein grape produces a rich and hearty wine, which is often very similar to merlot. And the little town of Tramin is where the white Gewürztraminer grape shows the best results. This particular varietal is very challenging for winemakers: It's a beast to farm, the higher tannin levels in its thicker skin dull its perfuminess, and it tends to get boozy quickly in the glass. On top of that, it's almost impossible to make it taste consistent year after year. But here, the winemakers have tamed it over time, making reliably good wines.

Alto Adige also produces some of the best examples of sauvignon blanc, because of the Austrian influence via Styria. It's really worth trying!

● Tuscany

→ **RED**
Sangiovese, canaiolo nero, cabernet sauvignon, merlot

WHITE
Trebbiano toscano

Pricey, powerful, super-hyped reds, with a few surprises still to be found.

A visit to Tuscany should be on everyone's bucket list—and not just for the food. I'm not going to go into all the individual regions that make up Chianti: There are too many, and this is where your phone comes in handy! I will tell you that the red sangiovese grape is the base of Chianti. Traditionally, it was blended with canaiolo nero and a small percentage of the white grape trebbiano to give it more freshness. Starting in the 1980s, they began blending sangiovese with the international varietals cabernet sauvignon and merlot to make the wines richer and more powerful. Then, in the '90s, winemakers started using oak barrels to make them even more marketable worldwide. Unfortunately, they began to lose their unique sense of place.

Today, there are still a few wineries that stick to tradition. Look for the Pian del Ciampolo from Montevertine, one of the best wineries in Chianti Classico. Look for Monteraponi wines, offering craftsmanship, a lower price, and great food-pairing wines with real elegance. Also look for wines from Fèlsina in Chianti Classico and Fattoria Selvapiana in Chianti Rufina.

Tuscany's flagship wine is Brunello di Montalcino, a clone of sangiovese grosso that was renamed. Brunellos are much more intense: You *want* food with them! The king of brunello is Soldera, and Casanuova delle Cerbaie is great as well. But those will cost you. I recommend starting a level below, with a Rosso di Montalcino. You can bring a bottle of it to a party if you want a medium splurge, or serve it with grilled steak at home.

Not far away is Montepulciano and its famed vino nobile di Montepulciano. Again, try starting with the "simpler" Rosso di Montepulciano and make your way up.

From the town of Bolgheri, on the Tuscan coast, comes Italy's most famous wine: Sassicaia. During World War II, the Incisa family planted cabernet sauvignon because their beloved Bordeaux weren't available. It was for family consumption only until the late 1960s, then slowly grew into the "Super Tuscan" cult, as more and more wineries planted cabernet sauvignon, merlot, syrah, and a little cab franc to create powerful, oak-aged wines from international varieties—all at top prices. Most Super Tuscans are a little too marketed for me, but there are certainly huge fans.

● Veneto

→ **RED**
Corvina, molinara, rondinella

WHITE
Glera, pinot grigio

Interesting Amarones amid an ocean of Prosecco and pinot grigio.

The area around Verona, the setting for *Romeo and Juliet*, is today mostly known for Prosecco, that light, super-sippable sparkling wine.

From this region also comes the fruit-forward DOC Valpolicella, which is a great wine for all sorts of simple Italian dishes. It's the little brother of Amarone, one of the country's most powerful *rossos*. (If you're looking for the Italian equivalent of a Napa cabernet, look no further. While they differ in flavor, they're matched in terms of concentration.)

The Veneto is also home to most of the country's commercial pinot grigios. They're soft, easy to drink—and often taste thin or almost diluted. They may have been marketed to perfection, but they rarely deliver much value in the glass.

ITALY

Spain

→ **Exciting young winemakers are rediscovering old and nearly extinct grape varietals, as well as revitalizing old-vine and abandoned vineyards— even entire regions.**

Spain is the largest wine-producing country per acre. Most of that wine is used for distilling into brandy, though, so it comes behind France and Italy.

Its diverse geography—ranging from the warm days and cool nights around Madrid to the wet and cooler Atlantic region of Galicia; from the white clay and limestone soil of Andalucia to the untamed, vertiginous volcanic slopes of the Canary Islands—results in a diversity of grapes and flavors. That means there's so much delightful wine to discover. Best of all for us drinkers, it's incredibly undervalued. There are some very traditional areas, like Rioja, Penedès, Jerez, and Ribera del Duero. But what interests me most is the massive change that's taking place both here and in Portugal. "New" winemakers are delivering super-interesting wines at super-attractive prices. My staff makes fun of me for constantly bringing up the latest new-to-me wine/grape/region from the Iberian peninsula, but I can't help it: Spain is endlessly fascinating.

The WINE REGIONS
of SPAIN

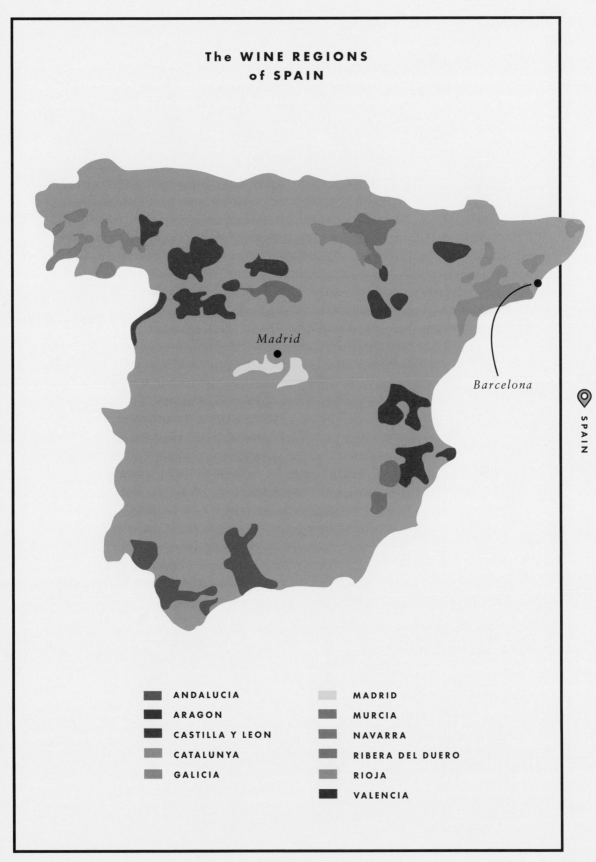

Madrid

Barcelona

SPAIN

ANDALUCIA	MADRID
ARAGON	MURCIA
CASTILLA Y LEON	NAVARRA
CATALUNYA	RIBERA DEL DUERO
GALICIA	RIOJA
	VALENCIA

● Andalucia

→ **WHITE**
Palomino fino,
Pedro Ximénez

The new Spain on full display, with lots of bright whites.

The incredibly limestone-rich soil around Cádiz—which is an unusual and striking white color—is perfect for the white grape palomino Fino, which is used for making Sherry. The grape's hearty, unique character is further shaped by the alternating hot, dry *levante* and humid Atlantic Poniente winds, which moderate the heat and keep the sugar and acidity in balance. The nutty, spice-bouquet aroma of the Fino- and Manzanilla-style Sherries is ideal with a plate of local Iberico ham and olives. Those who prefer deeply complex wines should try an Oloroso-style Sherry, which ages for many years.

A change has been in motion in recent years, with winemakers experimenting with nonoxidative whites (like sherry) and looking back to the 1800s to replant varietals that had almost disappeared, resulting in dry, citrusy whites with angular precision—what we call "nervosity"—that is comparable to a Burgundy chardonnay. At the wine bar, we love to pour Atlántida Blanco from Alberto Orte, a terrific bargain made from a white varietal that was brought back from near extinction. The white grape vijeriega thrives on the limestone-rich soils in certain regions, producing a wine of Burgundy-like quality.

● Catalunya

→ **RED**
Tempranillo, granatxa (granacha/grenache), carinyena (carignan)

WHITE
Macabeo (viura), xarel-lo, parellada, chardonnay

From large-scale Cava production to uniquely distinct reds, this diverse, dynamic area is one to watch.

Situated close to Barcelona in the northeast, Catalunya is most known for its sparkling Cava, which it pumps out in epic quantities. (So large that some producers are opting out of the DO or DOC Cava and simply labeling it as "sparkling wine.") Cavas are based on the whites listed above, but chardonnay and, slowly, pinot noir are also making their way into the appellation.

Wines from the steep slopes of the Priorat area are known for being powerful and high-alcohol, especially when made from granatxa. The area is now dialing it back to make more elegant, *terroir*-driven wines. One sip of a wine from Terroir al Limit and you'll understand how the area is repositioning itself. Penedès is also producing the rare white sumoll blanc grape. The remaining production is just twelve acres. The winery Heretat MontRubí, an excellent representative of the new Spain, might only release nine hundred bottles made from this varietal each year.

BRILLIANT SPARKLING WINE

→ **Penedès**, which is near Barcelona, is one of the country's major sparkling wine centers. One singular producer I want to point out is Pepe Raventós from **Raventós i Blanc**, who, in a bold move, stepped out of the recognizable Cava DO and created his own much higher-quality requirements. Taste his wines: affordable brilliance.

● Galicia

→ **RED** | **WHITE**
Mencía | Albariño, godello, doña blanca

Undervalued, interesting (and old-fashioned) wines.

The Atlantic northwest has become one of the country's hottest regions—at least when it comes to the new generation of winemakers. Albariño is mostly known in the Rías Baixas region, where the granite-based vineyards sprawl all the way down to the Atlantic. These wines have a zippy/crunchy acid, combined with a real savory finish—it's like a taste of the sea. There is a huge difference between the albariños grown farther inland and the ones grown on the coast. Also look for the term *sobre lias*, which indicates that the wine had extended contact on the lees. These albariños are much more powerful and expressive, unlike the light versions we got in the supermarket back in the day. If you're looking for a less expensive alternative to white Burgundy (think on the level of Puligny-Montrachet and Meursault), try something made with godello or doña blanca—often made into a blend.

The red mencía grape is undergoing a perception shift: Once known for its light, slightly herbaceous fruit—not unlike cabernet franc—it's now delivering an impressive range of styles, depending on the winemaker, at an incredibly good value. The wines from Valdeorras taste like Beaujolais, those from Ribeira Sacra evoke the Northern Rhône, those from Rías Baixas taste more green. One winemaker covering this region in a fascinating way is Raúl Pérez. Try his Castro Candaz Mencía from Ribeira Sacra; his entry-level, Bierzo-made Ultreia Saint Jacques; and, at the higher end, Ultreia de Valtuille, which is, unusually, made with naturally occurring *flor* yeast.

SPAIN

CULT REGION: CANARY ISLANDS

→ Definitely one of the cult regions, especially among those who tout "island wines" and the distinctive flavor characteristics of volcanic soil. Once known for low-quality plonk marketed to tourists, in recent years the Canaries have spawned winemaking projects like Envínate Táganan, which took over old, super-steep vineyards that had been seen as too tricky to work. (Google "Canary Island vineyards": They're so untamed, you'd never know they were vineyards!) The quality is incredible, and the grape mix is often of varietals you've never heard of—usually with the white listán blanco and red listán negro as the base. Also look for wines from Bodega Juan Francisco Fariña.

● Ribera del Duero

→ **RED**
Tempranillo (tinto fino, tinto del toro)

Posh, traditional area making big, rich reds.

Home to Vega Sicilia, Spain's most famous wine, this region stretches along the Duero River. The area is influenced by its high-altitude plateaus, whose chilly nights temper the warm climate, resulting in wines with rich, concentrated power and the finesse and brighter flavors you get from higher acidity. Ribera, as it's most often called, produces dark, lush reds. (The smaller region of Toro produces a style that's more powerful . . . and cheaper.) The region is currently having an identity crisis due to the trends that the new generation is launching on the peninsula.

FIND THESE WINES!

→ If you can track them down, try the wines from **Envínate Lousas Ribeira Sacra** in Galicia, currently one of the hottest wine projects in Spain. The wines are often sold out before they hit the US (that's why you need a good relationship with your wine store!). The grapes are grown with no pesticides on single parcels in various regions and hand-harvested, and the wines are exposed to minimal intervention in the cellar; sulfur is only added if needed. They have absolute cult status right now.

● Rioja

→ **RED**
Tempranillo, granatxa (grenache)

WHITE
Viura (macabeo)

Oak-aged reds: Are we in Bordeaux? Actually, you're not that far off . . .

The classic red Rioja, a historic appellation on the level of Bordeaux and Barolo, is a blend of the fruit-forward tempranillo and granatxa grapes, which gives the wine the acidity needed for aging. (The technique was introduced by the Bordelais centuries ago, so they have a long tradition of it in the region.) Winemakers in the area also use a lot of American oak, which lends the wines their distinctive vanilla aroma. The region also produces the dark, hearty, fruity style known as crianza, which can be drunk much sooner. (Riojas typically require some aging before they soften.) The riservas and gran riservas come at a higher price, but you can find interesting—and interestingly priced—Riojas from R. López de Heredia and Bodegas Hermanos Peciña. Try doing a tasting with a Crianza, a Riserva (aged three years), and a Gran Riserva (aged at least five) to give you an idea of what aging does to a wine. You'll also find a viura-based white, which can range from fresh to oaky.

Get to Know Spanish Grapes

→ Chalk it up to human nature, but we have a tendency to drink the same wines. Once you start looking for lesser-known varieties in regions you might not be familiar with, however, I promise you not only a great reward but great savings, too. Nowhere is this more true than in Spain. There is so much diversity, it's impossible to put Spanish wine into one box. Even the grapes themselves have a tremendous span within the varietal. You'll find the citrusy, refreshing albariño and the citrusy, powerful doña blanca; the round, slightly oxidative viura and the amazing godello, which gives you the elegance of a Burgundy chardonnay without the price of a Puligny-Montrachet. Here are some grapes to look for.

Albariño

Citrusy, fresh, lightly herbaceous

It might have a reputation as a cheap supermarket white, but this variety is about to explode in quality. Some albariños are rich and can have a lot of texture, while others are leaner. Some are very zesty and mineral, while those grown closer to the Atlantic have much more focus and precision, as well as an intriguing salinity. Try Rodrigo Mendez and Raúl Pérez's partnership, Bodegas Forjas del Salnes, as well as Nanclares y Prieto, Atalier by Raúl Pérez, or the high-end and limited Sketch (also by Pérez).

Garnacha

Red fruit, delicate tannins, balanced

This grape is widely planted in Spain, but no one really paid attention to it until now. It's more interesting than tempranillo, and has the acidity needed for aging. Don't compare Spanish garnacha to the Mediterranean-influenced grenache used in the famously powerful Châteauneuf-du-Pape; think of pure, uplifting wines that are more similar to pinot noirs. One of the most exciting projects right now is Comando G, in the cool elevation of Sierra de Gredos west of Madrid. The young, second-generation winemaker's La Bruja de Rozas is a delicious $21 bottle. Also keep Sierra de Gredos on your radar: Some really interesting wines will come from here in the near future.

Godello

Citrusy, focused, green apple

This white grape grows only in Galicia and responds especially well to its slate and clay soils. Depending on the way it's made, it can taste like an excellent Riesling or even a Puligny-Montrachet. Most of the godello is in the Valdeorras region. Try Rafael Palacios's Louro Godello.

Doña Blanca

Bitter almond, silky, medium-bodied

This neutral white, which is often blended with godello, was once used mostly for distilling, but it's been on the rise. It's very tight and closed, often requiring at least three years of aging before it becomes really interesting.

Mencía

Dark fruit, spice, savory

It's quite amazing to see a grape that has such a diverse range. Wines made from these red grapes work with a variety of cuisines, and it's hard to go wrong with a bottle.

Tempranillo

Fruity, fresh, ripe

Spain's best-known grape. It's especially popular in Rioja, where it's being blended with granacha (grenache in France), graciano, and mazuelo (carignan). The beauty of Rioja wines is that you can buy aged bottles for very little. That is, until the rest of the world catches on to how great they are.

Treixadura

Vibrant, zesty, mineral

A super-interesting white grape. It's bright and zippy and has a seashell-like minerality—a little challenging for some, but very fun. One of the absolute masters of this varietal is Luis Rodriguez of Luis Anxo Rodriguez Vázquez in Ribeiro. This humble pioneer is the shining star of Spain for what he's accomplished. Be sure to try his reds, too.

SPAIN

Portugal

➡ **I like to say that Portugal is the sleeping giant of wine.**

At the moment, I put it right behind Spain—my favorite. The **Douro** region, the home of port production, has many different microclimates and elevations, making for some fascinating reds and whites, such as touriga nacional and touriga franca (red). Also look for the grapes rabigato and gouveio for white. Because of the trend toward dry wines, port wine is in a recession. As a result, producers are moving toward dry whites and reds. The traditional producer Niepoort is an excellent example. The region's rising star is Luis Seabra, who works with minimal intervention to express the great *terroir* of the Douro.

Vinho verde is also undergoing a change from the effervescent, off-dry whites (Arinto, Loureiro) toward single-vineyard bottlings that express their *terroir* of schist and granite soil and still have that trademark touch of gentle fizz. These are great summer wines! Keep an eye out for the baga grape from **Bairrada**, which is very similar to nebbiolo because of its high tannins.

Dão is the most interesting region, tucked inland in the mountains. Gaen (Mencía) brings out Northern Rhône–like syrahs. Wines here have a finesse. Alentejo is a region that brings out a more approachable and richer style—I love these wines with stews! There is also historically a lot of amphora wine production around here. Vinho verde is the second-biggest appellation after **Alentejo**. It's moving rapidly from making supermarket wines into single-vineyard white wine bottlings. It's unique.

The WINE REGIONS
of PORTUGAL

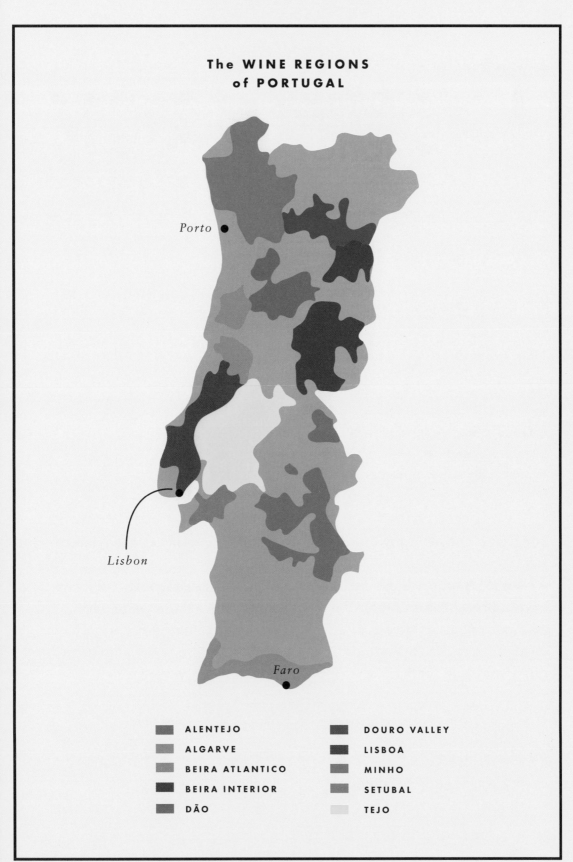

Porto

Lisbon

Faro

PORTUGAL

ALENTEJO

ALGARVE

BEIRA ATLANTICO

BEIRA INTERIOR

DÃO

DOURO VALLEY

LISBOA

MINHO

SETUBAL

TEJO

Germany

→ **The home of Riesling is full of surprises. The diverse climates and soils in Germany make for some incredibly exciting wines.**

German wines are also remarkable for their precision and clarity. I attribute this to how cleanly the winemakers work, whether it's using stainless steel tanks or old-school oak vats, a cellar so high-tech it could be a surgery room or an old-fashioned one with a dirt floor.

It's almost impossible to talk about German wine without paying homage to Riesling. The country produces the finest and purest examples of the grape, whether dry (*trocken*) or off-dry (*halbtrocken*)—especially the powerful GGs (Grosses Gewächs), which are Germany's equivalent of a French grand cru—and legally obligated to be dry! Today, the US market is looking for the traditional off-dry style, which tastes a little sweet, while the European market is screaming for dry wine. Needless to say, it has shaken things up a bit in the country.

I love dry Riesling with its focused, minerally, savory complexity, but I'm surprised that more people don't love the slightly off-dry, Kabinett-style Rieslings. They can be so great with food—Thai, sushi, Korean—and age incredibly well, yet they never get crazy expensive.

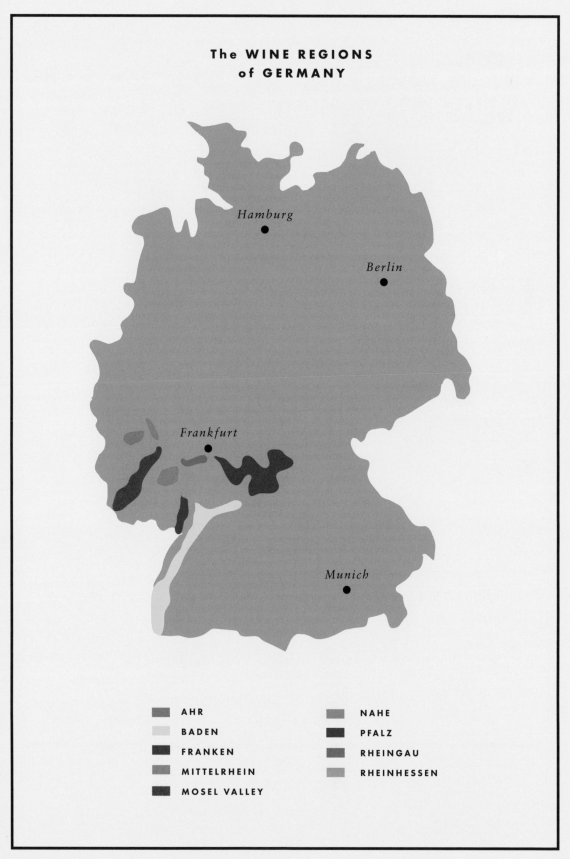

The **WINE REGIONS**
of **GERMANY**

Hamburg

Berlin

Frankfurt

Munich

GERMANY

AHR		NAHE
BADEN		PFALZ
FRANKEN		RHEINGAU
MITTELRHEIN		RHEINHESSEN
MOSEL VALLEY		

The sweeter Spätlese and Auslese styles are a bit out of fashion, which is why I'm stocking up on these wines from the '70s and '80s: They become even drier and more magically complex with age.

Germany is not all Riesling, all the time: Spätburgunder, a late-ripening clone of pinot noir with a black pepper edge, is also worth seeking out. Pinot noir has a long history in Germany due to the Cistercian monks of Clos de Vougeot, who made wine at their monastery in the Rheingau. Today, as the climate is getting warmer, Germany benefits from its northern position, especially around Franken, Ahr, Rheingau, Pfalz, Rheinhessen, and Baden. These pinots aren't comparable to their Burgundian siblings, as the different regional soil structures result in another expression of the wine's personality.

(In this case, it has a certain cold smokiness, like a fireplace that's just been extinguished, as well as a bit of black pepper spice to it.) They're definitely worth tasting. Look for bottles from Fürst, Keller, Benedikt Baltes, and August Kesseler.

In order to keep this book short, I won't talk about every region, but there is a lot to explore in Germany. Just don't let yourself be intimidated by the long words on the labels!

Mosel Valley

→ **WHITE**
Riesling |

The northern Mosel Valley is home to the world's steepest vineyards, where the sun hits the vines at a perfect ripening angle in this cool climate, allowing the winemakers to produce the finest and purest expressions of Riesling. The steepest vineyard is Bremmer Calmont, which slopes at 65 degrees. (Even I, as an Austrian who loves to hike, find it tough-going!) My favorite winemakers in the region are Franzen and Stein.

The valley also has two side streams. Ruwer is home to the benchmark wineries Karthäusterhof and Maximin Grünhaus. The Saar region is colder, resulting in wines with naturally higher acidity levels, which is why they always have a touch of residual sugar to soften them. (As the vintages have become warmer over the years, winemakers have been fermenting the wines to be more dry.) Try the wines from Florian Lauer, which drink like an aromatic version of Chablis in terms of their minerality. This region is known for wines with a significant amount of residual sugar (i.e., off-dry and sweet).

The Saar is also known for the most famous of all Riesling producers, Egon Müller of Scharzhofberg, who makes wines on a completely different level. He doesn't care about today's trend toward dryness; he makes wines like his father did, which means that almost all of them have residual sugar. His Trockenbeerenauslese (dry berry selection, made with botrytized grapes) is *the* most expensive white wine in the world—even more expensive than Montrachet, and it will certainly outlive it in aging, too. This is a bucket-list wine for every serious wine drinker, as Müller makes very, very little: often only one hundred bottles yearly.

Nahe

→ **WHITE**
Riesling |

This relatively small area is home to some of the greatest producers, including Dönnhoff, Schäfer-Fröhlich, and Martin Tesch. The wines from this area combine the qualities of the Mosel and Rheingau and offer you a great deal of value in the glass. Rieslings from the Nahe have the raciness of the Mosel and the substance of a Rheingau wine. It's an area that focuses more on quality than on quantity.

Rheingau

→ **RED** | **WHITE**
Spätburgunder | Riesling

German wine is typically associated with the historic Rheingau. The region is warmer than the Mosel, and therefore its wines are more powerful and have more weight on the palate. The quartzite soils that form the Taunus mountain range deliver expressive mineral wines. Try a bottle from Johannes Leitz or from his former cellar master, Eva Fricke.

GERMANY

113

USA

→ **In the last twenty years, Americans have become extremely thirsty for wines from around the world, making the US the number one wine-drinking nation. But there's so much made here to be proud of.**

In fact, all fifty states, Alaska included, make wine. (Whether or not it's all good is open to debate.) Unrestrained by the strict laws that govern so much of winemaking in Europe, Americans are free to be creative and experimental. There are more than a few differences between Europe and the US, though. While European wine laws are super strict regarding what you can plant, it's much more free-spirited in the US, which is why you find a much broader diversity of grapes than you did only twenty years ago. Also different is that most wineries here have a mailing list or wine club, which allows people to buy directly from the winemaker—sometimes they don't even have to work with distributors. And while wines from the US are often perceived as big, bold, overextracted, and generously oaked, it is no longer the standard. Young winemakers traveled and worked all over the world and have brought their knowledge back home to produce a much more balanced style of wine. Just look at all the *pét-nats* coming out of California, the creativity that's happening in Santa Barbara County, and how many interesting chardonnays have been appearing in Oregon! And one look at the shift in quality in New York State's Finger Lakes region and the Hamptons will tell you all you need to know: America is making some very exciting wines.

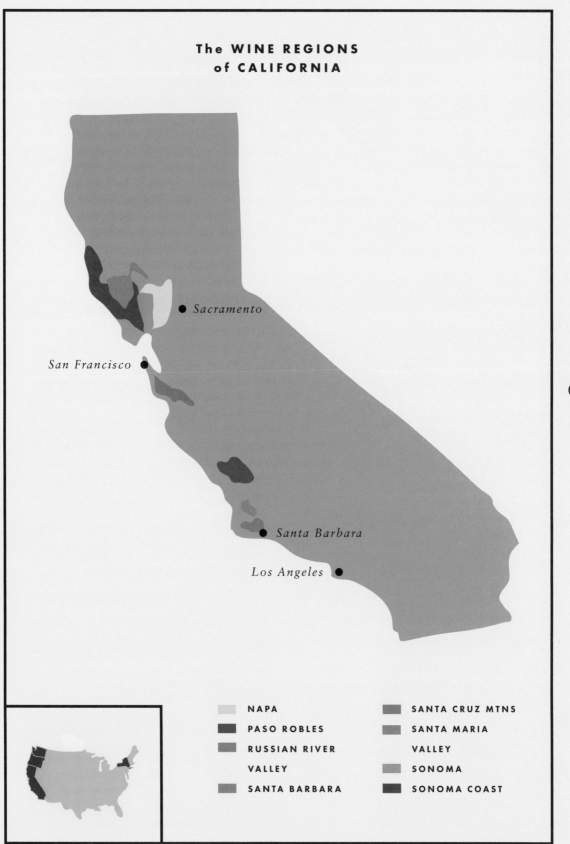

The WINE REGIONS
of CALIFORNIA

- Sacramento
- San Francisco
- Santa Barbara
- Los Angeles

USA

NAPA

PASO ROBLES

RUSSIAN RIVER
VALLEY

SANTA BARBARA

SANTA CRUZ MTNS

SANTA MARIA
VALLEY

SONOMA

SONOMA COAST

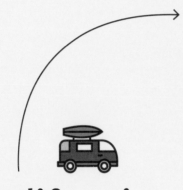

California

→ **RED**
Cabernet sauvignon,
pinot noir, merlot,
zinfandel, syrah

WHITE
Chardonnay,
sauvignon blanc

Freshness and elegance are on the rise in the sunny land of creamy, buttery, oaky chardonnay and big, bold cabernets.

California is a giant of wine production. When we talk about California wine, we think mostly of Napa and Sonoma, where people started farming grapes in the early 1900s. The bulk of it, however, comes from the hot, flat Central Valley, where E. & J. Gallo has reached an enormous industrial scale. Young winemakers are heading for cooler climates, especially ones with fog, in an attempt to break the stereotype of sun-baked wines with outsize personalities. That hardcore A/C every evening results in wines with surprising freshness. (Plant pinot noir in Napa and it will be soulless and sunburned, with round, flabby flavor. Plant it on the foggy Sonoma Coast or up high in the Santa Cruz Mountains, and you have something with personality and soul.) It's an exciting step forward.

NORTH COAST

○ Napa

→ **RED**
Cabernet sauvignon,
merlot

WHITE
Chardonnay,
sauvignon blanc

Napa Valley became one of the world's most famous wine regions in the late '70s, thanks to the Judgment of Paris competition, in which several of the region's wines beat out the French. Today, Napa's wines are known for their rich, bold, concentrated personalities, with the best-known being from Stags' Leap, Oakville, Rutherford, Mount St. Helena, Mount Veeder, and Los Carneros. It's easy to generalize the region's vintages because it's consistently sunny, but the area is much more complex than that, thanks to variations in fog, exposure, and elevation.

Be sure to check out Cathy Corison's wines, as well as those from Enfield, Massican, Sky, and Stony Hill.

● Russian River

→ **RED**
Pinot noir

WHITE
Chardonnay

The region's warmer growing conditions make for weightier wines, whose lushness can earn them lots of accolades, depending on where they're grown. They also age incredibly well. Try the Joseph Swan Vineyards Pinot Noir Cuvée de Trois: It's smooth, rich, and beautifully balanced.

Sonoma Coast

→ **RED**
Pinot noir

WHITE
Chardonnay

Sonoma is less touristy than neighboring Napa, without the Segway tours and gift shops. The Sonoma Coast AVA is right on the Pacific and home to the best producers. That coolness and fog make ideal conditions for growing chardonnay and pinot noir.

You can't miss Hirsch Estate, which pioneered the region for winemaking. It's also totally worth it to dip into some Arnot-Roberts wines.

CENTRAL COAST

Santa Cruz Mountains

→ **RED**
Pinot noir, cabernet sauvignon

WHITE
Chardonnay

The area between Silicon Valley and the Pacific coast has an elevation of 2,000 feet—and a much more relaxed attitude than Napa, making it a great place to visit (and less expensive, too). Ridge is producing probably one of the most underrated California cult wines, Ridge Monte Bello. (It was a Ridge wine that ranked fifth in the famous Judgment of Paris competition in 1976, in which blind tasters selected a—gasp!—California wine as being the world's best.) If you want to be a bit more adventurous, visit Bonny Doon Vineyard, where Randall Grahm experiments with several unusual varietals. Worth a try!

Santa Barbara

→ **RED**
Pinot noir

WHITE
Chardonnay

The movie *Sideways* was set here. Immediately after the film became popular, sales of merlot plunged, while pinot noir rose like Icarus (without the getting-burned-by-the-sun part). The county is home to the well-known AVAs Santa Maria Valley and Sta. Rita Hills. This is where you get the most value for pinot noir and chardonnay worldwide.

This county is one of *the* regions in California right now. Exciting things are happening thanks to young start-ups and investors, and the climate is perfect for pinot noir and chardonnay: The cooling fog rolls in from the Pacific at night and is burned off by the sun by late morning. It's that rather consistent combination that has attracted many winemakers. World-renowned sommelier Rajat Parr runs both Sandhi winery (whites and reds) and Domaine de la Côte (pinot noir). The famed Burgundian Étienne Montille of Domaine Montille recently purchased land, which bodes well.

Jim Clendenen of Au Bon Climat and Clendenen Family Vineyards is a classic producer. The latter's the Pip Pinot Noir is an incredible value from a prime region. Also try the whites from Tatomer, which specializes in dry Rieslings—as well as what I consider among the best Grüner Veltliners outside of Austria.

USA

Washington State

→ **RED**
Cabernet sauvignon, merlot, syrah

WHITE
Chardonnay, Riesling

Large-scale production with some bright spots.

The majority of the state's winemaking is east of the Cascade mountain range, which does a great job of buffering the weather. The desertlike growing conditions are aided by irrigation from the rivers. Bordeaux blends are a specialty here, but syrahs tend to do really well, too. This is also the home of large-scale Riesling production, mainly fueled by Chateau Ste. Michelle.

Oregon

→ **RED**
Pinot noir

WHITE
Pinot gris, chardonnay

The less-commercial alternative to California, known for its pinots and, increasingly, its great chardonnays.

Oregon is often falsely compared to California. It's a cooler, rainier state, therefore requiring much different farming. (Many vineyards here are biodynamic.) Oregon's pinots are much earthier, spicier, and more powerful than their more rounded, fruit-forward neighbors to the south. Pinot gris is also fairly popular here, while chardonnay is delivering some really exciting wines.

The most prominent and productive AVA is Willamette Valley, which has several sub-AVAs. Try chardonnays from Evening Land Vineyards and Lingua Franca, an interesting new collaboration between the Master Sommelier Larry Stone and top Burgundy producer Dominique Lafon. Classic Oregon pinots can be found from Bergström, Cristom, Domaine Drouhin (a Burgundy producer), and the historic Eyrie Vineyards.

New York

→ **RED**
Cabernet franc, merlot

WHITE
Riesling, chenin blanc, chardonnay

Rosés and Rieslings in New York State? Really.

New York's winemaking is concentrated in two different regions. In the glitzy Hamptons, you'll find passionate winemakers bottling interesting chenin blancs, cabernet francs, and some very trendy rosés. Look for Wölffer Estate, Paumanok, and Channing Daughters. Meanwhile, up north in the rural, folksier Finger Lakes region, the cooler growing season and heat-retaining lakes make for some Rieslings to watch, especially from Dr. Konstantin Frank, Hermann J. Wiemer, Ravines, and Boundary Breaks. Clement Wines is producing some of the state's most interesting reds. If you like dry wines, try Empire Estate Riesling.

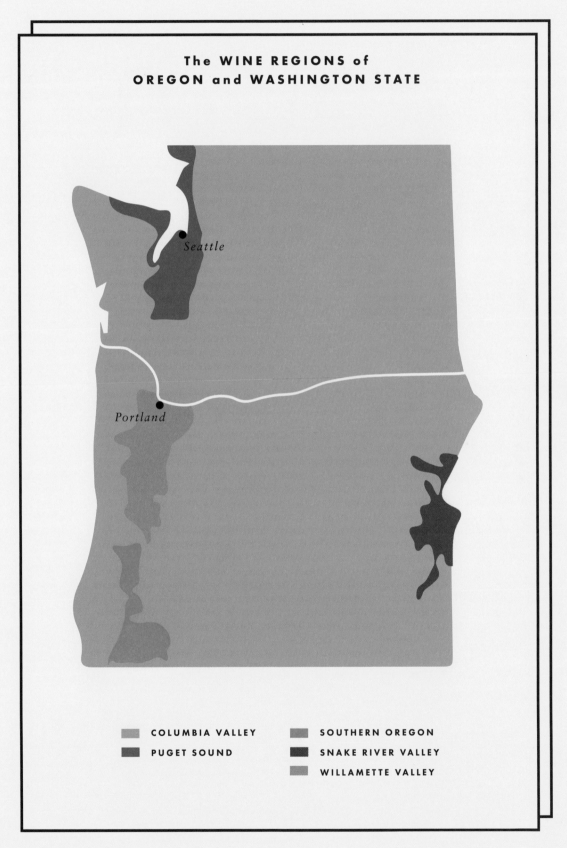

The WINE REGIONS of OREGON and WASHINGTON STATE

Seattle

Portland

USA

COLUMBIA VALLEY

PUGET SOUND

SOUTHERN OREGON

SNAKE RIVER VALLEY

WILLAMETTE VALLEY

South America

→ There's a wine revolution going on in <u>Argentina</u> and <u>Chile</u>.

The traditional, lush styles of wine were influenced by the rich soils washed down from the Andes, paired with the warm climate and cooling elevation. French winemakers, looking for affordable land and labor (and something to do during the winter and spring, when South America is in full summer and fall), invested heavily here. South America also has the advantage of having original ungrafted vines, since the phylloxera disease that wiped out vineyards across Europe in the late 1800s never made it as far as Chile.

Like most young winemaking countries that abandoned their traditions in favor of globally friendly wines (bigger, bolder, more oak), they've been righting the balance in recent years, recovering indigenous grapes and reassessing their identity. Still, Argentine reds have a concentrated, hearty fruitiness and distinctive purple hue, while their Chilean counterparts have a eucalyptus tone that can be quite entrancing.

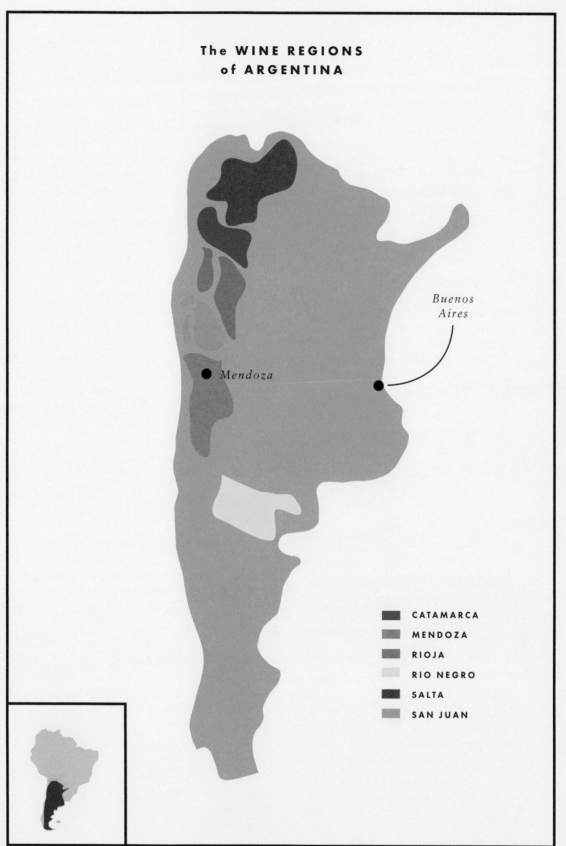

The WINE REGIONS
of ARGENTINA

Buenos
Aires

SOUTH AMERICA

● Mendoza

CATAMARCA
MENDOZA
RIOJA
RIO NEGRO
SALTA
SAN JUAN

Argentina

→ **RED**
Malbec, cabernet
sauvignon, bonarda

WHITE
Torrontés,
chardonnay

The homeland of powerful, affordable malbec and zippy torrontés.

Argentina revolutionized its wine production—and drinking—in the late 1990s, turning away from its indigenous pink-skinned grapes, used for light, farmer-style table wines, toward serious winemaking. The desertlike climate and sandy soil somehow create strong growing conditions. The country's malbec grabbed the mantle from California cabernet thanks to its similar qualities—think inky, bold, spicy, powerful—and much more sensitive price. While formerly a little heavy-handed with the oak, the winemakers have managed to dial it back in recent years.

The breathtakingly beautiful northern **Salta** region—at 10,000 feet, it's home to one of the world's highest vineyards—is producing some fine examples, especially at Bodega Colome. The dramatic altitude leads to thicker-skinned grapes that lend their purple hue to wines that have both a juiciness and a delicacy. (These wines will also stain your teeth purple after an hour of tasting!) The white torrontés grape is showing its best results up in Salta, with its fresh, floral, citrusy notes.

The most prominent region is **Mendoza**, where malbec plays a major role and where the wineries tend to be large-scale. You'll find different expressions of malbec elsewhere, such as the powerful, spice-driven versions in **Luján de Cuyo** and the more Burgundian-style malbecs high up in the stunningly beautiful **Uco Valley**. Bonarda is a local red specialty that caught my attention during my visit there. While it gets little respect from winemakers, I found these simple, fun, easy-to-drink wines very tasty—and they didn't cost a whole lot.

Going south in **Patagonia**, you can find the forward-thinking Italian Piero Incisa della Rocchetta (of the family that created the first Super Tuscan wine) biodynamically farming pinot noir to create many different labels. Try his Zin Azufre ("no sulfur"). He also recently started a chardonnay project with Jean-Marc Roulot, the star from Meursault/Burgundy. Their wines won't be cheap, but from what I've tasted, it's like having a high-end Corton-Charlemagne from Argentina for much less money.

The idea in this country has always been to make one's own wine, so small-production wineries are far more common than they are in the much more industrial Chile. The trend is to go into high-altitude regions such as **Tupungato** and the mountains of the Uco Valley, where they're on to a new style of malbecs that express the *terroir* (rather than the winemaker's ego). The wines now have more grip and freshness, which would have been unthinkable even five years ago. Try the wines from Matias Michelini from the Uco Valley—perhaps the country's most progressive winemaker.

The WINE REGIONS of CHILE

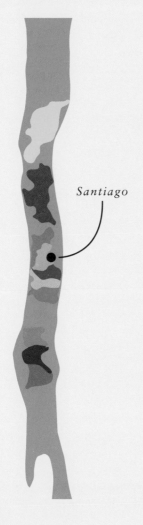

Santiago

■ ACONCAGUA

■ ATACAMA

■ BÍO-BÍO VALLEY

■ CACHAPOAL

■ COLCHAGUA

■ COQUIMBO

■ CURICO

■ ITATA VALLEY

■ MAIPO VALLEY

■ MALLECO

Chile

→ **RED**
Cabernet sauvignon, merlot, carménère, país

WHITE
Chardonnay, sauvignon blanc

From industrial to revolutionary.

In recent decades, Chile was very attractive to foreign investors thanks to its high plateaus and abundant sunshine; and there was plenty of water for irrigation. The phylloxera louse, which destroyed many vineyards around the world in the 1800s, never made it this far south, so many of the vines were appealingly ungrafted. The result of all that know-how and investment from a few powerful families was a slew of industrially produced, French-influenced wines made from international varietals.

Luckily, a change is taking place as a new generation pushes south into the Andes and closer to the cold Pacific. Dry farming (no irrigation), old vineyards, and biodynamics are what they're going for. **Maule**, **Bío-Bío**, and **Itata** are the key regions for this new wave. Look for Pedro Parra wines, especially his Imaginador, a cinsault-based red from vines planted in granite soil. It's unique and profound.

In the mid-2000s, a couple of pioneers, including a Burgundian, produced old-vine carignan and were drawn to the país grape. Both varietals continue to produce straightforward young farmhouse wines called *vino pipeño*. These inexpensive, highly enjoyable wines are often produced from ungrafted old vines, which are super-rare to find anywhere else. I love the pure, concentrated fruit and herbaceous eucalyptus notes of the reds in this country. The new Chile is coming!

SOUTH AMERICA

South Africa

→ **Synonymous with mass-produced chenin blanc, South Africa is also bottling wines with character and soul.**

Winemaking here dates back to the 1600s, although most of the wines were made for distilling, as well as a rather commercial side of pinotage production. Nowadays, there is tremendous breadth and change afoot. Fancied-up regions like **Stellenbosch**, **Paarl**, and **Franschhoek** have picture-book vineyards and beautiful tasting rooms. But, as in other countries, there is a generational change occurring, as young winemakers go back to the country's roots, taking extra care in farming and opting for regions with cooler temperatures. Hannes Storm in Walkers Bay is a great example: He's producing some really fine pinot noir and delicate chardonnay that taste almost like Burgundy. In **Swartland**, look out for wines from Badenhorst, whose Family White Blend reminds me of a light version of white Hermitage. Sadie Family wines are also really sought after.

The WINE REGIONS of SOUTH AFRICA

SOUTH AFRICA

Cape Town

OLIFANTS RIVER	CAPE SOUTH COAST

COASTAL REGION

1 SWARTLAND
2 STELLENBOSCH
3 CAPETOWN
4 PAARL
5 FRANSCHHOEK
  VALLEY

CAPE SOUTH COAST

1 OVERBERG
2 WALKER BAY
3 SWELLENDAM
4 ELGIN

KLEIN KAROO

BREEDE RIVER VALLEY

Austria

→ Dry wines, sustainably made.

RED
Zweigelt
Blaufränkisch
St. Laurent

WHITE
Grüner Veltliner
Welschriesling
Riesling Italico
Riesling
Chardonnay
Sauvignon blanc

Austria has reinvented itself twice in the last thirty years. The first revolution was away from mass-marketed wines toward better quality. The most recent transformation stemmed from a generational shift, as the children who had learned winemaking from their fathers and grandfathers did internships around the globe and put their knowledge into practice when they took the reins. The result is a lot of creativity and movement away from traditional winemaking styles in favor of stainless steel tanks and lower-alcohol, less-concentrated wines. Austria has also received attention for its organic, sustainable, and biodynamic farming practices of late, but it's always been a pretty green country: Rudolf Steiner, the father of biodynamic farming, was from here. Even though the labels rarely tout their practices, you'd be hard pressed to find a winemaker spraying her vines with pesticides.

Austrian wines are always dry. Grüner Veltliner is the signature varietal that put this tiny country on the wine map in the late '90s, with its yellow fruit components ranging from fresh to powerful. The widespread Welschriesling (not related to Riesling) also delivers a range of wines: In **Styria**, it is responsible for a crisp, light wine; it's also the main varietal used in sweet wine production around **Lake Neusiedl**, an area that is ideal for the botrytis growth necessary for sweet wines,

The WINE REGIONS of AUSTRIA

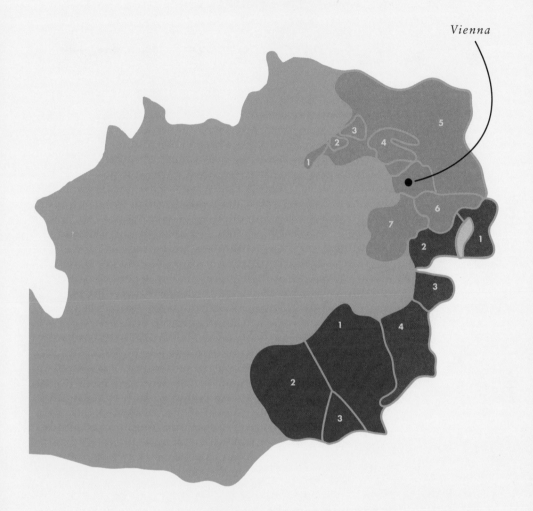

Vienna

AUSTRIA

LOWER AUSTRIA

1 WACHAU

2 KREMSTAL

3 KAMPTAL

4 WAGRAM

5 WEINVIERTEL

6 CARNUNTUM

7 THERMENREGION

VIENNA

BURGENLAND

1 NEUSIEDLERSEE

2 LEITHABERG

3 MITTELBURGENLAND

4 EISENBERG

STYRIA

1 VULKANLAND STEIERMARK

2 WEST STEIERMARK

3 SÜD-STEIERMARK

comparable to a French Sauternes or a Hungarian Tokaji. (My shameless plug for that region is Kracher winery, but I'm biased: I make wine with them!)

While the most traditional region is the **Wachau Valley**, **Kremstal** and **Kamptal** are making equally good wines. Just south of **Vienna** is the **Thermenregion**, home to the indigenous white grapes Rotgipfler and Zierfandler. The latter is delivering really impressive wines thanks to the area's limestone-rich soils. Try the ones from Stadlmann.

The aforementioned Styria is called the Tuscany of Austria thanks to its rolling hills (though it's much greener!). It's where chardonnay (called morillon) and sauvignon blanc find ideal conditions, resulting in enormous purity in the glass. They have a slightly greener acidity. Not as lemonish as Sancerre—more like a Granny Smith apple. In terms of new winemaking styles, the area is on the rise thanks to the knockout single-vineyard sauvignon blancs being made by Tement, as well as those made by Katharina Lackner-Tinnacher under her own label. Christoph Neumeister's wines are stunning in their crystal-clear precision. In a challenging year, the winemaker has been known to go out into the vines with a coffee spoon to scoop out rotten grapes from the cluster in order to guarantee perfect, healthy fruit. It's insane labor, and you can taste it. Rising temperatures in the country have led to increasingly interesting red wines, too.

The **Burgenland** region is also home to the red Blaufränkisch, a noteworthy grape that produces juicy wines evocative of dark berries and spice. Depending on how it's made, it can be between a Côte-Rôtie and a Burgundian pinot noir. In this region, look for Roland Velich's Moric Blaufränkisch, as well as reds from the up-and-coming Hannes Schuster, Wachter-Wiesler, Markus Altenburger, Paul Achs, and Prieler. Also try the natural red wine cuvées from Claus Preisinger.

DAC (Districtus Austriae Controllatus): The origin of a wine indicates where the grapes used for its production come from.

Australia

→ **Moving (way) beyond Yellow Tail shiraz to make fascinating chardonnays, Rieslings, and cabernet sauvignons.**

While Australian wine growing got started in the 1830s—that's pretty recent in the wine world—it's a huge part of the country's society. Australians love their high-octane, concentrated shirazes and are proud of them just the way they are. Four large companies dominate the market, but many small producers opted for cooler climates, where they're bottling really diverse and interesting wines that, unfortunately, have yet to make it to our shores.

Australia is much more than shiraz (syrah in French), which grows so well in the hot **Barossa Valley**, as well as in the cooler **Yarra Valley**, **Geelong**, and **Adelaide Hills**. Other varietals are thriving: sémillon in **Hunter Valley**, Riesling in the **Eden** and **Clare Valleys** (the latter is also home to age-worthy shirazes at Wendouree), grenache in **Barossa**, cabernet sauvignon in **Margaret River**, and pinot noir in **Tasmania**, **Yarra Valley**, and **Mornington Peninsula**.

One thing to notice when you buy an Australian wine: They prefer screw caps over corks pretty much across the board, so don't assume that cap denotes Yellow Tail quality in the bottle.

The WINE REGIONS of AUSTRALIA

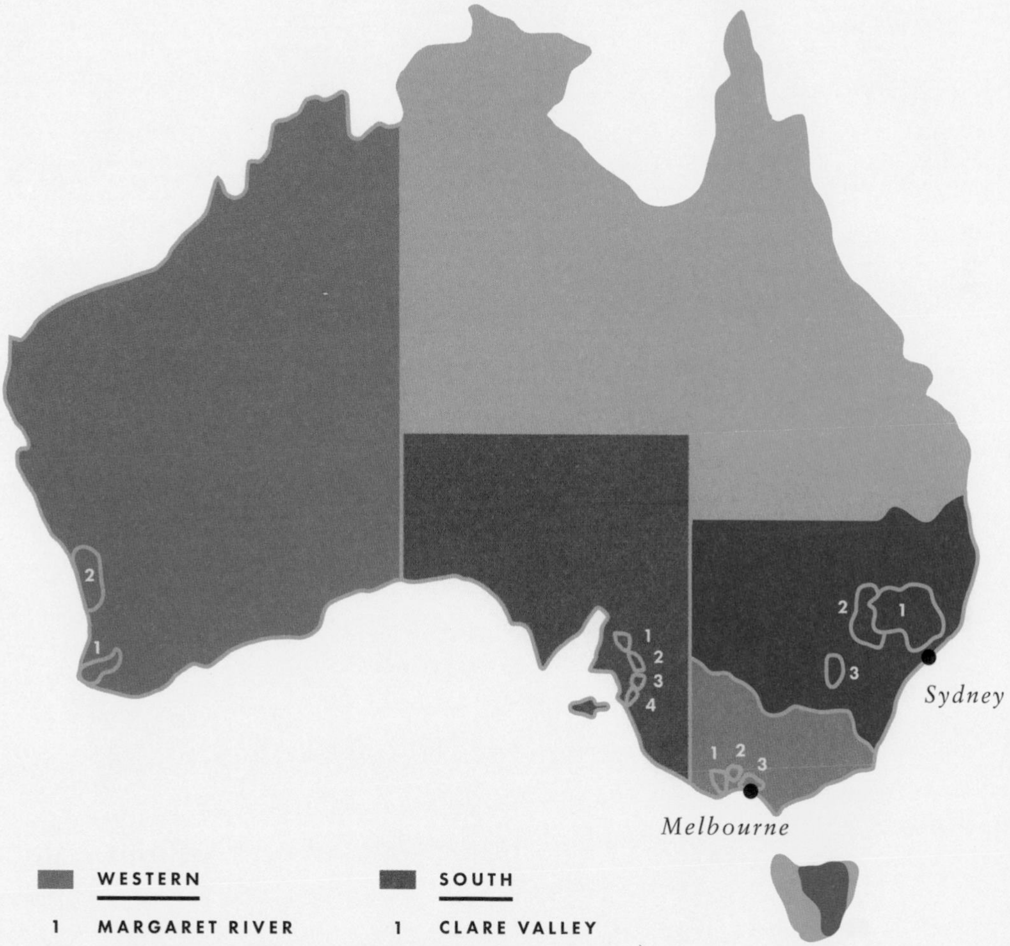

AUSTRALIA

Sydney

Melbourne

WESTERN

1 MARGARET RIVER
2 SWAN DISTRICT

TASMANIA

NEW SOUTH WALES

1 HUNTER VALLEY
2 MUDGEE
3 ORANGE

SOUTH

1 CLARE VALLEY
2 BAROSSA VALLEY
3 EDEN VALLEY
4 ADELAIDE HILLS

VICTORIA

1 GEELONG
2 MORNINGTON
  PENINSULA
3 YARRA VALLEY

New Zealand

→ **Loud and proud sauvignon blancs.**

RED
Pinot noir

WHITE
Sauvignon blanc
Chardonnay

The great sauvignon blancs of France's Loire Valley have a distinctive zestiness. But in New Zealand, it's much more about the fruit punch. Black currant, cat pee (you'll know what I'm talking about once you smell it), exotic fruit . . . there is an abundance of flavors, making it the polar opposite of its French cousin.

It is by far the most planted varietal in New Zealand, and you'll find it on pretty much every wine list around the globe. That's quite a statement for such a small country, which produces just one percent of the world's wine!

Marlborough winery Cloudy Bay's successful sauvignon blanc was reviewed in the trusted wine magazine *Wine Spectator*, putting New Zealand wine on the map. Now you'll find many others releasing sauvignon blancs that are straightforward and supercharged with flavor. They're hugely popular because they're so concentrated and loud. (Yes, that's a wine term.)

For pinot noir, wine lovers seek out the earthy, spice-driven, concentrated wines coming out of the colder **Central Otago** area.

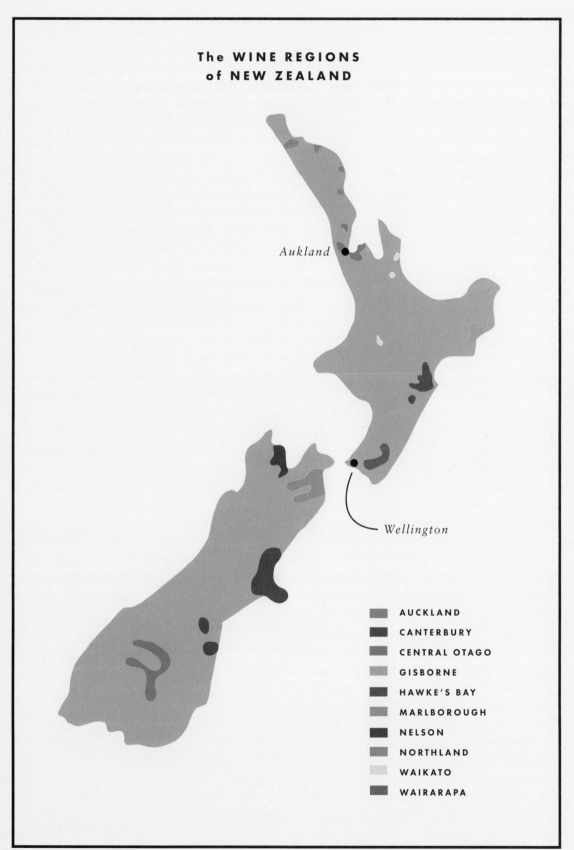

The WINE REGIONS of NEW ZEALAND

Aukland

Wellington

NEW ZEALAND

AUCKLAND

CANTERBURY

CENTRAL OTAGO

GISBORNE

HAWKE'S BAY

MARLBOROUGH

NELSON

NORTHLAND

WAIKATO

WAIRARAPA

Regions to Watch

→ In a world with an increasing number of wine lovers, it makes sense that wine prices are on the rise. What was once possible as an occasional splurge is now way out of reach. As wine writer Eric Asimov recently told a reporter, "In the '80s or '90s, it was a splurge for me to buy a first-growth Bordeaux or a grand cru Burgundy, but I could do it. Now I'm the wine critic of the *New York Times*. That might be as far up in my profession as I can be. And I can't afford those wines."

Luckily, as I explain on page 169, it's a myth that the more expensive a wine is, the better it is. There are areas around the world that might be overlooked or are still on the rise where you can find great wines at sane prices. Just open your mind and taste. Ask sommeliers what they're into: They will always drink affordable wines and take pride in being ahead of the curve. But don't wed yourself to the countries highlighted here. Keep on reading and tasting!

France

Savoie
Interesting whites

Right Bank Bordeaux
More affordable merlot–cabernet franc blends

Côte Roannaise
Delicious, easygoing gamay

Marsannay and Givry
Affordable alternative to Côte de Nuits pinots

Mâcon
Affordable whites

Greece

Santorini
Assyrtiko is their version of Chablis

Macedonia
Xinomavro is a really rich, powerful red

Spain

Andalucia
Nonoxidative whites, Burgundy-like vijeriega

Canary Islands
Cult "island wines" with incredible quality

Galicia
Wines of very different styles based on the mencía and albariño grapes; very high value

Penedès
Raventós i Blanc makes incredible non-Cava sparkling wine

Portugal

Douro
Super-interesting area

Dão
Look for the nebbiolo-like baga grape, which also grows in Bairrada, as well as the syrah-like Jaen

Alentejo
Approachable, richer style of reds

Vinho Verde
Moving from supermarket wines to single-vineyard bottlings

Chile

Maule, Itata, and Bío Bío
Inexpensive young farmhouse wines called *vino pipeño*

Germany

Rheingau
Spätburgunders (pinot noir) comparable to Burgundy

Mosel
Rieslings from producers Franzen, Lauer, and Eva Fricke

Argentina

Tupungato
Exciting high-altitude wine

Uco Valley
A new style of malbecs that express the *terroir*

Unsung Heroes

*Here are some of the people whose wines—
and philosophies—I really admire.*

Dominique Moreau

**Champagne Marie Courtin
(Champagne, France)**

Moreau's elegant single-vineyard, single-varietal, single-harvest Champagnes made from biodynamically grown grapes are still considered revolutionary almost two decades after she launched.

Elisabetta Foradori

**Azienda Agricola Elisabetta Foradori
(Fontanassata, Italy)**

Elisabetta redirected her family's estate away from commercial varietals and invasive farming practices to make wines that are truly evocative of her corner of Trentino.

Raúl Pérez

**Bodegas y Viñedos Raúl Pérez
(Bierzo, Spain)**

Pérez is making wines in several regions in Spain, all to incredible effect.

Julien Sunier

(Beaujolais, France)

This natural producer is making excellent Morgons and Fleuries from 100 percent gamay.

Michael Moosbrugger

Schloss Gobelsburg (Kamptal, Austria)

His Rieslings and Grüner Veltliners reflect the care of his minimal-intervention winemaking and organic farming.

Rajat Parr

**Domaine de la Côte
(Sta. Rita Hills, California)**

One of several winemaking projects of this sommelier and author; its elegant pinot noirs remind me of the finest French examples.

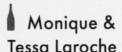

Guillaume d'Angerville

Domaine du Pélican (Jura, France)

The former banker took over his father's fabled Volnay estate in Burgundy and rose to the occasion. Now he's making fascinating wines in the Jura, too.

Arianna Occhipinti

Occhipinti Winery (Sicily, Italy)

Arianna has become a beloved figure for a new generation of wine lovers. Anyone who has met Arianna will instantly vouch for her contagious positive attitude and her equally expressive wines.

Monique &
Tessa Laroche

Domaine Aux Moines (Loire, France)

Monique and Tessa are an under-the-radar mother-and-daughter team that has a long track record of quality. They are making superb wines today.

Let's Talk About Natural Wine

➡️ **Nothing divides wine drinkers today like natural wine.** Even nonprofessionals have such strong opinions; the topic borders on political, with rabid factions on the right and left. Me? I have to confess that I was always critical of natural wine. As much as I respect the men and women making it, as well as the taste and opinions of my peers and young sommeliers who are in favor of it, the volatility (volatile acids) that causes the flavors to change quickly; the ciderish, kombucha-like flavors; that aroma of mouse cage that you sometimes get—none of these aspects are what excite me about wine. It is an interesting trend, and I'm eager to observe how these wines develop.

➡️ **As defined on page 42, natural wine is wine from organically and/or biodynamically farmed grapes that's bottled in small quantities by free-spirited producers (what I love most about it).**

Nothing is added or removed in the making of the wine. None of the chemical additives or processing aids frequently employed by conventional winemakers throughout all steps of the winemaking process come into play, and the juice is allowed to ferment using naturally occurring yeast with minimal—ideally no—intervention, such as filtration. What goes into the bottle is considered a living, untainted organism, perfect in its imperfections.

One of the natural camp's biggest arguments against mainstream winemaking is the addition of sulfur dioxide (SO_2). What's not talked about is that sulfites result naturally in any fermentation process. You can also find them in apples, green asparagus, and dried fruit. They're even in french fries! To add a touch of sulfur before bottling is, so far, the best way of preserving wine and ensuring that the bottles can ship worldwide. The sulfur binds yeast, oxygen, pigments, sugars, and other compounds that can have a negative impact on wine over time. It also allows it to age gracefully. (The belief that sulfites give you a headache is a myth, by the way. What really causes headaches are biogenic amines such as histamines and tyramine, or the overconsumption of alcohol. No way around that!)

Unsulfured wines have a touch more generous fruit and will appear to be more drinkable on glasses one and two. However, the fruit starts to taste wilted the longer the bottle stays open. I talked about this with Jean-Louis Dutraive from Domaine de la Grand'Cour, one of the absolute stars of Beaujolais and a person full of life. He said that he fills some bottles without SO_2 for his personal consumption but finds that the last glass is not the best.

It's this inconsistency that causes me to be critical of natural wines: As someone whose livelihood—and those of his staff—is dependent on the happiness and return visits of his customers, it's hard for me to champion a wine that can behave erratically from one glass to the next.

I also take issue with the fact that the kombucha-like character of some natural wines obscures what grape it was made from. I recently served my coauthor, Christine, and her friends a natural sauvignon blanc. They were unable to tell me what varietal it was made from— and sauvignon blanc is the most distinctively aromatic grape! The country of origin was impossible to determine, too. For me, being unable to identify what the wine is made from or where it was produced—an unintentional result of not adding sulfur—takes away so much of the pleasure of drinking. And yes, I realize what a cranky old man I sound like!

The Sneaky Experiment

I was reminded of that ultimate philosophy of pleasure when Christine and I took some young foodies, plus Sarah Thomas, a super-talented young sommelier at Le Bernardin, to a research dinner at my favorite Thai place in Queens. We started with sparkling wines, continued with a Sandhi 2015 Bentrock Santa Barbara chardonnay, and moved over to a natural wine that Sarah brought, followed by a dry and an off-dry German Riesling. It was fascinating to observe how everyone's eyes lit up when I revealed that the wine they had just tasted was natural. They said they found it interesting, different, and new. To me, the wine was volatile and smelled mousy, and I said so. Suddenly, I realized that I had cast myself out of the conversation by going against it. But after dinner, I noticed one little detail: All the bottles were empty . . . except the natural one. I asked everyone the ultimate question: "Would you order a second bottle?" The answer was no!

Because in my opinion, the best wine is always finished right after the appetizer, and you immediately order another.

Going to Extremes

It would be arrogant to brush off the situation, but it sparked my interest, so I wanted to learn more. I reached out to a couple of leading people in the industry and asked them about natural wine. The first person I called was my friend Rajat Parr, a superstar sommelier and rising winemaker (he made the aforementioned Sandhi chardonnay): I noticed that he had been posting pét-nats (pétillants naturels) on Instagram. According to Raj, whose interest in natural wine was sparked in 2015, he finds these wines interesting, inexpensive, and easy to drink. He said there are "a lot of fucked-up wines out there," but the trend will continue and wines will become better.

Since we're friends, I decided to ask him some tougher questions. Does he no longer like "sound" wines from, say, Roulot, Domaine de la Romanée-Conti, Egon Müller, Château Latour—you know, the classics we studied? He still does, very much so, and agreed that you can't be a young wine professional and not know the classics. Natural wine is a specialty, he said, but you can't fully understand it if you don't know the base.

I moved on to one of the biggest personalities in natural wine, journalist Alice Feiring, whom I very much respect, even if I have a very different opinion and palate. I thought we were going to clash—I thought she was 100 percent antisulfur, etc.—so I was surprised to hear that her definition of natural wine is simply "organic viniculture, nothing added, nothing taken away, and very minimal sulfur."

While I see natural wines' volatility as a flaw, Alice sees it as a charming characteristic. "I like how expressive they are, and that every taste is going to be different," she said. "I like the adventure and that it's not a boring conversation with one bottle. I think the most important thing with natural wine is the emotional response."

She, too, is disturbed by the current trend in the natural wine world toward "kombucha wines," or bright, sour wines with an almost fizzy factor. "Now I'm the one that feels like an old fart when I see people go, 'What is this? It's kombucha!' I'm like, I like kombucha, but when kombucha gets mousy? That's disgusting."

In her book *The Battle for Wine and Love*, Alice lamented the "Parkerization" of wine, in which winemakers around the world began making uniform wines—concentrated, highly extracted reds that were dark in color and high in alcohol—in an attempt to get high scores from the influential critic Robert Parker. (Who, it must be said, did a tremendous amount to put American wine on the global map.) Now she sees a similarly worrisome reduction in natural wine to a certain style that doesn't take into account all the different styles and flavors and aromas possible in natural wine. (An effect that Christine, who joined us, dubbed "Actionization," for the Vice Munchies personality Action Bronson's influence in getting millennials into the *vin de soif* style, which is easy-drinking, ciderish, and cloudy.) "People are trying to make [natural wine] a brand," Alice predicted.

While Actionization could be seen as the extreme consequence of Parkerization twenty years later, Alice is heartened to see what she calls a market correction—one that's having an impact on conventional winemakers. More people are returning to natural yeast fermentation, which wasn't the case even ten years ago. . . . And all the best producers have decreased their level of sulfur. So natural wine is redefining great wine, basically returning it to sanity."

What was most interesting was that we ended with an open dialogue, and therefore had the liberty to reflect afterward. Alice wrote me that it was very insightful for her to see how far apart our starting points of learning wine were: "Because of my alternate route with very little formal education, I was much freer to accept different flavors. Right now there are these kids knowing only these natural wines. They don't know the difference between Chablis and Meursault. And worse, they don't care!" She took the words out of my mouth! Alice even inspired me to host an impromptu natural wine night at Aldo Sohm Wine Bar, which grew into a flight on the menu.

Finding the Middle Road

A few days later, I took a bike ride with Bobby Stuckey, a Master Sommelier from Boulder, Colorado, who co-owns Frasca Food and Wine. I told him about my experience in Queens and said I felt like a right-wing conservative talking to far-left liberals. He thought it over and said, "It's actually the opposite, since natural winemakers are the old-school traditionalists." (Controversial, I know!)

My takeaway from these conversations, as well as what's been going on in food and wine media, was that there is too much of a conflict and not enough dialogue.

The key is to stay open: to evolve and learn. I agree that sometimes winemakers go too far in their quest for perfection. There was a time when using unlimited pesticides in vineyards and SO_2 in the bottle was acceptable. There was too much research done into yeast, and, as a result, it seemed like wines around the world suddenly tasted the same. I understand the countermovement of the market away from highly commercialized wines that are overextracted, overoaked, and overdesigned toward wines that favor craftsmanship and individuality. While they might not be natural, per se, there are exceptional noncorporate winemakers who are constantly evolving, adopting less-intrusive farming methods and less-manipulative winemaking techniques to produce beautiful, sound bottles.

At the other end of the spectrum, the rawness of natural wine can be limiting. I believe that the truth lies in the middle of the two extremes. Just as I'm learning by tasting natural wines and talking to their makers, I hope that conventional winemakers will take note of what young drinkers are so thirsty for—nonindustrial wines with soul—and return to their roots in every way.

As Alice put it so well, the way to judge a wine is based on your emotional response to it, not getting dogmatic. "You can't overstate the importance of deliciousness," she said. "Otherwise, why drink it?"

MY TOP 10 NONCORPORATE WINEMAKERS

▷ **Domaine Roulot**
(Meursault, Burgundy, France)

▷ **Pierre-Yves Colin-Morey**
(Chassagne Montrachet, Burgundy, France)

▷ **Domaine Gérard Boulay**
(Sancerre, France)

▷ **Château Pontet-Canet**
(Pauillac, Bordeaux, France)

▷ **Envínate** (Spain)

▷ **Borgo del Tiglio** (Friuli, Italy)

▷ **Johannes Leitz**
(Rheingau, Germany)

▷ **Bernhard Ott**
(Wagram, Austria)

▷ **Arnot-Roberts**
(Sonoma, California)

▷ **Lingua Franca**
(Willamette Valley, Oregon)

MY FAVORITE— YES, I SAID IT—NATURAL WINEMAKERS

▷ **Thierry Allemand**
(Cornas, France)

▷ **Jacques Lassaigne**
(Champagne, France)

▷ **Giuseppe Rinaldi**
(Barolo, Italy)

▷ **Christian Tschida**
(Burgenland, Austria)

▷ **Giusto Occhipinti/COS**
(Sicily, Italy)

2

How
to
Drink

▶ Now that you understand the hows, whats, and wheres of wine, it's time to move on to the whys and experience how those factors play out on the tongue. Learning what you like is the fun part, of course. What else has such a delicious learning curve? (Okay, besides maybe becoming a chocolate expert.) Just as it takes lots of practice to get to Carnegie Hall, you have to drink hundreds of bottles before you become a wine expert. But you don't have to drink quite that much to be able to understand which grapes, countries, and even regions resonate with you—you just have to have a good memory. That's because being able to communicate what you like—and, perhaps, more important, what you don't like—to a restaurant sommelier, to the person behind the wine counter at the shop, even to a friend who's offering to bring over a bottle for dinner is what will help them guide you to that sweet spot that much faster.

In this section, you'll learn how to taste (hint: it doesn't start with your tongue!), shop for, order, serve, and store wine someplace other than above your fridge or in your stove. Who knows? Maybe you're even ready to start a collection—that is, if you're lucky enough to have the temperature-controlled space. There are lots of charts for the visually inclined, as well as shortcuts to help you speed up the learning process. My goal isn't to turn you into a wine geek like me. Rather, it's to tune you in to all those amazing things going on in your glass. Ready?

Aldo's Philosophy of Drinking

➤ **It's been amazing to watch wine become a lifestyle product in America over the last fifteen years.**

A what? You know: something that signals your tastes and personality to others. Something that's just part of your everyday life. Back in the day, Americans drank cocktails at meals. A two-martini lunch was perfectly normal. You'd never do that now! These days, you see people in movies sipping a glass of wine with a meal, or chatting on the couch after a crummy day at work, or catching up with a friend on the porch. Even airlines tout their wine lists, curated by celebrity sommeliers. In the '90s, the *idea*

of a celebrity sommelier would have had us aspiring somms doubled over with laughter.

When I was growing up in Austria, wine was always there. It was on the table at pretty much every meal, and we kids got to have a taste as soon as we'd moved on from milk. For adults, an apéritif of white or sparkling wine before a restaurant meal was just the way you did it—and come to think of it, it's pretty much still what I do today: a glass of Champagne before the food (the German expression for this translates to "making the palate green"), a glass of white with my first course, red with my main, and perhaps a sweet wine to round out dessert.

I've made wine my life on so many levels. Five days a week, lunch and dinner, I observe how people approach and experience it—for pleasure or adventure, status or connoisseurship. For me personally, though, wine represents joy. Its ultimate gift is how it brings people together. It stimulates conversation like nothing else. You get something going and it brings everyone into the mix, whether you're sitting with friends and opening a bottle of Champagne or having a glass solo at the bar. In my experience, it's almost guaranteed that when you have a glass of wine, you'll have a conversation in no time. Now that our heads are always stuck in our phones, these kinds of connections are increasingly meaningful.

There's also a cultural component of wine that I find fascinating: It evokes memories. Whenever I'm lucky enough to be able to drink a very old bottle, I take a moment to pull out my phone and check to see what was happening in, say, 1961, when that Cheval Blanc was harvested. What was the world going through? What has (or hasn't) changed? Some vintages give you the chills: Once I tasted a wine from 1945, which made me think about the great pains that must have been taken not only to make the wine during that year but also to hide it from looting soldiers. In Austria, there are very few remaining bottles dating from before 1950, because of the Germans and Russians who came through. Wine might just be a liquid, but to me, it's history in a bottle.

At home, I'm a very moody drinker. That is, I drink according to how I feel in the moment. Most nights after work, I have a beer and go to sleep. (True story.) Sundays, however, are for wine. I keep about five hundred bottles in the basement of my building, and more in a wine-storage facility. Whether I pull something out of the "cellar" or reach for the $16 bottle of Raisins Gaulois that I bought at the neighborhood wine store depends entirely on what my partner and I are cooking, what the occasion is, even the weather—temperature and humidity are big factors in determining what I feel like drinking. Sometimes I'm feeling curious and want to explore something new,

whether it's a natural winemaker I've never heard of or part of the intense Spanish trip I'm on right now. If the bottle doesn't work out, I might save it to try again the next day, or use it to cook with. I don't get upset; I learn what I can from it and move on.

On Sundays, I also love to get a group together for dinner at SriPraPhai, an awesome, no-frills Thai place in Queens that lets you BYO. It might be a bunch of sommeliers who each bring a bottle or three to discuss for hours. Or I love to go with my neighbor and cycling partner, Murray, who has been learning about wine with me. He and his wife let me bring the wines (and boxes of glasses) and order the food. It's fun to watch them react to the different combinations. Sometimes we have an all-Champagne evening—Champagne being perfect with Thai food—sometimes all-Riesling (ditto). These nights are about discovery and conversation: Like good wine with food, it's the perfect pairing.

And there doesn't have to be a super-special occasion for me to open a great bottle at home. If I've had a good day and I'm feeling like that '74 Ridge cabernet sauvignon would be perfect with short ribs, that's reason enough. (And believe me, it was perfect.)

How to Taste Wine (and Form an Opinion)

► Talking with friends while drinking a bottle of wine is one thing. Stopping to smell, taste, and even look at what's in the glass in front of you is an entirely different experience. Once you learn how to "listen" to a wine, you'll be fascinated by the stories it tells. My tasting ritual is pretty wonky and detailed, so I'll break it down to the essentials.

Throughout this section you'll find a lot of key words, or descriptors, to use when talking about wine. Identifying them will help you become not only a better taster but a better customer, too, as these are the terms that sommeliers and wine-store people are listening for when they're figuring out a wine for you.

First, Look

➡ **Tilt your glass so the wine slopes up the side,** preferably holding it up against a light background, such as a white tablecloth or the back of a menu. (Ideally you do this in daylight for the truest color, since most restaurant lighting lends too yellow a cast, but you don't need to geek out that hard . . . yet.)

TILT GLASS

If You're Drinking Red . . .

Look at the color: **the more violet the shade, the younger the wine.** It can also tell you a bit about the nebbiolos, gamays, and pinot noirs, for instance, which are lighter, while merlot, cabernet sauvignon, and malbec are inky. These days, many winemakers are following the market preference for darker wines, which some people (mistakenly) associate with higher quality.

Next, **how intense is the color and clarity from the center of the glass to the rim?** The darker the wine at the center, the thicker-skinned the grapes. Purple wine might mean a long maceration. As the wine ages, you will notice a lighter orange hue around the rim. A watery-looking rim indicates a warm climate or a hot vintage. Tiny bubbles around the edge are a sign of CO_2, which could either be a flaw or a young Beaujolais, which has a little effervescence to it.

If You're Drinking White . . .

Whites, particularly **those aged with oak, get more golden as they age**—though a yellowish wine could also indicate oxidation or a riper grape, which will translate to a richer, fuller-bodied wine with a higher alcohol level, depending on how it was fermented. A greenish tinge tells you it's very young. Cloudy whites—those that were unfiltered and unfined— tell you that you're most likely looking at a naturally inspired wine. (Same goes for reds.)

WHAT ARE WINE LEGS?

→ Legs, tears, whatever you call them—those clear liquid streaks or droplets that run down the glass after you swirl it or that creep up the glass from the edge of the wine after it's been sitting for a few minutes—tell you about the wine's alcohol level. (If you think about it, alcohol is a gas, so it evaporates. Those little tears trying to escape are just that.) The sharper and narrower they are, the higher the alcohol level (or it could be a sweet wine). Wider tears mean a lower alcohol level or that it's from a cool climate or vintage.

A S K
A L D O

Next, Smell

➤ Your nose is your most important tasting organ. Without our sense of smell, we couldn't even perceive raw onion! **With your mouth slightly open, dip your nose into the glass and inhale.** What are the aromas you experience? Are they clean, or are there flaws like oxidation or cork taint? The whole flavor story of the wine is in what you smell. The more complexity, the better.

I like to smell twice: The first time, I'm looking for raw characterizations. Is it mushroomy? Is there oak? Fruit? Spice? Flowers? The second time, I swirl the glass to open up the wine, then start adding specifics to my characterizations: "I smell cherries, licorice, violet," and so on. It's like forming a first impression of someone and then getting to know them better.

Some French people believe you should swirl counterclockwise, because they think it makes the wine smell different than if you swirl clockwise. Try and decide for yourself!

Should I Be Swirling My Glass?

At the risk of sounding like the stereotypical judgmental sommelier, I can tell a lot about a customer by how he or she swirls. Some swirl so hard I think the wine's going to spill. Others grip the glass by the bowl. Some even slosh it back and forth. All amateur moves! If someone holds the stem and raises the glass a couple of inches off the table before swirling, or even slips the bottom of the glass between their index and middle fingers to control the swirl on the table, doing it just twice, I know they're a pro.

But you know how I spot a real wine expert? They sniff first. People have a tendency to swirl the glass, stick their nose in it, say something like "Strawberry!"—swirl again— "Raspberry!"—and so on. But to me, this is like sprint/stop/ sprint/stop. Why not gather your impressions more fully? I prefer to sniff the wine, get those raw characterizations I mentioned earlier, then swirl and take a second deep, concentrated inhalation, really focusing and capturing the full range of impressions.

Aromas of Wine

*Aroma very often translates to flavor. See what speaks to
your palate to help guide you toward the right wine.*

*Many white
wines have
aromas that fall
in this area.*

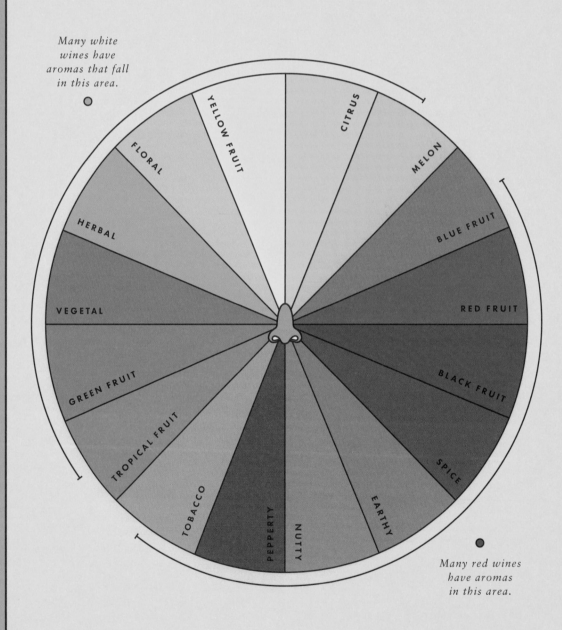

YELLOW FRUIT

CITRUS

MELON

FLORAL

BLUE FRUIT

HERBAL

VEGETAL

RED FRUIT

GREEN FRUIT

BLACK FRUIT

TROPICAL FRUIT

SPICE

TOBACCO

PEPPERY

NUTTY

EARTHY

*Many red wines
have aromas
in this area.*

GRÜNER VELTLINER ——— ◯ ◯ ● ● ◯ ◯ ◯ ◯ ◯ ◯ ◯

CHENIN BLANC ——— ◯ ◯ ● ● ◯ ◯ ◯ ◯ ◯ ◯ ◯

RIESLING ——— ◯ ● ● ● ● ● ◯ ◯ ◯ ◯ ◯

GEWÜRTZRAMINER ——— ◯ ◯ ● ● ◯ ◯ ◯ ◯ ◯ ◯ ◯

SAUVIGNON BLANC ——— ◯ ● ● ● ● ● ● ◯ ◯ ◯ ◯

CHARDONNAY ——— ◯ ◯ ● ● ● ● ● ◯ ◯ ◯ ◯

VIOGNIER ——— ◯ ● ● ◯ ◯ ◯ ◯ ◯ ◯ ◯ ◯

ALBARIÑO ——— ◯ ● ● ● ◯ ◯ ◯ ◯ ◯ ◯ ◯

PINOT GRIGIO ——— ◯ ◯ ● ● ● ◯ ◯ ◯ ◯ ◯ ◯

DOLCETTO ——— ● ● ● ● ● ◯ ◯ ◯ ◯ ◯ ◯

NEBBIOLO ——— ● ● ● ● ● ● ● ◯ ◯ ◯ ◯

GAMAY ——— ● ● ● ● ◯ ◯ ◯ ◯ ◯ ◯ ◯

GRENACHE ——— ● ● ● ● ◯ ◯ ◯ ◯ ◯ ◯ ◯

SANGIOVESE ——— ● ● ● ● ● ◯ ◯ ◯ ◯ ◯ ◯

PINOT NOIR ——— ● ● ● ● ● ● ● ◯ ◯ ◯ ◯

TEMPRANILLO ——— ● ● ● ● ● ◯ ◯ ◯ ◯ ◯ ◯

SYRAH ——— ● ● ● ● ● ● ● ◯ ◯ ◯ ◯

CABERNET SAUVIGNON ——— ● ● ● ● ● ● ◯ ◯ ◯ ◯ ◯

MERLOT ——— ● ● ● ◯ ◯ ◯ ◯ ◯ ◯ ◯ ◯

Now, Taste

➡️ **Take a sip and hold it in your mouth for a few seconds,** allowing it to touch every part of your mouth. Spit or swallow. Your tongue will tell you about the characteristics of the wine. I'm a very structured taster, which means I have an internal tasting grid that I go through in the same order every time. It allows me to have a set of reference points rather than dive into chaos. For you, being able to describe what you like from among essential characteristics (pages 154–160) is enormously helpful when buying and ordering wine.

MY TASTING CHECKLIST

☐ How **sweet** or **dry** is it?

☐ How **acidic**? (Does it leave a refreshing tingle along the sides of your tongue, or a vinegar-like jolt? Does it make your mouth water? That's another sign of acidity.)

☐ Are the **tannins** subtle and rounded, or do they bite into your tongue and dry out your cheeks like a cup of oversteeped tea?

☐ Then there's the **alcohol**: After you've swallowed and exhaled, does it burn the back of your throat like a whiskey, or leave a gentle warmth?

☐ What's happening with the **fruit**?

☐ Do you **taste** what you smelled?

☐ Finally, are the **elements in balance**? This harmony, in which no one aspect dominates, indicates a good wine.

A VISUAL GUIDE to the FLAVOR REGIONS of YOUR TONGUE

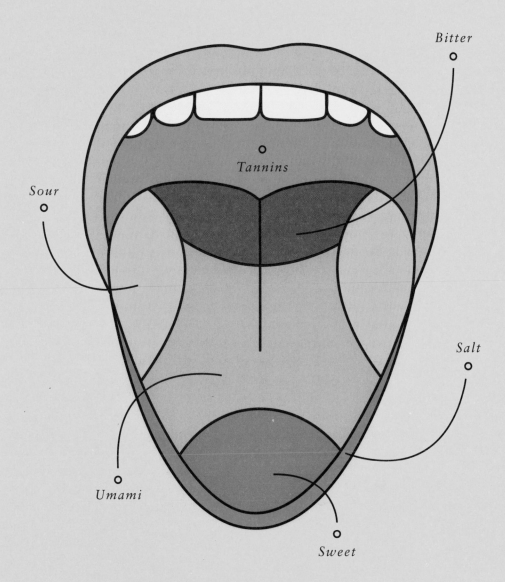

Bitter

Sour

Tannins

Salt

Umami

Sweet

WINE VOCAB FOR THE WORLD

→ I believe that most of our scent and flavor references are highly personal and are mostly developed during childhood, that time when we put everything into our mouths. (Wooden spoons, dirt, leather, you name it.) **Because wine is still primarily European, a lot of the descriptors that are used are eurocentric. But they shouldn't be the only ones:** If you grew up in a non-Western culture, use whatever words are evoked by a taste or smell. What some experience as strawberry might be your lychee. The language of wine will only get more interesting as a result.

The Elements to Taste For

1
Acidity

→ This one's pretty basic: Acidity is that puckery feeling when you drink. It could be like lemon or lime, aggressive like a Granny Smith apple, or round and tart like a Golden Delicious. I look at how high the acidity is, as well as how fresh: Is it integrated into the wine? Take a young nebbiolo or Riesling, whose acid is often so high, it blows up the tannins and keeps your palate too busy to get to the fruit, a sensation sommeliers describe as "tight." (That's why those wines benefit from aging, which we say opens them up.)

The acidity in Chablis and Champagne is bright and zippy, as is common in white wines from cooler northern regions. There the wines aren't as dominated by the grapes' sugar production, so the freshness and delicacy of the fruit can shine.

Acidity makes a wine seem dry—i.e., it has little residual sugar. The less dry and acidic, the more sugar there is. It's like adding sugar to lemonade to make it palatable.

Acidic wines are also more food-friendly. Think about it: Acid cuts fat, and fat also needs a little bit of sugar just to coat it.

(MOST ACIDIC)

CHAMPAGNE

RIESLING

CHENIN BLANC

CHABLIS

ALBARIÑO

MUSCADET

SANCERRE

WHITE BURGUNDY

CHARDONNAY
(Santa Barbara, CA)

NEBBIOLO

GAMAY

PINOT NOIR *(Burgundy)*

SYRAH *(Northern Rhône)*

RIOJA

CABERNET FRANC

LEFT BANK BORDEAUX

GRÜNER VELTLINER

SAUVIGNON BLANC
(New World)

CHARDONNAY

PINOT NOIR *(Sonoma)*

CONDRIEU/VIOGNIER

MARSANNE/ROUSSANE

CABERNET *(Washington State)*

ZINFANDEL

MALBEC

(LEAST ACIDIC)

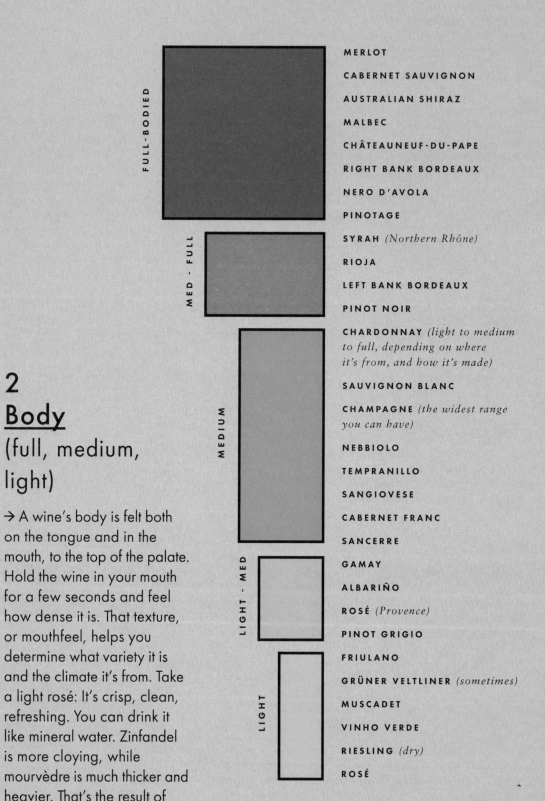

MERLOT

CABERNET SAUVIGNON

AUSTRALIAN SHIRAZ

MALBEC

CHÂTEAUNEUF-DU-PAPE

RIGHT BANK BORDEAUX

NERO D'AVOLA

PINOTAGE

SYRAH *(Northern Rhône)*

RIOJA

LEFT BANK BORDEAUX

PINOT NOIR

CHARDONNAY *(light to medium to full, depending on where it's from, and how it's made)*

SAUVIGNON BLANC

CHAMPAGNE *(the widest range you can have)*

NEBBIOLO

TEMPRANILLO

SANGIOVESE

CABERNET FRANC

SANCERRE

GAMAY

ALBARIÑO

ROSÉ *(Provence)*

PINOT GRIGIO

FRIULANO

GRÜNER VELTLINER *(sometimes)*

MUSCADET

VINHO VERDE

RIESLING *(dry)*

ROSÉ

FULL-BODIED

MED - FULL

MEDIUM

LIGHT - MED

LIGHT

2
<u>Body</u>
(full, medium, light)

→ A wine's body is felt both on the tongue and in the mouth, to the top of the palate. Hold the wine in your mouth for a few seconds and feel how dense it is. That texture, or mouthfeel, helps you determine what variety it is and the climate it's from. Take a light rosé: It's crisp, clean, refreshing. You can drink it like mineral water. Zinfandel is more cloying, while mourvèdre is much thicker and heavier. That's the result of a heavier phenolic structure.

3
Alcohol

→ Alcohol is the fat of wine. What?! It's a flavor enhancer, to a point. With too much alcohol, the wine gets boozy and heats up your mouth till it's practically burning. Think of a low-alcohol red like Beaujolais, which tastes leaner, versus a big, bold Napa cab, whose higher alcohol makes it richer and more powerful on the palate. That smooth, velvety jamminess also makes it easy to drink! Too much alcohol, though, and you just get that burning sensation in the back of your throat. That wine is deemed "hot."

Higher sugar means higher alcohol—ranging from 13.5 to 16%—and that usually indicates that the wine comes from a warmer climate. These days, as health becomes a focus, producers are making less-boozy wines—even in California, where 16.5% ABV isn't unheard of.

(HIGH ALCOHOL)

ZINFANDEL

MOURVÈDRE

GRENACHE

NAPA CAB *(to a degree)*

RIGHT BANK MERLOT

BRUNELLO

NERO D'AVOLA

RIBEIRA DEL DUERO

TORO

AUSTRALIAN SHIRAZ
(medium to high)

MALBEC

GEWÜRTZTRAMINER

VIOGNIER

CHENIN BLANC

CHARDONNAY *(medium to high)*

GRÜNER VELTLINER

PINOT GRIS *(Alsace)*

SANCERRE *(medium to low)*

CHABLIS

RIESLING
(depending on style)

ALBARIÑO

PINOT GRIGIO

CHAMPAGNE

ROSÉ

MUSCADET

VINHO VERDE

(LOW ALCOHOL)

4
<u>Tannins</u>

→ Tannins are picked up by the center of your tongue and can be experienced as bitter or astringent. Some people think tannins and a wine's "dryness" go hand in hand, but it's really just that tannins dry out your palate—that feeling that you need a sip of water. They don't affect the wine's sweetness, either. A young Barolo or Bordeaux can be overtannic in its youth because of the juice/skin/seed ratio, but it will soften with age. However, if a wine has green, harsh tannins because it was pressed with green seeds instead of mature brown ones, it will never mature well, no matter how long it's aged.

5
<u>Sweetness</u>
(dry, off-dry, sweet)

→ Put most simply, dry is the opposite of sweet, and off-dry is between the two. You'll feel it right on the tip of your tongue. But just because a wine isn't sweet doesn't mean it doesn't have any sugar in it: There's no such thing as a wine with 0 percent residual sugar. There aren't that many yeast strains that can ferment out all the sugar, and if they could, that wine would be brutal to drink. The way we perceive dry versus off-dry wine is often influenced by the acidity. (We often think Champagnes, which have a lot of acidity, are dry, but they often have 10 grams of sugar, which is a lot!)

(HIGH TANNINS)

NEBBIOLO

CABERNET SAUVIGNON

CARMÉNÈRE

SANGIOVESE

PINOT NOIR *(Old World)*

TEMPRANILLO

GRENACHE

MERLOT

MALBEC

BARBERA/DOLCETTO

GAMAY

PINOT NOIR *(New World)*

ZINFANDEL

(LOW TANNINS)

If your wine is too tannic, decanting or aerating is often very helpful: The fruit will evolve a little more quickly. See page 212 to learn more.

6
Flavors

→ Remember those aromas from page 150? Now it's time to see if they translate to your tongue. Like aromas, flavors are very personal and come from your memory bank. You don't have to get super geeky and be like the person in the documentary *Somm* who said that one wine tasted like "cut tennis balls and garden hose." But, hey, if that's what it evokes for you, go with it. The flavor spectrum is endless. Below are just the basic categories. Keep in mind that sometimes flavors have nothing to do with the grapes themselves—minerality is impacted by the soil the grape is grown in, and an oaky flavor is, of course, caused by the vessel in which the wine was aged.

Herbal

I like to mentally divide these green flavors into soft herbs (mint, thyme, etc.) and woody herbs and plants, such as rosemary and eucalyptus.

Fruit

Do you taste red fruits like strawberry, raspberry, cherry, red plum, or red currant, or dark fruit like plum, blackberry, black currant, black cherry, or even olive? (There are also jammier dried fruit and more exotic tropical fruit, tree fruit, and melon.)

Mineral

This popular term comes from the soil the grapes are grown in. The resulting flavor profile can be like wet stone, volcanic stone, chalk on a chalkboard, the scent of rain on asphalt, or the cold, smoky tone of an extinguished campfire. You get the idea. It is said in wine circles that American sommeliers taste for fruit, while European ones taste for soil. It's true that I look for the latter flavors, which, I think, are more helpful for identifying where the wine is from.

Earth

This is where you get into mushrooms, truffles, leather, autumn leaves, moss, and the like.

Oak

You hear this one all the time, too. It's the result of wine that's been aged in oak or in a tank with oak chips. The flavors that arise can include vanilla, warm woodfire smoke, toasted bread, even dill. That last one is most associated with American-grown oak.

SOHM SECRET

Finally, I ask myself one last tasting question: How much would I pay for this wine? It helps me put the bottle into perspective.

Finally, Reflect

➡️ Take a moment to observe the wine's finish and **sit with your experience**. Some wines, like rosé, are simple and refreshing. Others, like a mature Bordeaux, stay with you on the palate, revealing additional layers of flavor for sometimes ten seconds or longer. These are high-quality wines that you want to pay attention to and reflect on, rather than chug while you talk with friends. In the wine world, it's not about power—it's about the length of the finish.

GIVE IT A CHANCE!

➔ Even when I taste a wine I don't like, I still keep observing it over time. Why? The minute the cork is pulled, it's like giving birth—and you don't give birth to a fully developed eighteen-year-old! There are waves of flavor as a wine opens up over the course of a meal. It might start out pretty animalic (i.e., musky) in smell and then have really pretty fruit before closing down completely. An hour or two later, it might open up again to feature bright raspberries. There is no magic time chart or formula: You won't know until you try it—and try it again.

Suggested Wines by Preference, Mood & Occasion

SUGGESTED WINES by

Preference

"I like" and "I'm looking for" are the words I hear most often. Here are some of the most common likes—and my corresponding suggestions, from big-picture to granular.

	I LIKE...	BIG PICTURE	YOUR BOTTLE
1	**Bold Reds**	You're looking at cabernet, malbec, or zinfandel	● Luca Malbec
2	**Funky Reds**	Ask for a natural wine	● Reds from Jean-François Ganevat
3	**Cheap Reds**	Get to know Spanish wines	● Arlanza La Vallada, Olivier Rivière
4	**Very Dry White Wines**	Go to cool coastal regions like Muscadet, Rías Baixas, Sonoma Coast	● Orthogneiss muscadet from Domaine de la Pépière
5	**Full-Bodied Whites**	Grenache blanc should do the trick	● Le Cigare Blanc grenache blanc, Bonny Doon
6	**Oaky Whites**	Napa chardonnay all the way	● Patz & Hall (Sonoma Coast)
7	**Low-Acid Whites**	Take a viognier	● Les Vignes d'à Côté, Cave Yves Cuilleron
8	**Cloudy Whites**	Look at amphora wines	● Pithos Bianco, COS
9	**Mineral Whites**	Stay in Europe	● Chablis, Domaine Louis Michel & Fils
10	**Salty Whites**	You want an albariño or a Mediterranean white	● Leirana albariño, Bodegas Forjas del Salnes

SUGGESTED WINES by

Mood

I always say that I'm a moody drinker. That doesn't mean I'm a brooding drunk; rather, a change in the weather or a bad commute home can influence what I want in the glass more than anything on the plate.

	MOOD	BIG PICTURE	YOUR BOTTLE
1	It's hot and muggy out and I want something refreshing	Albariño, rosé (try one from Long Island), or something from Santorini	● Thalassitis Assyrtiko, Gai'a Wines
2	I'm feeling like some serious-thinking-required wines	Splurge on a Northern Rhône syrah, an old Piemontese red, or even Marsala	● Marsala Superiore 10-Year Riserva (NV), Marco De Bartoli
3	I've had a long day and I want a mini splurge	Pop a half bottle of Champagne	● Roederer Estate sparkling wine
4	It's the perfect fall day	A Barolo from Northern Piemonte is just right for the food	● Spanna Colline Novaresi, Antonio Vallana e Figlio
5	It's a blizzard out. Help!	Time for a full bottle of Champagne . . .	● Christophe Mignon pinot meunier
6	I'm in the mood for something delicious but don't want to think too hard	Red Bordeaux, California pinot noir, Tuscan red	● Pinot Noir, "The Pip," Clendenen Family Vineyards
7	I'm looking to go natural	Amphora wines, Friuli wines, pét-nats	● No Sapiens, Bichi

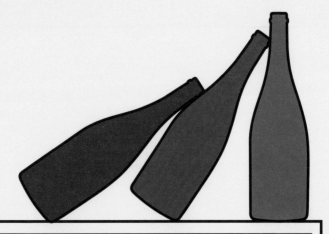

IF YOU LIKE X WINE...

TRY (Y) TO MAKE YOUR WAY TOWARD (Z)

WHITES

Grüner Veltliner ▷ Pinot grigio ▷▷ Albariño

Napa sauvignon blanc ▷ South African sauvignon blanc ▷▷ White Bordeaux

White Burgundy ▷ Santa Barbara chardonnay ▷▷ Godello

California chardonnay ▷ Australian chardonnay ▷▷ Italian chardonnay

Brand-name Champagne ▷ Grower Champagne ▷▷ Crémant

Pinot grigio ▷ Arneis from Piemonte ▷▷ Argentine torrontés

New Zealand sauvignon blanc ▷ Austrian sauvignon blanc ▷▷ Alto Adige Sauvignon blanc

REDS

Argentine malbec ▷ California zinfandel ▷▷ Languedoc-Roussillon carignan

Bordeaux cabernet sauvignon ▷ Super Tuscan ▷▷ Northern Rhône syrah

Pinot noir ▷ Spanish garnacha ▷▷ Northern Piemonte nebbiolo

Beaujolais nouveau ▷ Morgon ▷▷ Pinotage

Merlot ▷ Carménère ▷▷ Alto Adige teroldego

Syrah ▷ Ribeira Sacra mencía ▷▷ Austrian Blaufränkisch

SUGGESTED WINES by

Occasion

What you drink often depends on the why and where: You're not going to bust out a Bordeaux at a barbecue, just as you're not celebrating your thirtieth birthday with random Prosecco (I hope).

	OCCASION	BIG PICTURE	YOUR BOTTLE
1	Dinner party with a mystery menu	Grüner Veltliner is always easy, as is a sparkling crémant	● Grüner Veltliner Lois, Weingut Fred Loimer
2	Cocktail party	Prosecco, rosé, Chablis	● Domaine de Triennes rosé
3	Picnic	Light reds like Beaujolais or sangiovese	● Éclat de Granité Côte Roannaise Domaine Sérol
4	Thanksgiving	Light pinot noir from the Sonoma Coast, gamay, light zinfandel	● Pinot Noir, Barda, Bodega Chacra
5	Tuesday non-occasion wine	Half bottle of something fun	● Chianti Classico, Fèlsina
6	Sunday-night stew	Hearty reds from Spain	● Rioja Crianza, Señorio de P. Peciña
7	Labor Day weekend	Domestic rosé	● Ode to Lulu Rosé of Mourvèdre

THE BEST WINE FOR THE OCCASION

Budget ($) and Splurge ($$$)

▽	▽	▽	▽	▽
Birthday party	**Big birthday**	**House party**	**Hostess gift**	**BBQ**
($)	($)	($)	($)	($)
A magnum of Raventós sparkling looks good!	Sandhi Santa Barbara chardonnay	Vietti Nebbiolo Perbacco	Fèlsina Chianti Classico	Lapierre Raisins Gaulois
($$$)	($$$)	($$$)	($$$)	($$$)
Magnum of Krug	Joseph Drouhin Meursault	Fass 4 Grüner Veltliner, Bernhard Ott	Gaja Barbaresco	Saint-Joseph, Domaine Jean-Louis Chave

Wine Myths Debunked!

☒

The lighter the color, the lighter the wine.

Nope. Sometimes a pinot noir, which can be fairly light and translucent, has over 14% ABV.

☒

The heavier the bottle, the better the wine.

It's purely marketing! It might look more expensive, but it doesn't give you any information about what's inside. They didn't spend the money on the wine—they spent it on the bottle.

☒

The longer I decant a wine, the better it becomes.

Mmmm...see my thoughts on decanting on pages 212–213. Once you aerate the wine—in other words, expose it to oxygen—what goes out of the glass will never come back in.

☒

Screw-cap wines are of a lesser quality.

Not necessarily! In fact, corks can be more of a liability for winemakers in terms of a bad one potentially tainting the wine.

☒

All chardonnays are creamy and buttery and heavily oaked.

Chardonnay is such a versatile grape— it's like a chef with an ingredient: It all depends on what she does with it.

☒

Expensive "brand name" wines are worth it.

Spending $150 on a bottle of wine from a famous château doesn't guarantee that it will be life-changing. For the most part, they need to age for years, so you might not like the way it tastes if you open it right away. For the money, I'm more interested in exploring lesser-known regions and grapes to find a great value.

☒

You can't age white wine.

While it's true that most whites, especially lower-priced ones, are best consumed within a year or two after bottling, more complex grapes like Gewürtztraminer, chenin blanc, Chablis, and Riesling can age beautifully for over a decade.

Buying & Ordering Wine

▶ By now, you have the tools that you need to be able to steer a sommelier—or, more likely, a server—toward helping you choose a bottle you'll enjoy at a price that won't panic you. Even if you freeze and forget everything you've just read, remember: It's better to be honest and say that you're a beginner than to pretend you're the next Robert Parker, that famous critic. That's when you start spewing embarrassing things like "I don't like chardonnay, but I love white Burgundy." (They're the same thing! See the list on page 57 to avoid other mix-ups.) And at the end of the day, relax: It's only wine! You might be out $50 or so, but it's not like you bought the wrong car.

Say What You Like

In terms of flavor, you have a variety of adjectives (and experiences) and a range of regions with which you can create the road map to your ideal bottle.

Tip!

Take photos of the bottles you like and save them to their own folder for **easy access.** If you get really into it, download the **Delectable app**, which helps you sort—and shop— your favorites.

"I like light, bright whites with a lot of minerality, like the ones my friend brought back from Greece last summer. Like, zero fruit. Do you have anything like that?"

"I love California cabernets, but I'm ready for something a little more adventurous."

"I really enjoyed this bottle [hand them your phone, where you magically have a photo of it—see tip below]. It was cloudy and kind of fizzy and totally weird."

"I know I don't like merlot or Australian shiraz: They're kind of overpowering and heavy. Is there a lighter red you recommend?"

Communicate Your Price Range

The easiest way to do it is to simply say what prices you want to stay between. If that's still too uncomfortable, ask about two or three wines in that range: "How is this pinot grigio [point to $45 bottle] here? And what about that one [point to $60 bottle] there?"

Tip!

Try to avoid the word **fruity,** which some wine professionals interpret as sweet. You might end up with a Riesling that you won't enjoy. Instead, say "aromatic" for a sauvignon blanc.

Say What You're Eating

Whether you're having salmon or tuna could actually make all the difference. If you're at a wine shop looking for a bottle to go with dinner, tell them what you'll be eating. Wine professionals welcome the challenge! In fact, my coauthor, Christine, gives the staff at Terry's, her local shop, her dinner party menu and a price range, then sends her guests there to pick up the bottles that were chosen, thereby eliminating the guesswork. At a restaurant, it's even easier, of course.

On Wine Prices . . .

What determines the price of a bottle?

Materials

▷ The **bottle**
▷ The **cork**
▷ The **label**

Production

▷ **Labor**
▷ **Land** (the steeper the vineyard, the more labor required)
▷ **Yield** (how rare the wine will be)
▷ Investment in **facilities**
▷ Whether **oak barrels** were used

Shipping, importing, distribution, taxes, and customs

No one is the Steve Jobs of the wine world: In order to make a small fortune in wine, you have to invest a big one.

ASK ALDO

Why do some wines cost thousands of dollars?

Labor, high real estate, the rarity/iconic factor (a great vintage, a cult wine, a limited number of bottles produced, etc.), and the market. The winery sets the price but seldom gets all the money, unless it's sold directly to the consumer, which doesn't happen very often.

How often does the price of a bottle equate to value?

This is such a tough question! Wines become more complex, more layered (and more demanding to the drinker) as you go up the price chart. If you're asking if you should splurge for that $50 bottle of wine at the shop versus the $20 one, yes, you should, depending on the occasion. Higher-priced wines may deliver on greater complexity, but sometimes you want an easier, less challenging wine to enjoy. The $20 range is also ripe for great values, particularly from emerging regions. Ultimately, it's all about your taste preference and what you're looking for in the moment.

Short of carrying super-detailed vineyard maps around, <u>how do you identify a good deal</u>?

Thanks to the internet, you can comparison shop on the spot. Where it starts to get tricky is when you're looking at aged wines.

Pricing Rules of Thumb

Less than $12
Save it for cooking.

$15 to $20
Easy to drink, nothing complicated. Chugging wines!

$20 to $50
You can find some really good wines in this range, especially if you look to emerging regions.

$50 to $75
You can drink very well from established wineries.

$75 to $100
Drinking super-good. #selfcare

Everything over $100
Splurge! Warning: You might spoil your palate.

Remember: At a wine shop, you'll always get more for your money when you look beyond the fancy wine regions.

BEST VALUES FOR
THE BOTTLE
(aka Wines That Overdeliver)

- ☐ Spanish reds and whites
- ☐ Portuguese reds and whites
- ☐ Loire whites
- ☐ Central France (Côte Roannaise)
- ☐ Savoie
- ☐ Northern Rhône reds
- ☐ Santorini whites
- ☐ Any region you think is an underdeveloped area—that's where they're moving in right now
- ☐ Aged Rieslings
- ☐ Sherry
- ☐ Grüner Veltliner is always too cheap IMHO!
- ☐ Sicilian reds are super-interesting
- ☐ Crémants can be very interesting
- ☐ Santa Barbara County and Santa Cruz Mountains have some of the best deals in the US
- ☐ Chile is changing—look to Itata/Bío Bío
- ☐ Canary Island reds and whites

WINE PRICES

173

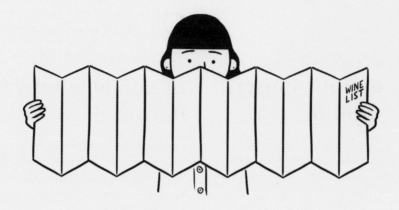

Choosing a Bottle in a Restaurant

→ It's easy for me to say, but **don't be intimidated!** You're paying for the experience of being in a restaurant, so why not get the most of it? By that I mean it's the sommelier's job to know not only every bottle on the list, but every dish on the menu as well—and, most important, how they go together. Your job is to be able to explain what you're looking for as clearly as possible, and to give clear price parameters.

If you're the alpha tasked with ordering for the table, take a moment to gauge your friends. Lead the conversation to find out what they like and don't like. What's the most they're willing to spend? Don't be the jerk who orders an expensive bottle of Champagne when everyone else wants cheap red.

▲ When it comes to price, let your finger be your guide.

The old rule of, um, thumb still applies: While talking to the sommelier, point at the number you want to pay while saying, "I'm looking for something at this price." That way, your date won't know how much (or little) you spent.

TRY TO AVOID...

O Saying **"in the X-dollar range,"** as servers will often go above it by about 20 percent. Instead, say, "Give me a bottle in the X-to-Y range." Or give them your top number and add "or less."

O Asking for something **"in the medium range":** What's medium to a sommelier at a good restaurant could be $200! Such a misunderstanding can be painful at the end of a great evening.

■ Use the Magic Words.

Ask any sommelier "What are you most excited about?" or "What's drinking really well right now?" Not only will they steer you toward the wines they're proudest of, chances are you'll also make a fun discovery and a new friend. Tell them a few things that you like and set a price range, then give them a chance to show you what they've got. I especially do this when I have dinner with my partner at a restaurant with a huge wine list.

⬤ Tell your server or somm what you're thinking food-wise.

It can get confusing, since many servers take your wine order before the food, but it's best for everyone to take a minute to check out the menu first: If two people are having fish and two are planning to order steak, this might not be the time to spring for a bottle for the table—one that goes with everything, like Champagne. You can also order a bottle of Champagne or a crisp white to start while everyone decides: It helps refresh the palate— and set the mood. It also buys you more time to look at the menu!

▼ Do your homework.

If you need to impress your date or guests, you have two options: You can look at the wine list and menu online ahead of time to determine your goalposts and select a backup or two, keeping in mind that wine lists aren't updated as often as food menus. Or you can arrive twenty minutes early to talk to the sommelier, identifying a white and a red option. Maybe have a glass of Champagne while you wait to help ease the jitters . . .

IN A RESTAURANT

How to Spot a Wine List Bargain

Game the List
Don't pick the most expensive bottle, and don't go for the cheapest. Stay in the middle ground and you'll be just fine.

→ "What's your best deal on the list?" can be a sommelier's least favorite question. Here's an extreme answer: When one client asked me that, I jokingly pointed him toward an ultra-rare $10,000 magnum of Montrachet from the cult winemaker Domaine de la Romanée-Conti. He said, "Are you crazy?" And I replied, "With all due respect, you asked me for the best deal. If you even can get a DRC, you will pay at least $15,000 for it at any auction. So you already have a $5,000 savings! And if it's corked, we'll even take it back. This, sir, is the best deal."

But seriously . . . **For me, the safe spot for a restaurant bottle is usually between $65 and $90.** And don't think that just because a wine is $50, it's an afterthought. Quite the contrary: Anyone can choose a good $300 bottle. You really have to work to find a wine that, after the triple markup from the wholesale cost, sells for $50. Any good sommelier enjoys the challenge!

That said, I don't advise going lower than $35 a bottle in a restaurant in the States. Quality-wise, you're better off ordering by the glass in that case.

ASK ALDO

What If There's No Sommelier?

At restaurants where the server sells you the wine, I've learned one thing: Ask what's been getting the best feedback. You won't make a big new discovery, but the chances are high that you'll be okay.

Tips for Ordering by the Glass

Show your enthusiasm.

Ask questions! Tell your sommelier you're curious about wine. You want to build that human connection, just as you do at the wine store. If you're curious and excited and humble, people will want to help you. More than once I've poured enthusiastic newbies some top-shelf leftovers just because they were so clearly into learning about wine.

Ask if anything special is open.

Sometimes a customer sends back a wine that he or she didn't like. And sometimes those bottles are excellent. It also gives you a chance to try a more expensive bottle at a by-the-glass price.

Ask what the sommelier is drinking right now.

This gives him or her a chance to show off trendier items on the list. You'll definitely spark something!

Don't like it? Send it back with constructive criticism.

Say, "This doesn't hit my sweet spot. It's too dry/ too aromatic/has a cloudy flavor, and so on. Can you please pour me something else?" While there is no rule as to how many pours you can reject when ordering by the glass, I would say that over three or four requests is rude.

And yes, that $20 glass is far better than the $12 glass. Sorry!

How I Create a By-the-Glass List

My job is to get the widest variety of wines that will work with the restaurant's cuisine, without offering *too* many choices.

In addition to the menu, which changes seasonally, I try to read the audience: What are they looking for, adventure or comfort? What are they willing to spend? In terms of variety, I want to offer an aromatic wine, an off-dry wine, and different textures. I want something geeky, something tannic, something juicy and lush. I strive for that diversity, in both reds and whites so that I can cater to the majority of customers' palates.

IN A RESTAURANT

SENDING BACK A BOTTLE

→ **Some people think they can send back a bottle because they don't like the way it tastes.** Unless the wine has a serious flaw (cork taint, mousy, oxidized, an unwelcome fizziness from secondary fermentation in the bottle), **I'm sorry to say that this is a no-no.** If this happens with a glass of wine, no big deal. But if you order a bottle, you should stick to it—especially if you chose it without the sommelier's advice.

You do have room for negotiation if, say, you told the sommelier that you wanted an oaky, buttery chardonnay and he poured you a petit Chablis. That's a bad recommendation, as they're 180 degrees apart on the flavor spectrum.

When Is It Better to Buy a Bottle?

→ If there are four of you, always order a bottle that you can have by the glass, because they calculate the glass cost differently: It's determined by dividing the bottle price by four to allow for spillage . . . but you can get up to five glasses out of that bottle, depending on how it's poured.

I prefer to order by the bottle because I don't have to wonder how long it's been sitting open, losing its freshness. Also, it helps me keep track of how much I've had to drink!

The Joy of the Half Bottle

Half bottles are a fun way to try a wine that might not be attainable in its full-size glory, or for when you want to drink a little more than just one glass. (The selections are usually a step up from by-the-glass offerings.) Say two of you are celebrating and want to drink a white and a red, but your budget won't allow for two full bottles. Half bottles tend to cost 30 to 40 percent less—not 50 percent, unfortunately, since the cork and labor still cost the producer the same. Bonus: You'll be sober enough to enjoy that half bottle of sweet wine or Champagne with dessert!

Wines with Bad Raps

The wine world—not unlike, say, food or fashion—is subject to trends. Here are the wines that some snobs might currently make fun of and which, like all things, will eventually make their way back into favor. Of course, for me, this is where I hunt for bargains.

	WINE	REPUTATION	DESERVED?
1	**Zinfandel**	Big, bold, chunky	The market drove this until people got tired of it. Writing it off isn't right.
2	**American chardonnay**	Creamy, oaky, buttery	Not at all! Look toward the Sonoma Coast and Oregon for unoaked versions.
3	**Merlot**	The movie *Sideways* damaged its reputation	Some of the world's greatest reds are merlots, like Pétrus and Le Pin.
4	**Lambrusco**	Cheap; bad hangover	Sorry, but what can be better with charcuterie?
5	**Beaujolais**	Too young, too cheap	Great makers are rewriting the reputation.
6	**Pinot grigio**	An ocean of plonk	Some really interesting examples to be found.
7	**Marsala**	Cooking wine	Generally deserved, but some cult producers are changing that.

Ask Me Anything!

(sommelier edition)

Are you a "supertaster"? How do you remember the flavor of so many wines?

I typically avoid this term, which refers to a person who has more concentrated taste buds, because I prefer to let others talk about my qualifications. In terms of memorization, it comes from many years of training and building up a repertoire of saved flavors that I can call upon easily.

What's that silver necklace that sommeliers wear?

It's called a *tastevin* (tas-tuh-van), a traditional sommelier's tool that anyone can wear. The moment we open a bottle tableside, we taste it using one of these. In the old days, winemakers used them in dark cellars, working by candlelight to see if a wine was cloudy or clean. Those bumps showed the reflection, and one whiff from it would let them know if the bottle in question was corked.

What was it like training, competing, and winning Best Sommelier in the World?

Grueling! In terms of training, I studied every free minute for ten years and had multiple trainers, who drilled me on timed service exams in subjects like decanting. The competition was grueling, too. I was tested to the bone for two days, from nine a.m. until seven at night, with random breaks that made it even more difficult to sustain the adrenaline. The categories: theoretical knowledge, tasting, service skills, how do you present yourself, how do you recommend wines, service, and pairings. Oh, and you weren't allowed to compete in your native language, which is why I originally moved to the States: to improve my English!

What's the most memorable wine you ever had?

Oof! I've had many memorable wines because I'm a spoiled brat, but it was a 1980 La Tâche that changed my life when I was twenty-three. That really got me into Burgundy. I had tasted many mature Bordeaux, but when I tried that, I went, "Wow, this is a whole different thing!"

You make wine seem so fun that I want to quit my day job and become a sommelier. Good idea or bad?

The grass is always greener! Yes, there's a certain artistry to our job, but the hours are long, and we work when everyone else is off. That sets the group apart right there. Making money in wine is not easy. So if you're on Wall Street, you might want to stay put.

What advice do you give to the sommeliers you mentor?

Learn to listen and to read your customer, which takes years of experience. Also, the fish has to like the bait, not the fisherman: When you recommend a wine, the customer has to like it—don't just sell them what you like. (Which, for sommeliers, tends to be acidic wines that few others enjoy.)

What's the most expensive wine you've ever tasted?

I drank a 1900 Margaux, which was worth $15,000 to $20,000. I've had old Romanée-Contis, old La Tâches. The price tag is meaningless to me, though: Do you really want to look at a painting longer just because it has a certain value assigned to it?

What's your favorite wine?

I can't tell you that! It's like asking who your favorite person is, or your favorite food. I love braised short ribs, for example, but in the summer it would never dawn on me to eat them.

Which level of sommelier are you?

No level! I'm just a regular sommelier, not part of the Court of Master Sommeliers.

Do you drink wine all the time?

Actually, at the end of the day, I enjoy a beer. ☺

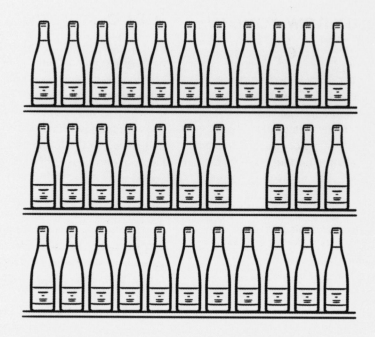

Choosing a Bottle in a Wine Shop

→ Price-wise, at least, the stakes are lower when you're trying to find the right bottle to drink at home: **Retail markup is just 1.6 times the wholesale cost, versus 2.5 to 3 times for restaurants.** That said, in my opinion, it takes a little more work to find the right store and tune the employees in to your taste. But it's more than worth it. Here's how.

Find your new favorite local wine shop.

It's no longer mandatory to go to a place with a flickering neon "LIQUOR" sign. Interesting wine stores are opening all over the country, whether they're attached to cheese shops in Portland, Maine, or opened by expat Brooklyn sommeliers in upstate New York. I find wine stores by asking sommeliers and chefs at my favorite restaurants, as well as through following my favorite sommeliers and wine writers on social media. (If they're not tagging, chances are they're following some good spots.) Or sometimes friends will ask me to walk through their local wine store with them to pick out some things—or tell them to go elsewhere!

Build a relationship with the store manager and salespeople.

This is essential. Sign up for their mailing list to learn about tastings—and go to them! Sure, they're sales pitches, but they're a great way to get to know the people at the store and tell them what you like. Explain that you're new to wine but you're really curious and want to learn. Don't be shy about it! Their job is to help turn you into a regular. Your loyalty will be repaid with special discounts, insider allotments, out-of-range delivery, and other frequent-buyer perks. Your salesperson might even know a couple of wine people and get you into their tasting group.

Buy a sampler.

Ask your new friend(s) to put together a mixed case, giving you a combination of flavors so you can get to know your palate. Try starting with whites: There should be a pinot grigio from Friuli, a sauvignon blanc from Sancerre, two chardonnays (a buttery one from Chablis, plus a creamy California chard), a Kabinett Riesling, and an albariño. Take notes, then download them in person: "This was too acidic, that was too tart, this was too sweet," and so on. Then try it with reds: Ask for a Sonoma Coast pinot noir, a cabernet sauvignon from Bordeaux, an Argentine malbec, a Rioja, and a Beaujolais like a Fleurie. If your tastes are in tune with the store's, they might have a monthly mixed sampler you can subscribe to at a good price. Speaking of which, the beauty of buying a case is that you should always get a 10 percent discount! It's also fun to share the case with a friend so you can learn together while splitting the cost.

Avoid the internet.

Yes, you can probably find a better deal in, say, rural North Dakota using Wine-searcher.com. But once you factor in shipping, you're probably only saving a few bucks per bottle—that is, if the bottle arrives intact. You can't return a corked wine to Arkansas, but your local merchant will take it back. Besides, you're building loyalty, remember? If it's simply about convenience and not about discovery, try to order from a reputable retailer.

IN A WINE SHOP

A  Few Tricks to Remember

☒

Don't buy the demo bottle.

(The one standing up.) You want wine that's been lying on its side, keeping the cork moist. This is especially important if you plan to store the wine for a while. If you don't see one, ask: Chances are, they have it in the back. The exception? Wine with a screw cap or crown cap.

☒

Don't buy the bottle in the window.

Light does terrible things to wine. Trust me.

☒

Don't spend less than $12.

Unless you're looking for cooking wine . . .

☒

Don't splurge on a $100 bottle of aged wine unless you know the shop well.

Who knows how it's been stored all these years.

☒

Some may say they'd rather pay $15 and get something "eh" than spend $20 and be disappointed. Break that rule!

Think about it: Why would you waste $15 on something that's 89 percent sure not to be good rather than spend the price of a Starbucks latte more to have a 50-50 shot of it being really good? One of the wine distributors that I buy from told me that people don't ask them for a $20 cab—the likelihood that you get one is slim. A better ask: "a bold $20 wine."

☑

You can often find steals on older wines in the suburbs and beyond.

Because the wine shop couldn't sell it back in the day, they never adjusted the price. One of my somms found a $400 bottle of Diamond Creek at a liquor store in Queens for $75. The owners were just happy not to have to keep dusting it!

IT'S WHAT'S INSIDE THAT COUNTS!

A Word on Wine Labels

➡️ **Labels can be confusing.** Most of the world's winemakers list the grape variety on the front. In most of Europe, they list the region where it was grown, leaving you to figure out the grape based on that region's rules. While others just put a cool drawing, a made-up name instead of just the vineyard, and maybe "Vin de France" on the back. One thing the label will always tell you is the alcohol level. (I choose not to buy wines over 15% ABV, but that's just my taste.) And on a Riesling, you know if it's dry or off-dry if it's not specifically written. Here are some guidelines.

The fancier the label, the less likely I am to pick up the bottle.

Sure, it can be fun and approachable, but to me it's a sign that the producer is so high-end, it's not as concerned with the craftsmanship in the bottle. Winemakers are farmers! They don't have tens of thousands of dollars to spend on slick label design.

It used to be that the term *vieilles vignes*, or "old vines," was a sign of quality.

Yes, but it's also a sign that the wine will cost more.

Some say it's more important where the grapes were grown, not where the wine was made.

Well, yes and no. You can have crappy white Burgundies from fantastically great real estate, because the winemaker screwed it up. Again, I think of it like a chef: You can have the best fish, but if the cook botches it, you're out of luck.

It used to be the more specific the label, the better the indicator of the wine's quality.

But natural winemakers have turned labeling on its head, listing only, for the most part, where the wine is from and the designation "Vin de France." This rebellious act means that the winemaker willingly downgraded the wine to bypass the strict winemaking requirements. ("Vin de France" is the lowest designation, btw.)

ASK ALDO

What's up with the points systems?

Tricky subject! Let's say that those wines can be interesting, but each reviewer has a different palate. It's about finding the right critic for you, and reading their producer profiles. (For more, see page 243.) And usually, those 100-point wines need to age awhile before they're drinkable. Personally? I don't look at points a whole lot.

Here's a key to some of those French terms on the label:

➤ Domaine

This is good! It means the wine was made by one producer who owns the land. The moment they buy grapes from elsewhere, it's no longer labeled a *domaine*.

➤ Château

It might evoke beautiful castles, but this word is pretty insignificant, especially in Bordeaux. A château can be a fancy castle or just a regular house. There's no regulation on it, and it can be misleading. The words *mis en bouteille au château* let you know the wine was bottled there.

➤ Coopérative

A group of winemakers that produces and sells wine from grapes grown by its members. It helps to centralize such processes as bottling, storing, and selling. Some people assume that cooperatives are big and therefore not good, or that they mix all the grapes together to make one big soup. Not true. For young winemakers in many regions, where it's almost impossible for someone just starting out to get the loans to buy land, they ultimately have no other choice but to purchase grapes.

➤ Vineyard

This means that the grapes come exclusively from that vineyard. The moment you have a single vineyard (SV), it denotes quality.

ASK ALDO

Why do so few Champagne labels have the vintage on them?

Because the base wine for most Champagnes is a combination of different vintages—a little from last year, perhaps; maybe even some from five years ago or more. (And if you think about it, any bottle of Champagne is automatically at least three years old!) That's why you'll see "NV," or non-vintage, on the label. Some houses, like Dom Pérignon, wait up to ten years before releasing a vintage, made from a single base. If you ever have the chance, it can be fun to taste a few years from one house—or the same year from a few producers: When stored properly, Champagnes age beautifully.

The Joy of the Half Bottle: Part 2

You'll find many half bottles in my cellar. Because when I'm home alone for the night, I don't want to open (and waste) a bottle. And when my partner and I are cooking, two bottles are too many. My tolerance isn't what it used to be! But a bottle and a half? Perfect. I also keep a lot of half bottles of Champagne on hand: They're perfect for a toast, and it makes any occasion seem like a special splurge. Luckily, you can find plenty of really decent producers on the 375 mL train.

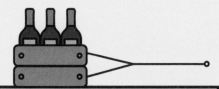

IN A WINE SHOP

Finding a Good Bottle in a Bad Shop

→ My barber was running behind, so I offered to grab a bottle of something to drink—a decision I regretted as soon as I stepped into the nearest liquor store. What could I possibly find in that ocean of mediocre pinot grigio and rosé? As crazy as it sounds, even they had a Grüner Veltliner chilling in the cooler. I bought a sleeve of plastic cups at the counter, and everyone was happy.

Ninety-five percent of the time, you can buy a $15 Grüner and it'll taste good. In fact, you don't have to spend more than that. It's one of the best food-pairing wines, typically everyone likes it, and you don't have to spend more than $25 to get a good one. No Grüner? Your next best options are a Chablis or Sancerre.

IMPORTERS TO RECOGNIZE

→ That importer label on the back of the bottle can be a great indicator of the quality of what you might find inside. That's because importers select their winemakers based on a personal philosophy. Here are some I gravitate toward:

☐ **Louis-Dressner**
Helped bring the natural movement to the US.

☐ **Kermit Lynch**
Synonymous with old-school, independent French producers with soul.

☐ **Olé Imports**
Finessed Spanish and Portuguese wines that can also appeal to the general palate very well.

☐ **Jose Pastor**
His label tips you off that this is going to be a geeky, cutting-edge Spanish wine.

☐ **Polaner**
Boutiquey, cutting-edge portfolio. There's no better Champagne "book" out there.

☐ **Rare Wine Co.**
Old-school, classic wines to treasure.

☐ **European Cellars/Eric Solomon Selection**
Boutique importer. Highly mineral wines from small, niche, European producers. Really interesting wines.

☐ **Terry Theise**
Riesling, Champagne, Austrian, and German wines. He has a tendency to like residual sugar.

BOXED, BAGGED & CANNED WINES

→ These options offer a much more fun, more up-front way of drinking out of the box (literally). A can of Ramona grapefruit-flavored Sicilian white? It must be summer. These wines are more about instant pleasure than long-term investment—your weeknight/party wine. When hosting a party, I like those bag-in-box wines. Not only do they help eliminate waste, leftovers will stay fresh for weeks in the fridge.

Wine at Home

▶ There's something indulgent and ceremonial about being served wine at a restaurant. But personally, I find it much more satisfying to drink at home, whether it's with friends, neighbors (I turned my downstairs neighbor, Murray, into a Champagne addict), my partner, Catherine, or even just enjoying a half-bottle on a rare night by myself. I can see why it might be intimidating to up your game. There are so many types of glasses, corkscrews, even bottle-stoppers, it can be hard to know what's best. (In my opinion, the simpler the better. Unless you have room for a million trendy gadgets and glass shapes, stick with the classics.)

Now that you've figured out what wines to bring home, this section will tell you how to store, open, pour, and preserve them (with some tips on how to wash those life-changing new wineglasses). Once you're feeling confident, you can host a wine tasting with friends to speed up the learning process. Because as I've said, drinking is knowledge. What else can you say that about in life?

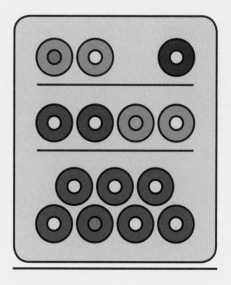

Storage 101

➡️ Loving good wine is one thing. Taking care of it properly is another. **Wine is a delicate, living substance, which means it's sensitive to temperature, light, even being in a bottle that's been standing up for too long.** Wine needs to be stored in a cool, dry, dark place. (Ideally, of course, this is a temperature-controlled cellar.) Short of investing in a wine fridge, the smartest thing to do is to use your local wine store promiscuously and drink as you go, storing nothing. But humans are gatherers, collectors . . . hoarders. We can't help it! (I know: I have over five hundred bottles in my basement, yet I still come home with cases, which my partner no longer finds endearing.) And so in this case, I think it's best to start with what *not* to do.

☒ Don't leave your bottle standing up for more than a week.

Really! The cork will dry out, leading to oxidation, which results in less-than-pleasant-tasting wine. (And remember: Don't buy the standing bottle at the store; ask for one that's been lying horizontally, which might be kept in back.) Wine should always be stored horizontally, with the label facing up. If the wine has a screw top, crown cap, or glass cork, don't worry about laying it down.

☒ Don't keep your wine in the kitchen.

It's too hot! Wine starts to get really unhappy at around 78 degrees, and starts to "cook" at 90 degrees. When I first moved to New York, I stored my wine in my oven, since I never used it. Boy, was that embarrassing when the *Wine Spectator* journalist asked to see where I stored my wine . . . (Even if you don't use your oven, chances are, you're still cooking on the range top, which gives off not-insignificant heat.) And don't stick it on top of the fridge, either: The fridge not only gives off heat, but those constant vibrations disturb the wine over the long run.

☒ Don't store your whites and Champagne in the fridge for longer than a few days.

The humidity is too low in there, meaning the cork dries out and all sorts of bad things happen. Over time, the wine absorbs fridge odors through the cork, too. Also, the fridge is too cold for storing your whites and Champagnes, which are rather fragile, not to mention that wine is sensitive to light! And yes, you can taste the difference between a perfectly stored bottle and the one stored in the fridge for a month.

☒ Don't store your wine on the top shelf of your closet.

Heat rises. If you must keep it in a closet, at least put it on the floor.

☒ Don't leave your wine near sunlight.

It cooks it. And not in a good way.

☒ Your apartment/ house is probably too hot, no matter what you think.

The ideal storage temperature for wine is 55°F, with about 75 percent humidity. *That sounds like my basement*, you're thinking? Great . . . as long as it's not musty or moldy: Those odors make their way into the bottle over time. So probably not there, either!

☑ Which leads us to . . . the <u>wine fridge</u>.

If you realize that you are becoming serious about wine, and buying bottles that you care enough about that you want to maintain them in good condition until you drink them—whether it's in six months or sixteen years—you should start researching wine refrigerators right now. You can get a decent one that holds twelve bottles for under $100 and hide it in your closet or basement, or get one that holds thirty-six and show it off in your kitchen. (Craigslist can be a good source, as can green building supply sites, which cheaply sell appliances that contractors have ripped out of model homes.) Again, you want it set at 55°F, with 75 percent humidity.

STORAGE

How to Build a Wine Wardrobe

→ The scary storage stuff on the previous pages didn't put you off and you've got a nice, cool place to keep six to twelve bottles? Excellent. Then you've got room to start building a base. At first it's a good idea to give yourself a range of styles, going from light- to full-bodied. This is where it can be helpful to ask your wine store to put together a mixed case for you, like the sampler mentioned on page 183. Here are the notes I'd be sure to hit.

Whites

Have something crisp like a Chablis or a Sancerre, and something richer like a new-style chardonnay from California or Oregon. Include a sparkling wine or Champagne, and maybe something dry like Grüner Veltliner, depending on what you like to cook. (For food-pairing ideas, see pages 250–257.) If you're really passionate about rosé, have a bottle or two of those, of course.

Reds

Again, going from light to full: Have a Beaujolais, such as a Morgon or Fleurie, a malbec, a Right Bank Bordeaux for your $40 splurge, plus a Chianti Classico or a nebbiolo d'Alba. Rioja is easy to find with a little age on it without breaking the bank. Include a pinot noir from Sonoma, since everyone loves them.

THE BEST / CHEAPEST PARTY WINES

TO MAGICALLY HAVE ON HAND

If you a) get invited to lots of dinners and parties, b) are very organized, and c) have a little wine-friendly extra space, you should always have a few extra bottles lying around. It will save you the headache of trying to find a decent wine shop when you're already late.

Whites

Grüner Veltliner

○ Lois, Weingut Fred Loimer

○ Am Berg, Bernhard Ott

○ Gobelsburger, Schloss Gobelsburg

Chablis

○ Petit Chablis, William Fèvre

○ Chablis Vieilles Vignes, Domaine Louis Michel & Fils

○ Chablis, Drouhin-Vaudon

Loire

○ Menetou-Salon Morogues, Domaine Pellé

○ Orthogneiss, Domaine de l'Ecu

○ Pouilly-Fumé Domaine, Jonathan Didier Pabiot (not cheap, but superb)

Sauvignon blanc from Northern Italy

○ Marco Felluga, Collio

○ Ronco del Cero, Venica & Venica

○ Winkl Sauvignon Blanc, Cantina Terlano

Reds

■ Raisins Gaulois, Marcel Lapierre

■ Éclat de Granite, Domaine Sérol

■ Viña Almate, Alfredo Maestro

■ Nebbiolo Perbacco, Vietti

■ Béla-Joska Blaufränkisch, Wachter-Wiesler

Sparkling

▷ De Nit Extra Brut Rosé, Raventós i Blanc

▷ Brut Nature Méthode Traditionnelle, Domaine François Chidaine

▷ Blanc de Blancs, Gruet

▷ Timido Brut Rosé, Scarpetta

Temperature Is Important (Very!)

➤ It may seem minor, but **a few degrees change everything.** Try the same glass of red wine at two temperatures and you'll see: It's like drinking two different wines. Just as too much cold can mask the flavor of white wine—a good thing when you're drinking something that's low quality or too old—a red wine that's a few degrees too warm can blow up the alcohol and tannins and strip even the finest Bordeaux of its delicate aromas and nuances. It's not like you can just add an ice cube and start over. (Why not go all the way and add club soda and a lemon? Just kidding. I respect personal preferences.) Here's how to get it right.

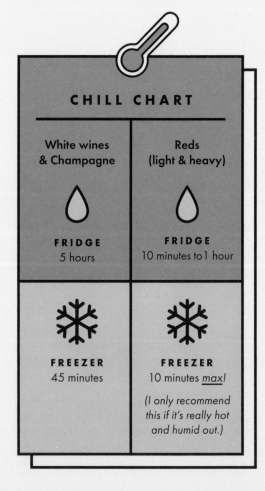

CHILL CHART

White wines & Champagne	Reds (light & heavy)
FRIDGE 5 hours	**FRIDGE** 10 minutes to 1 hour
FREEZER 45 minutes	**FREEZER** 10 minutes _max!_ (I only recommend this if it's really hot and humid out.)

On Chilling

Reds

People always say that red wine should be room temperature. But what does "room temperature" really mean? Is it an air-conditioned room in summer or a heated room in winter? (Let's not even get into how humidity affects temperature . . .and wine.) **I like my reds slightly cool:** I find it restrains the alcohol, putting it more into the background, and allows the fruit to become more layered. That's why if it's not coming from a cellar, which is always kept at 55°F, I'll put it in the fridge for ten minutes to an hour. If you want to get geeky about it, I like to serve lighter reds like pinots and gamays at 55°F, and heavier ones, like cabernet and merlot, at 60°F. You can gauge this with a thermometer or the temperature dial on your fridge.

Whites, Rosés, and Champagne

If you put your bottle in the fridge 24 hours before you plan to drink it, you have nothing to worry about. If you're starting at room temp, it needs four to five hours, minimum.

When I don't have that much time, I don't bother with ice buckets or wine sleeves. **I use the freezer instead.** Keep it in there for thirty minutes to an hour, max; forty-five minutes for Champagne (because the bottle is thicker). Otherwise, it's cleanup time.

FRIDGE TIP 1

If I get caught up in conversation and forget a bottle in the fridge for too long, I simply run it under hot water for twenty seconds. Or just pour it into the glass, swirl, and wait (and taste).

FRIDGE TIP 2

While it may seem convenient, don't store your wine in the fridge for the long haul—just a few days max. See page 193 for more.

Skip the Bucket

I rarely use an ice bucket at home—it sweats all over the table, and it makes the label on the bottle look messy, which I don't like. Instead, I put a cork or Champagne closer in it and stick it back in the fridge until my guests are ready for another glass.

B.T.W. (Bring the Wine)

I have one of those stretchy neoprene bags for transporting wine to friends' houses. I always keep a couple of wine sleeves (made of the same squishy material as ice packs) in the freezer, then slip one on each bottle—yes, even red—before I go. If I have a long subway ride ahead of me, I'll freeze the already refrigerated bottles for twenty minutes before I leave and carry them in an insulated bag. By the time I arrive, they're perfect.

TEMPERATURE

FACT Just by pouring wine into the glass, you immediately gain 3°F—especially if you have a big glass.

How to Open a Bottle of Wine

→ This is the only wine opener you need. Learn how to use the **basic waiter's wine key**, and you're set: It's what you'll find in almost every kitchen drawer, from your friend's house to that Airbnb in Paris. Whether you opt for a basic version from the liquor store or a fancy one from French knifemaker Laguiole (I'm biased: it's what I use) is up to you. Just make sure it has a sharp knife—aka foil cutter—and a long worm. Yes, that's what the corkscrew part is called in somm-speak.

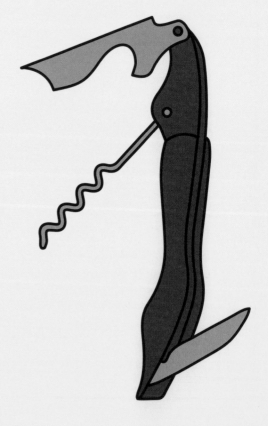

1 — **Using the knife, cut the foil all the way around, just beneath the ridge of the lip.** Remove the foil. I do this because there's always a drop at the top of the bottle after you pour, which eventually makes its way into the next glass. Do you want that droplet resting in foil that's been home to who knows what microorganisms for how long? Exactly.

2 — **Poke the tip of the corkscrew just off center into the cork, going in at a slight angle.** Cork quality varies, and it diminishes with time. By not going straight down, you avoid crumbling the cork or snapping it in two should it be fragile.

3 — **Turn the corkscrew and the bottle in opposite directions** until you can no longer see the curled part of the corkscrew. Going all the way down won't give you an advantage.

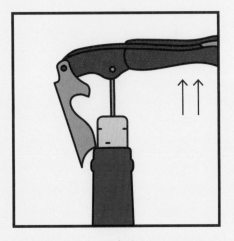

4 — **Lower the step until the angled part is "hooked" onto the lip of the bottle.** Then, while holding down the step for leverage, pull up on the handle of the wine key until the cork comes out. (Some corkscrews are "double-stepped," requiring you to move the step to a second height as the cork comes out.) **Unscrew the cork and set aside.** Pour yourself a taste!

...Help!

(Yeah, we've all been there.)

 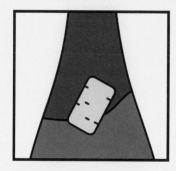 

Whoops! The Cork Ripped in Half...

. . . and now the corkscrew won't reach that far. Strange but true. It happens! Check to see if you have another corkscrew lying around: Some have longer worms. (As a professional obsessive, I always work with two corkscrews in my pocket for exactly this purpose.) No? Use the handle of a wooden spoon or a skewer to push it all the way in. Then proceed as in the next step.

Ummm, My Cork Fell In.

Congratulations: You've got a swimmer. If a chunk or two falls in, don't worry. If it crumbles into tiny pieces, however, set a fine-mesh strainer or a piece of cheesecloth over a funnel and pour the wine into a decanter (another bottle will work fine, too). This is mostly an issue with older wines. The wine is still okay!

The Cork. Won't. Budge.

A tight cork is actually a sign of quality, but it sure doesn't feel like it. The only thing to do is to pass the bottle around and turn it into a strength contest. Or take it to your weightlifting neighbor downstairs and ask politely. Not great for the ego, but the first glass should soothe it. If this happens with Champagne, you can try removing the cage, putting your wine key in the cork, and carefully opening it like (very-high-pressure) wine.

TIP! **If your cork is covered in hard wax, things can get messy fast.** Not only will you end up with tiny bits of wax all over your kitchen, you'll most likely be pulling them off your tongue, too. So stand over a trash can and, holding the bottle at a 90-degree angle, use the blade of a knife to start chipping away at the top of the bottle. (If you're even more of a neat freak, cover the top with a kitchen towel and knock it with a knife; the towel will catch all those bits.) If the wax is soft, just put the wine key right through the wax and proceed; once the cork is out, use your knife to make sure the edge is clean.

The Injury-Free Guide to Opening Bubbly

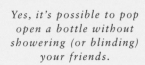

Yes, it's possible to pop open a bottle without showering (or blinding) your friends.

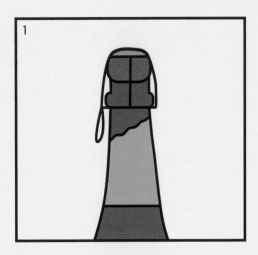

1 — Using the knife on your wine key or a small knife, **cut the foil, just below the cage, all the way around** that wire thing holding the cork and remove the foil.

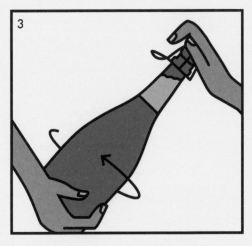

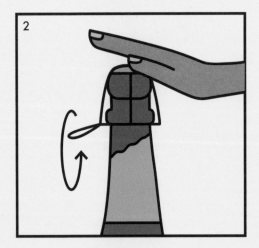

2 — While cupping the cork with the palm of your hand, **open the cage and loosen it a little bit, but don't remove it entirely** (leaving it on gives you extra grip). Keep holding the cork!

3 — Most people turn the head of the bottle. I turn the bottom. **While continuing to apply downward pressure on the cork with one hand, give the bottom of the bottle a gentle spin or two with the other hand.** The CO_2 will do all the work for you! As the cork pops out (you'll notice it doesn't make much noise), keep controlling it with that downward pressure to avoid the fountain effect. (If you end up with a shower anyway, quickly touch the spouting neck with a kitchen towel: It should go down.) You can also put a kitchen towel over the cage to protect your hand—it can get a little slippery.

SO YOU WANT TO SABER?

This (extremely) dangerous party trick won't go away. In fact, celebrating Napoleon-style has become so popular that upscale knife makers like Laguiole are selling fancy swords just for this use. Once you've removed the foil and cap, it's pretty much a one-two strike. Here's how to do it without killing anyone. (I hope.) But seriously: Be careful!

Supporting hand holds bottle here

Dull side of blade faces the cork

Wound spot

The seam

Dominant hand here (with a firm grip)

Direction of force

STEP 1
Make sure you're not pointing the bottle at anyone—or any windows, mirrors, or lights.

STEP 2
Using your fingernail, find the two seams running up to the top of the bottle. Got one? Turn it so that it's centered in front of you. Now trace the seam to where it joins the curve of the lip: That's called the wound spot.

STEP 3
With the dull side of a long knife pointing up toward the lip, glide it up and down the seam a few times to practice. (It doesn't have to be a saber. You could even use a metal spoon! Just don't use the sharp side of your knife. It's less about the force than where you hit it.) When you're ready, use the power from your forearm to quickly and forcefully strike the wound spot with the blade. Prepare to pour! (And clean up.) Just be careful of that razor-sharp neck . . .

 NOTE: At the risk of sounding like a dad, the average Champagne bottle has double the pressure of a car tire. If your sabering goes wrong, you're in big trouble. I've seen some really gruesome accidents.

The Glass Matters, Too!

➤ Sure, it's great to drink rosé from a tumbler on the beach. But you're doing yourself a huge disservice. Just as even a great Bordeaux will taste meh in that tumbler, a so-so merlot can blossom into something borderline beautiful in the right glass.

That's because a well-designed wineglass is crafted to concentrate the aromas specific to that style so they hit your nose—and tongue—just right, therefore elevating the flavor. And a top-of-the-line glass is handmade with a lip so smooth that the wine falls right onto the tip of the tongue, where we taste sweetness. (Even a tiny ridge at the lip can create a slight bubble, meaning that the wine falls farther behind on your palate, where we experience bitterness.) To me, a glass is like a microscope, magnifying the flavors.

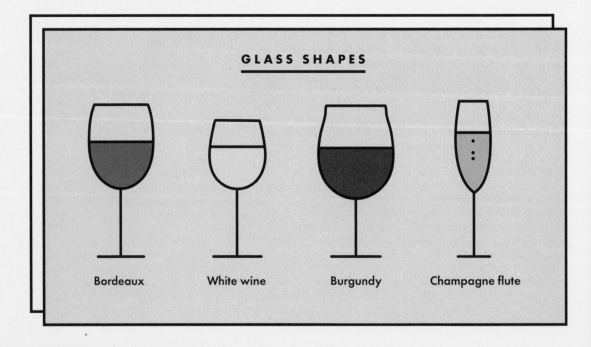

GLASS SHAPES

Bordeaux   White wine   Burgundy   Champagne flute

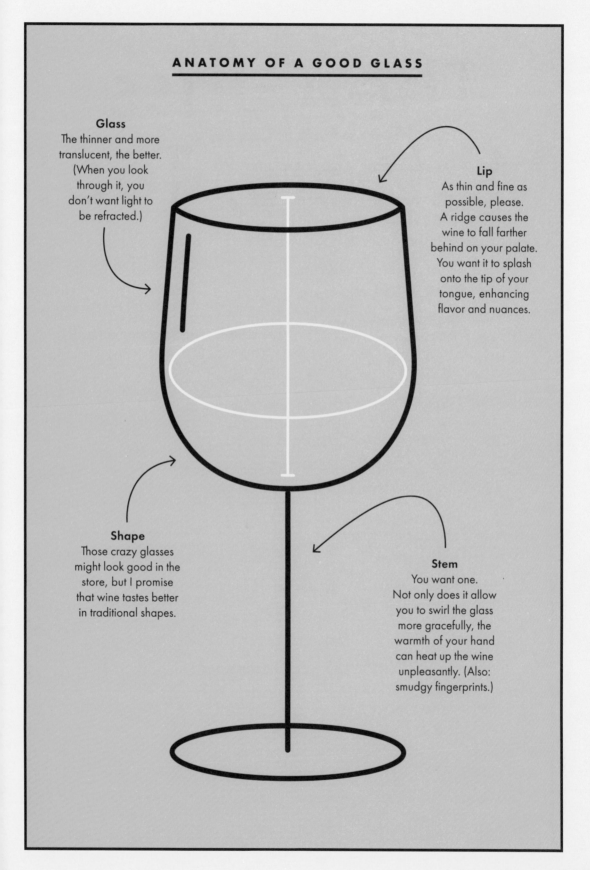

ANATOMY OF A GOOD GLASS

Glass
The thinner and more translucent, the better. (When you look through it, you don't want light to be refracted.)

Lip
As thin and fine as possible, please. A ridge causes the wine to fall farther behind on your palate. You want it to splash onto the tip of your tongue, enhancing flavor and nuances.

Shape
Those crazy glasses might look good in the store, but I promise that wine tastes better in traditional shapes.

Stem
You want one. Not only does it allow you to swirl the glass more gracefully, the warmth of your hand can heat up the wine unpleasantly. (Also: smudgy fingerprints.)

How to Pick a Glass

Do You Really Need Six Kinds of Glasses?!

My fellow wine-loving Austrians, the Riedel family, first explored this question in the 1980s, introducing a range of glasses scientifically calibrated to enhance (and mute) flavors in different styles of wine—a big bowl to open up the tightness in a minerally chardonnay, a narrower nose to concentrate the red fruit of a Bordeaux, and so on. When I started working in wine, I lived near the Riedel factory and went to public tastings, where I immediately saw professionals and nonprofessionals responding to the shape of the glasses. Needless to say, I ended up with a *lot* of glasses for a twenty-three-year-old.

If your cabinet space is as vast as your budget, it's great to have a glass wardrobe. Now that I'm older, I've become much more of a minimalist. I also have a better sense of what I like to drink at home. And so now

I have "just" three glass shapes, all from Zalto, for whom I am a brand ambassador:

→ The **white wine glass** for Champagne and really light rosés

→ The **Universal glass** for whites and reds

→ The **Bordeaux glass** for bigger wines like Burgundies and Barolos, because it's wide enough that you can tweak it for Burgundy varieties

→ Oh, and I have a few **Champagne flutes**, because my partner, Catherine, insists . . .

It takes a while to figure out what kinds of wine you drink most. I recommend buying one or two of a particular wineglass style and building your way up to six to eight—keeping in mind that wineglasses break. When you're just starting out, try the Universal glass by Zalto; the Riesling or Chianti Classico glass by Riedel; or the Spiegelau red wine glass. These are the most versatile shapes from the best brands. Then add other shapes when you become more drawn to a certain style of wine. And yes, it always makes sense to have a six-pack (or four) of IKEA glasses for parties.

. . . IN WHICH I MAKE A CASE FOR A $60 GLASS

If you care about wine, you should care about the glass. It's like the speaker for your music: Cheap earbuds sound different from Bose headphones, which sound different from a super high-end home system with a giant subwoofer. I'm always surprised when people will spend $60 on a bottle of wine that they'll drink in a couple of hours, but they won't spend $60 on a Zalto Universal glass that they will use to enjoy countless bottles of wine—at any price. (The Universal was created to work with a wide range of wines.)

ASK ALDO

TRY THIS!

Drinking the same wine from three different glasses (of varying shapes, glass thicknesses, lip-styles) is an eye-opening experience. I did it for Jenn Sit, the editor of this book, one day at the wine bar, and she was blown away. Try it at home, solo or with a friend.

① Choose a style of wine that you drink most—maybe it's chardonnay, maybe it's a big red—and buy a bottle.

② Buy one "good" glass that corresponds to the style. At the higher end, I recommend Zalto, Spiegelau, and Riedel. Keep the sticker on in case you want to return it!

③ For the other two glasses, grab your go-to wineglass from your cabinet, as well as a tumbler.

(Or, if you want, buy a second style of wineglass that you're curious about, again keeping the sticker on.)

④ Taste from each glass. How is the aroma different? The flavor? Where does the wine fall on your tongue? And, more important, which makes the wine taste best to you?

⑤ You can also try this at a restaurant that has good stemware: Ask the sommelier to set up a "glass tasting" for the bottle you've ordered.

TIP

When I'm taking my wine team to Brooklyn for a picnic, or hosting twenty friends on my roof, I order a bunch of **Govino plastic glasses.** Figure two per person.

Why Are People Drinking Champagne Out of Wineglasses?

Coupes were it in the '70s. Then, after drinkers realized all that surface area caused the bubbles to quickly fizz out, flutes ruled until, say, 2010. But these days, with the rise of grower Champagne, serious wine people are enjoying their bubbly from white wine glasses.

It's not just a trend—something contrarian that drives your parents nuts. It's reality. The climate is becoming warmer, resulting in sweeter grapes. Makers of grower Champagne have been working on concentrating the flavors, and it was discovered that a flute's narrow nose cages the flavors. The slightly wider surface of a white wine glass allows them to shine.

The only way to decide for yourself is to try. Taste it in both glasses. Form an opinion. *Then* you can judge.

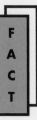

FACT

The #1 way to decide if a glass is for you: Does it make you want to drink out of it?

Washing Tips

In the machine...

I load all of my glasses in the top rack in the dishwasher, putting them closer to the middle so their stems can lean to the side. (The first time I did this, I made sure that they did in fact fit on top, crouching down to look while I slowly slid the rack in.) Longer-stemmed glasses can go on the bottom, too: Just make sure that you don't cram heavy plates all around them. If your dishwasher has one of those stem holders that folds down from the side, now's the time to use it.

I like to use Jet-Dry in my cycle; otherwise the glass gets fatty and doesn't dry. (Before I started doing this, I noticed that fat residue on glasses caused Champagne to look flat, even though it tasted bubbly. What's the point of Champagne without bubbles?!)

After the cycle is done, I like to keep the door closed for as long as possible. Then I gently slide out the drawer in case anything shifted. If needed, I use a towel to dab off that drop that always seems to collect at the base of the stem.

In the sink...

Rule #1: If you're drunk/tired, leave the glasses until the morning! Just dump out any remaining wine and pour a splash of water into red wine glasses.

The biggest cause of breakage is gripping the stem too tightly while you soap up overzealously, thereby twisting the glass in two.

I like to start with an empty sink and a small bowl of warm, soapy water, rather than squirting soap into each glass. Make sure you clean the outside and the rim, and get—gently—down into the bowl. Rinse thoroughly with warm water.

DRYING

I dry them by hand with a clean cloth, working my way up from the stem.

STORAGE

☐ Glasses build up greasy kitchen residue as they sit, which is why **I don't like open shelving**—at least not for all of my glassware.

☐ Keep the glasses you use most, both in terms of number and style, at an easily accessible height. Your "entertaining" glasses can go somewhere else, whether it's on a higher shelf or under the cabinet, still in the box. There's no point in taking up prime real estate with six huge chardonnay glasses if you only use a couple of them once a month.

☐ If your glasses have been sitting for a while, gently wipe the outside with a clean, soft cloth. (Yes, I keep one just for this purpose.) If they're really smudgy, wash them the morning of a party so you're not handing friends slippery glasses as they arrive.

☐ Storing your glasses bowl-side up is the most stable way.

Pouring Wine

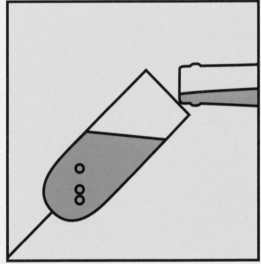

For Everything (except Champagne)

→ Tilt the bottle until the lip is about an inch above the center of the glass. Pour 5 ounces—a little less than ¾ cup—into the glass. Then, when you're ready to stop pouring, use your wrist to give the bottle a half twist as you pull it up and away. Wipe away any dribbles that may have gotten on the outside of the glass or bottle.

For Champagne

→ It's kind of like pouring a beer so it doesn't foam over: Tilt the glass toward the bottle about 45 degrees as you lower the bottle almost 90 degrees to meet it, angling the lip so it's practically resting on the rim as you pour just below it. (This will help tame the bubbles so the glass doesn't fizz over.) Pour until the bubbles are a few inches from the rim, then use your wrist to give the bottle a half twist as you pull it up and away. Hold the glass upright until the bubbles die down enough to allow you to pour more. Repeat as needed.

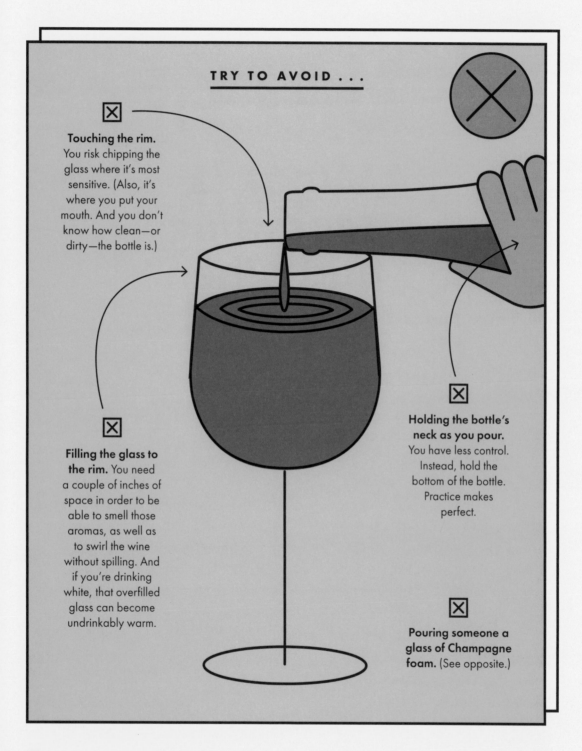

TRY TO AVOID . . .

Touching the rim. You risk chipping the glass where it's most sensitive. (Also, it's where you put your mouth. And you don't know how clean—or dirty—the bottle is.)

Filling the glass to the rim. You need a couple of inches of space in order to be able to smell those aromas, as well as to swirl the wine without spilling. And if you're drinking white, that overfilled glass can become undrinkably warm.

Holding the bottle's neck as you pour. You have less control. Instead, hold the bottom of the bottle. Practice makes perfect.

Pouring someone a glass of Champagne foam. (See opposite.)

Before You Pour, Do This

It sounds crazy, but I pour about an ounce of wine into my glass and swirl and turn it around so all the surface gets covered, then put that wine into the next glass and repeat as needed. (I'll use a tablespoon of wine for every six glasses.) That's called seasoning the glass. What it does is remove any soap residue and dishwasher drying agent, which can affect the taste of your wine. Paranoid? Sure. But it works. Who wants to drink chemicals? When you're done, pour out that wine and move on.

What Is Decanting, and When Do I Do It?

➡ Decanting is done for two reasons: **First, it aerates the wine, or exposes it to air**, thereby opening up the fruit aromas and toning down the tannins that hide them, essentially mimicking the aging process. **Second, with an older wine, it separates the wine from the sediment that has accumulated in the bottle.**

Young Bordeaux, Barolos, Riojas, Brunellos, and California cabernets have a lot of fruit-masking tannins when you first open them, making them good candidates. Both older reds and tight whites can benefit

from a little oxygen bath. But I never decant without tasting the wine first. If it tastes closed or "tight" (the different fruits are quiet) or watery (a sign of high tannins), it needs a little decanting time.

Even a glass pitcher will do. You just want to increase the surface area exposed to air (aka aerating the wine, which also happens simply by pouring, as well as by swirling it in the glass).

Some sommeliers refuse to decant for sediment, while others can't stand having any sediment in their glass. I say do what you prefer.

How to Aerate Using a Decanter

First things first: Always take a sip of the wine before you decide to go the decanter route. Does it taste tight or watery? If so, then proceed. Pour the contents of the bottle into the decanter, aiming so the wine streams down the side instead of directly into the center. Keep in mind that you've sped up the oxidation process, so you want to drink the wine within an hour or two.

But wine is mysterious! Each bottle ages differently and the optimal timing for aeration can be hard to predict. Plus, I'm more interested in experiencing the evolution—the curve. Sometimes at Le Bernardin, I'll only decant half the bottle and pour the other two glasses for the client to see how it tastes right from the bottle. When you pour wine, you give birth. Do you want to get a full-grown adult right out of the bottle?

● If you want to **aerate your wine**, you need a wider decanter to allow for air. (A pitcher or even a big mason jar will do in a pinch.)

● If you're **decanting for sediment**, use a narrower decanter.

● **Don't buy those wine-aerator thingies.** They might promise to "age" your wine by injecting oxygen into the glass, but I promise you: It's a gimmick. There are two simpler ways to expose your wine to a little more oxygen: Pour it from a few inches above the glass, or simply swirl it in your glass a few times.

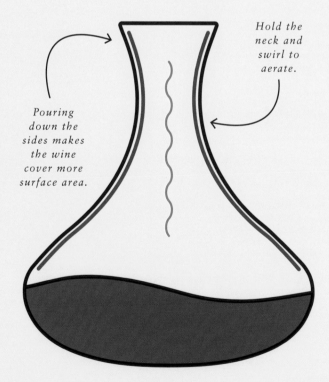

Pouring down the sides makes the wine cover more surface area.

Hold the neck and swirl to aerate.

▷ **How to decant for sediment?** YouTube! (It's highly unlikely that you'll open wine at home that's old enough to have sediment.)

Wines to Aerate

- ☐ Young Barolos and Brunellos
- ☐ Young Rhône-style blends
- ☐ Young Riojas
- ☐ Young California cabernets
- ☐ Young Bordeaux
- ☐ Super Tuscans
- ☐ Reductive wines

Wines to Decant (Because of Potential Sediment)

- ☐ Bordeaux, Barolos, and Riojas older than 10 years
- ☐ Old California reds

How to Host a Wine Tasting

➤ The best way to learn is to taste as much as possible. Having friends over to try up to six different wines will help you build your knowledge—as well as have a great time. Here's how to do it.

Set a theme.
Here are some ideas:

→ **Pick a varietal, a country, a region**—or any combination therein—that you're interested in, and choose six bottles within a given price range that everyone will be comfortable with. It could be six cabernets from California, or cabernets from California, France, Chile, Argentina, Australia, and Italy.

→ It's always fun to do **Old World versus New World:** Do you like a creamy, buttery Australian chardonnay, or a crisp, light, mineral-driven Chablis? Pinot noir, cabernet, and Riesling also work well for this, as do sparkling wines. (You could also try doing it with multiple varieties for contrast.)

→ And, hey, what is the **best rosé?**

→ You could even **host a movie night and show scenes from** *Sideways* while you do a tasting from that area. (Skip the dark parts and focus on when they go to the first wine tasting and when they go to the restaurant. Maybe you don't want to show the scene where he steals money from his mom . . .)

Do some <u>research.</u>

Learn what you can about what sets these wines apart, because there will definitely be questions. Have a printout handy. A map can be helpful, too.

<u>Give guests some paper and a pencil</u> to take notes if they'd like.

When tasting in a group, great questions typically surface, and you'll want to take notes. You can also scribble down which wine you liked, which you disliked, and why.

There's no ideal number of guests . . .

. . . but however many you invite, **make sure that you're all drinking from the same kind of glass.** Otherwise you'll all taste different things. If you're short on glasses, put out a bucket or bowl for people to pour their wine into between bottles. (Note: Don't rinse out your glass between bottles. Water changes how you perceive the wine.)

<u>Order the wines</u> according to the alcohol level, from lowest to highest.

(You'll find that info on the back label.)

Go one bottle at a time.

Give each guest a small pour, enough for three or four sips—you want to have a little left in the bottle so you can go back and taste again at the end if you'd like.

<u>Taste</u> and <u>discuss!</u>

What flavors from page 159 did you notice? What did you like? What was disappointing? What would you buy again? Remember, there is no right or wrong at a tasting. It's about the experience. Keep in mind that we all perceive things differently. When you talk about your experience, your friends will bring up interesting new observations. This is a good moment to retaste and check to see if you missed something.

Tips  for a Successful Tasting

For next-level tasting ideas, see page 228.

You can give guests parameters for what to bring . . .

(say, a Washington State pinot for under $30), or buy the wine yourself and **have everyone Venmo you.** Be sure to let the wine-store staff know what you're doing so they can guide you.

When you're just starting out, don't taste more than six wines.

By the seventh, your senses fatigue and the wines all start to smell and taste the same. You don't run a marathon the first time you go out for a jog!

Give guests a glass of sparkling wine while you wait for everyone to arrive.

This helps clean the palate and set the mood.

Water and Tasting

The best way to avoid a hangover is to drink double the amount of water to wine, but when you're doing a tasting, water can throw you off course. For one thing, taking sips of water between different wines kind of changes your palate. Try to minimize your water intake during the tasting. Some people like to rinse out their glass between wines, but you change the structure of the wine with water. And unless you're wiping the glass dry, you're ultimately diluting the wine.

Avoid food.

Having food during the tasting—especially fatty foods like cheese and charcuterie—will change the flavors, so try to avoid them until the end. I like to finish with a big pot of stew and some bread.

Don't forget to put out a bucket or container for people to pour their unfinished wine into.

You can also put out mugs—nothing transparent!—for those who prefer to spit.

When you're done . . .

offer everyone a glass of a crisp, acidic white or sparkling wine—even a beer—to cleanse the palate.

Don't feel like hosting? Outsource!

○ Ask the sommelier at your favorite restaurant or wine bar to do a tasting for you—or even just a flight of three or four glasses. Tell her specifically what you're looking for and set a budget ahead of time.

○ Ask the crew at your wine store to connect you with a tasting group.

How to Preserve Leftovers

➤ Sometimes finishing a bottle is just a bad idea. How to make sure it's still drinkable the next day? There are plenty of gadgets promising to extend the life of your bottle, but few actually work. Here are my preferred techniques, in order.

Drink the wine and be hungover.

(See my tip on page 217.)

Put the cork back in and put the bottle—red or white—in the fridge.

This slows down the oxidation process, which is what starts depleting the wine's fresh flavors and making it taste musty. (Think of an apple: Once you cut it and expose it to oxygen, it starts getting brown and mushy; the flavor changes, too.) I keep on hand a couple of glass or rubber stoppers that I've saved from other bottles—I prefer the way they look.

For Champagne, invest in one of those hinged closures they sell at the counter at the wine store.

It's the best way I've found to keep the bubbles relatively intact overnight.

Drink more half bottles!

While experts agree that half bottles don't age as well, if you're by yourself and a full bottle seems ambitious, that half comes in handy. It's often hard to get half bottles of high-end wines. Luckily, I prefer drinking half bottles for simple pleasure rather than a big occasion.

PRESERVATION MYTHS

Putting a **silver spoon** in an open bottle of Champagne maintains the bubbles. *This is false.*

Vacuuming gets rid of all the oxygen. *No. It's just creating a vacuum in which some oxygen is still present (and therefore oxidizing your wine).*

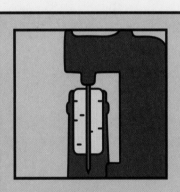

For professionals, the **Coravin**, which inserts a superfine needle into the cork and allows you to extract the wine glass by glass, is worth the $300 price tag. We use it for expensive wines by the glass at the wine bar, but I admit I never use mine at home: I always drink the whole bottle!

3

How to Evolve Your Palate

▶ I guarantee you that the more wines you taste, the more your taste will change. Sauvignon blanc and malbec are perfectly nice grapes, but at a certain point, if you start to care about wine, you'll crave more complexity and character. It's hard to go back to Prosecco once you've tried a great Champagne. (Sorry!) But, of course, both are worthy of their own time and place.

Think about it this way: Unless you've grown up next to an ocean, you probably don't love your first oyster. But you build up to it. And then, if you're curious, you try different kinds, noticing the difference between a Kumamoto and a Malpeque, West Coast versus East Coast. It's the same with wine. You're probably not going to love Bordeaux right off the bat (it may seem too tannic, which covers your taste buds and feels watery or sourish; the wine isn't that at all, it's just our taste buds). The same goes for brut nature Champagne, which is too austere and demanding for a beginner, and Sherry, whose oxidative qualities can take time to know and love. But they're all definitely worth working toward. It offers, how shall I say, a happy marriage over the years, thanks to its consistent quality.

The point isn't to become a wine snob. It's to appreciate and find joy in the magic that is fermented grape juice. Here are some of the best ways to learn and grow.

Building a Flavor Library

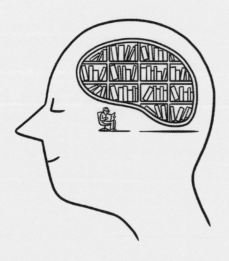

→ I'm a firm believer that all of the tastes we saved from our childhood are archived, like data ready to be retrieved. To help you put words to those flavors, I recommend reading wine writers' tasting notes to expose you to the vocabulary. (See suggestions on page 243.) Don't worry, you don't have to study them. Just observe what words they use. Here are some other techniques.

Taste more.

It goes without saying that the more you try, the more you learn. Start a wine group with friends: Host tastings and go to wine bars and restaurants together to share and compare bottles, or ask the sommelier to put together a flight for you. Attend tastings at wine stores: Not only will you taste a lot for free, you'll meet people who are also interested in wine. Maybe you'll start a wine group together.

Taste smarter.

Pay attention! Put away your phone and focus on the glass at hand. You're building a library of flavors and aromas, and those memories will never be stored properly if you're distracted by your email. Be in the moment: It's delicious.

Smell everything.

Again with the flavor library. I love to smell my food: I smell the bread, the butter, etc. Walking through the farmers' market, I inhale the scent of strawberries, tomatoes, and herbs. We taste with our noses first, so work on having as many available "flavors" to pull from as you can.

▽ Travel.

When I was starting out, I lived in Tuscany for three months to learn about Chianti. By the end, I could tell you what village it was from just by tasting. That's an extreme example, but being in the place where the wine was made gives you a much deeper understanding and appreciation. You don't have to go vineyard hopping to absorb the context—though I highly recommend taking a wine trip at some point. Just being in, say, Paris, Rome, or Barcelona, drinking a different wine (or three) every day and eating the local food it's served with, will bring things into focus. Better yet, take a wine trip with friends: Hearing other people's questions will open a new chapter of things you haven't thought of yet.

MY FAVORITE WINE TRIPS

☐ **Alto Adige, Italy**

Unpretentious, beautiful, and inexpensive. The winemakers here are much more welcoming than they are in, say, Burgundy. Visit Cantina Terlano, a large cooperative with a great stock of old wines, and J. Hofstätter, one of the best pinot noir producers in the picturesque town of Tramin. Bonus: You can go via Milan or Venice to get your culture fix.

☐ **Austria**

Friendly, food-loving, and totally green in terms of farming. Visit Nikolaihof in Wachau: Built around the second church in the Roman empire, the Romans dug the cellar! It also has a nice little tavern attached. Be sure to stay in Vienna, one of the few world capitals that are home to a significant number of winemakers. An evening at Weingut Wieninger is a must.

☐ **California**

So fun! Stay on the Sonoma side or go down to Santa Barbara. You want to go to the places that make it hard to get in! Try Hanzell, which is an institution, and head out to Hirsch for breathtaking views on the Sonoma Coast, stopping by Hog Island Oyster Co. for lunch.

225

▽ Never stop learning.

Find a critic whose palate you like and read his or her reviews regularly. Whether it's Jancis Robinson in the *Financial Times* or on her own Purple Pages website, Eric Asimov in the *New York Times*, Lettie Teague in the *Wall Street Journal*, or Antonio Galloni in Vinous online, there's a lot to be learned. The easiest way to find out who shares your taste is to buy a bottle that they awarded around 93 points—16 or 17 points from Jancis—and see what you think, the idea being that a 100-point wine will taste like a 100-point wine to anyone. Also follow interesting sommeliers on Instagram to see what and where they're drinking. It's a fun way to be led down new rabbit holes, especially when the sommeliers travel. Following your wine shop on Instagram keys you into tastings and new arrivals.

Turn to page 242 for more resources to expand your wine knowledge!

SIGNS YOU'RE BECOMING A CONNOISSEUR...

☐ You think about what wine you're going to have with dinner when you're eating lunch.

☐ You start traveling for wine.

☐ You start following sommeliers on Instagram.

☐ You get a subscription to Jancis Robinson.

☐ You sign up for more than one wine club.

☐ You start converting your basement into a wine cellar.

☐ You buy more than one "good" glass.

☐ You create a wine hashtag.

☐ You start tasting blind.

☐ You start looking at restaurants' wine lists online.

☐ You can tell if a Bordeaux is Left or Right Bank.

WINE PEOPLE I FOLLOW ON INSTAGRAM

@jancisrobinson / Jancis Robinson, wine critic, London

@rajatparr / Rajat Parr, winemaker, California

@pascalinelepeltier / Pascaline Lepeltier, sommelier, New York

@ess_thomas / Sarah Thomas, sommelier, Le Bernardin, New York

@bobbystuckeyms / Bobby Stuckey, cofounder, Frasca Food and Wine, Boulder, Colorado

@jaymcinerney / Jay McInerney, writer and critic, New York

@ericasimov / Eric Asimov, critic, *New York Times*

@pazlevinson / Paz Levinson, sommelier, Paris

@sorenledet / Søren Ledet, sommelier, Copenhagen

@weinwunder / Stephan Reinhardt, critic, Robert Parker, Germany

@marco_pelletier / Marco Pelletier, sommelier, Paris

Next-Level Wine Tasting

➞ Once you're ready to move beyond your evenings of, say, Oregon pinots and global chardonnays, things can get challenging—in a good way. Find a group of like-minded individuals who are willing to go there with you. And remember: The more people you include, the more wines you can try, splitting up the cost among you. Here are some suggestions.

▽ Go vertical.

Taste one producer from 2016 down to 2012 to see how the winemaker evolves and which vintages were tricky weather-wise, keeping in mind that warmer years are higher in alcohol, while colder vintages are more acidic. (In terms of finding the wines for these types of tastings, Winesearcher.com is your friend—just be sure to give yourself enough time for everything to arrive before the tasting.) If you really want to push it to the next level, print out a vintage chart. You can find them online in *Decanter* magazine, in *Wine Spectator*, or on Jancis Robinson's website. Look for one- or two-liners, such as "2015: Lots of rain. Hail in July. Finished up with a warm summer. Very early harvest." Stuff like that.

→ **Try:** Wines from Julien Sunier (Fleurie), Domaine de la Côte (pinot noir), Peter Lauer (Riesling).

⬤ Go vintage.

Try the same vintage from different regions within a country. You'll learn the breadth for the year, and it will teach you how weather ultimately impacts what's in the bottle: How do wines from a hot, dry year taste against those from a cool, rainy one? How is the fruit showing? What is the alcohol level? Where does the acid show up on the palate? Maybe Google hot vintages and cold vintages from different countries—or even the same one!—within a year to help you select three bottles from each type.

→ **Try:** 2017s (a very hot vintage) from German winemakers Leitz, Lauer, and Keller, against the 2016s (a cooler vintage).

◻ Get generational.

It can be fun to taste the wines of the son or daughter after they take over from their father. Chances are, their winemaking styles are as different as classical and indie rock.

→ **Try:** Alois and Gerhard Kracher (a range of varietals), Marcel and Mathieu Lapierre (Morgon), Didier and Louis-Benjamin Dagueneau (Pouilly-Fumé), Jonathan and Didier Pabiot (Pouilly-Fumé).

△ Move into a fancy region.

In order to build a base of wine references, you need to have some of the classics in your memory bank. And so eventually it will be time to venture into Bordeaux, Burgundy, Piemonte, and Rioja. Cost is definitely an issue here; maybe it means you all chip in to try three $60 Bordeaux instead of six $25 bottles. Or scale down and do one Left Bank Bordeaux and one Right Bank. Or, hey, if ten of you put in $50 each, you can buy a bottle of Margaux and each have half a glass. The key with this tasting is to expand your reference points by exposing you to what "the good stuff" tastes like. And if it turns out you're crazy about Barolo but it's way out of your budget, you can start exploring more attainable options, like a nebbiolo d'Alba or a nebbiolo clone such as spanna. Just don't blow your money on heavily marketed wines. I always say the nicer the bottle or the snazzier the website, the less attention was paid to the actual product.

→ **Try:** A second-tier wine like Echo de Lynch-Bages, Domaine Sylvain Pataille Marsannay, Maison Joseph Drouhin Chambolle-Musigny; Chianti Classico Riserva from Fèlsina, or a Super Tuscan like Le Pergole Torte from Montevertine.

WHAT TO DO WHEN WINE TASTES LIKE...

☐ **Cabbage**

That's wine that's been made in the reductive style, and it's actually trendy! If you're not into it, try decanting.

☐ **Madeira**

That kind of cooked, oxidated flavor can sometimes be tamed by a few hours in the fridge. Or serve it with cheese, which coats your palate.

☐ **Mouse fur**

This effect is caused by yeast called *Brettanomyces*, and is more common in natural wines. Some love "Brett," some hate it. Give it a run through a decanter and see if it helps.

☐ **Old cork**

Take it back to the wine shop where you bought it. They should give you a refund.

☐ **Vinegar**

Nothing you can do here. Why not use it to make . . . vinegar?

■ Taste blind.

This doesn't mean you blindfold your guests. It means you disguise the bottle with a paper bag, allowing you to move past any preconceptions and simply taste. If you want to pour everything ahead of time, try making a placemat on which you've numbered six wineglass-size circles so people can keep track and make notes. You can turn it into a group guessing game if you're feeling confident, or simply take notes and share later (or not). Is it New World? Old World? French? Italian? Can you even guess the grape? Does the wine taste like it has some age on it? At the end of the tasting, all will be revealed. One tip: Don't have spicy food or coffee before. It'll blow out your palate.

→ **Try:** Whatever you want!

● Taste for soil.

By far the geekiest of these tastings, but one of my favorites. When Le Bernardin sommelier Sarah Thomas asked me what I meant when I said that European sommeliers taste for soil while American sommeliers taste for fruit, I set up a tasting of Rieslings from Germany, where the *terroir* is diverse from region to region. We tasted wines grown in the red, blue, and gray slate found in the Mosel region, the sandstone in the Nahe, the quartzite of the Rheingau, and the volcanic soil of the Pfalz. Each tasted slightly different. You can also do this beautifully with shiraz from Australia or the Rhône Valley of France.

Try This App

José Andrés launched **WineGame**, an app that puts together a blind tasting for you, complete with questions, based on photos you take of your bottles. Warning: It's competitive. And addictive!

Using the Lunar Calendar to Decide When to Drink

➡ The lunar calendar has been used for centuries by farmers to determine when to plant and harvest. It can also be used to tell you what days are best for drinking wine.

In the early twentieth century, Rudolf Steiner, who created the biodynamic farming system, saw vines as being linked to the four elements: earth, water, air, and fire. Each element is favored when the moon passes into the constellations associated with it, thereby determining when a wine tastes best. You can take it with a grain of salt, but the winemakers I admire swear by it!

Even I will admit that some days, you taste a wine that you know well and nothing really strikes you, while other days, one wine is better than the next. Rather than blame it on the wine, think about it this way: We humans are susceptible to full moons, high pressure, and so on. So I don't know that the wines themselves change based on the planets; I think our perceptions just might.

○

The When Wine Tastes Best app puts the calendar at your fingertips. Consult it before you open a pricey bottle.

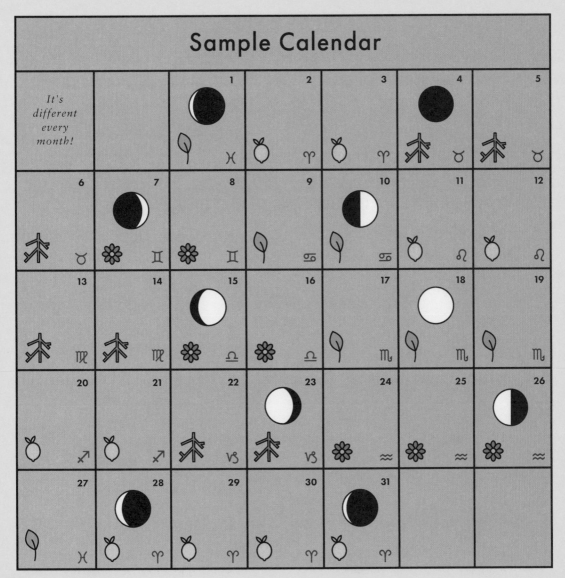

Sample Calendar

It's different every month!

Root Day
Not a great day to taste wine, as wines are perceived as being closed. Root days are in the earth signs: Capricorn, Taurus, and Virgo.

Leaf Day
A day when plants are busy producing chlorophyll, so the wine tastes less vibrant. These days are in the water signs: Cancer, Scorpio, and Pisces.

Flower Day
A good day to smell! Wine aromas will be enhanced. These days are in the air signs: Gemini, Libra, and Aquarius.

Fruit Day
The best day to taste wines, as they are the most open and fragrant. Fruit days are in the fire signs: Aries, Leo, and Sagittarius.

Intermediate Tasting Glossary

Here are some terms related to tasting and winemaking that will pop up as you advance in the world of wine.

AUSTERE A super-uptight wine that's pure acidity when you take a sip—you can't put your finger on what kind of grape it is.

BALANCED When the sweetness, acidity, tannins, alcohol, and body are in equilibrium.

BARNYARD Wine with volatile animalic components. In other words, it smells like manure, cows, urine—you name it.

BOTRYTIS (aka Noble Rot) A fungal infection that concentrates the sweetness, particularly in white grapes, adding caramely and fruity notes to what become dessert wines.

BRETT Short for Brettanomyces, a yeast that gives red wines an aroma evocative of horse sweat and barnyards—a popular characteristic of natural wines.

CHEWY Wine that's a bit more tannic than astringent.

CLOSED Wine that, while flavorful on the tongue, lacks aroma on the nose, but seems as though it will "open up" with time.

CORKED Wine that smells like a wet, damp cellar and has a white-mushroom character.

CRISP Wine that is pleasantly acidic. Mainly used with whites, rosés, and Champagne.

DRY Wine with very low sweetness—between 1 and 10 grams of residual sugar per liter.

EDGES Wine with "edges" is the tasting term for wine with a little bite, thanks to slightly elevated acidity and tannins, and occasionally minerality. The opposite of round.

FINESSE Wine that has elegant layers, twists, and turns. Nothing is too loud. Think of it as classical versus hip-hop.

FIRM Wine that has noticeable but not aggressive tannins.

FLABBY Wine that lacks acidity.

GRIPPY Wine with tannins that cling to the inside of your cheeks.

JAMMY Wine with concentrated fruit and a rich mouthfeel.

LINEAR Wine that tastes zippy and precise, with all the flavors seemingly attached on a straight line.

MADERIZED Wine that has been exposed to oxygen and/or heat for too long. Its brownish-yellow color and caramel flavor are evocative of the sweet Portuguese wine Madeira.

MERCAPTAN Chemical compounds formed by yeast during or after alcoholic fermentation that cause a rotten-egg smell.

MINERALITY Flavors that are evocative of slate, chalk, wet stone, or gravel. There are no trace minerals in wine; it is believed that these aromas are evocative of *terroir*.

MOUSY Wine that smells, well, like mouse fur or mouse cage. (Sorry to say, but it's a smell that most city dwellers are familiar with, as is anyone who had a mouse as a pet or in their classroom as a kid.)

MOUTHFEEL Describes a wine's texture or weight.

OFF-DRY Wine with low sweetness—between 17 and 35 grams of residual sugar per liter.

OXIDIZED Wine that's been exposed to too much air, resulting in a loss of freshness and fruitiness. This can happen by leaving too much in the bottle or glass overnight—or even a few hours, or over the course of years via a faulty cork or a bottle that's been stored upright for too long.

PALATE A person's tasting ability and preference and, more specifically, the regions on the tongue that perceive flavor.

REDUCTIVE Wines that did not receive enough oxygen during fermentation. The result is flavors of shaved white cabbage and white sesame.

RICH Wine that's massive on your palate. Lots of fruit, lots of spices, and a little residual sugar result in boldness.

ROUND Wine tannins that are smooth without being too soft.

SUPPLE A wine whose acids and tannins are harmoniously balanced.

TANNIC Wine that dries out the tongue and cheeks. Tannic wines are often great served with rich, fatty foods to help clean the palate.

VEGETAL Wine that has, well, vegetable aromas—most often of the greener variety like bell peppers, green tomatoes, and cabbage.

Age Matters

→ **People get worked up over whether a wine is from a good or a weak vintage.** That has merit if, say, you're ordering a wine from your birth year at a fancy restaurant, deciding if a younger bottle that you're considering buying at the wine store is age-worthy, or wondering why, say, a 2009 Burgundy costs so much more than a 2011. Me? I hate those charts telling you which vintages to pay any price for and which to avoid.

The quality of a vintage depends on that year's weather and when the grapes were harvested. Cool, rainy years yield more acidic, less flavorful fruit, while hot years result in high-alcohol sugar bombs. A year with frost or hail? Yikes. An ideal year means that the grapes have the perfect balance between enough rain, enough sun, no rot and fungus, and perfectly mature fruit—woody stems and fully developed brown seeds. But as anyone who's driven even a few miles from a rainy, cool part of the countryside to find themselves in a sunny, warm spot knows, every country—make that every region, and even vineyards *within* a region—is different. How can you quantify that in a chart?

Another thing to keep in mind is that many Burgundies and Bordeaux—the wines that collectors get most age-obsessed about—are judged and reviewed when they are *en primeur*, or newly made. How can the critics tasting them know that the wine will still be great in twenty to thirty years—the time that it takes for such wines to get into perfect drinking shape—or that a so-called bad vintage won't blossom into something beautiful, often in a shorter time? And remember that any winemaker can make a great wine in a stellar year, but a great winemaker knows how to make a good one in a terrible year. So if you're a bargain hunter, look at not-great years from renowned houses. I once did a tasting with the novelist and wine writer Jay McInerney and winemaker Guillaume d'Angerville of Volnay. We tasted all the way down to 1928—it was insane! What really surprised us, especially Guillaume, was that the so-called lesser vintages showed beautifully. So don't be ageist!

My short answer: I rarely store a wine that I paid less than $30 for. These wines are meant to be consumed young, when you'll enjoy the primary fruit flavors, such as pineapple, cherry, strawberry, green apple, citrus fruit, but also floral notes such as roses, or herbal/vegetal components like eucalyptus or bell pepper. Secondary flavors come mainly from the fermentation process. They include oak, vanilla, coffee, cedar, butter, and yogurt.

With aging, which varies from one grape variety to another, the primary and secondary flavors become more delicate as they head toward the background and let the tertiary flavors become more prominent: truffles, dried forest leaves, dried cigar tobacco, butterscotch . . . At this stage, the wine becomes an incredibly good-smelling bouquet. Every element will be in harmony, and the wine will stay on your palate for a long time. As you drink old wine, it will challenge you to think about what's going on. Young wine? You can chug it and won't really think about more than how much fun you're having. So, yes, age matters.

TRY THIS

→ Talk to your favorite wine-store person or a sommelier who knows your palate about trying wines with a touch of age. Don't start with a 1945 Château Mouton Rothschild! **Buy a five-year-old wine and get comfortable with it, then explore the same wine and/or region with ten years of age.** That way you'll get a reference point for how these wines evolve and learn from it.

Buying Aged Wine

➤ Purchasing a bottle that someone else aged sounds so easy, right? Well . . . Like us humans, wines have an aging curve. And because of the cork, not every bottle ages the same. When buying aged wines, you want to know the provenance. This is really hard, unless you're a professional buyer. Has it been consistently stored in a dark, temperature-controlled environment? Was it transported—both to the States and to the store—in a temperature-controlled container? Has it been kept on its side so that the cork has stayed moist? And so on. If you buy it at auction or online, how do you know that it hasn't been kept on top of someone's refrigerator in a hot kitchen for forty years? Unfortunately, you can't.

That's why you should always buy from a reputable store or auction house. Once the cork is old, it becomes soaked, allowing air to slowly come in and thereby accelerating the aging process. We professionals look at where the fill level is in the "shoulder" of the bottle. We also look at the label to make sure it hasn't been deteriorated by light or humidity. And, of course, if the bottle is displayed standing upright in a shop, move on.

A WORD ON VINTAGE CHARTS

→ With my apologies to vintage charts, I'm just going to say it: I hate them. They're useful for experienced collectors who plan to cellar wines. But if you start going online to pull up a vintage chart for, say, Burgundy, where there are so many side areas and valleys, each with its own microclimate, it's impossible to make a blanket statement that X was a perfect year for every winemaker in the region.

Those perfect years are, of course, the most expensive and the hardest to find. I prefer to look for so-called lesser vintages. Not only are they up to 50 percent less expensive, but you can often drink them sooner. And these wallflowers often blossom beautifully while no one's looking.

White vs. Red

We focus on aging reds more than whites, though whites can age really well. German, Austrian, and Alsatian Rieslings are magic. Chablis/white Burgundies, grower and vintage Champagne, and Loire chenin blancs age beautifully. Of course there are more, but these are great places to start.

A great Burgundy, Bordeaux, Rhône, Barolo, Barbaresco, and Rioja will pretty much always benefit from aging. The young tannins—derived from grape skins, stems, and seeds, as well as the wood tannins from oak barrels—make red wine often seem "watery" when you're tasting it. (This is especially true of Bordeaux.) The tannins somehow stretch a blanket over your taste buds, and the wine is perceived as watery on your mid-palate. Most people would write off that wine, but observe the tension on your palate, as well as how quickly the tannins disappear. Typically, such wines benefit a lot from aging, as the tannins soften and the fruit enters its full bloom.

. . . vs. Rosé

Rosés are meant to be drunk the year that they're bottled. If you happen to have forgotten that you had a rosé made from pinot noir, or from the fabled house of Tempier in Bandol for a year or two, you can still give it a shot.

THE VERY GOOD (I.E., VERY EXPENSIVE) YEARS

→ If you're wondering why a 2005 French red is double the price of a 2006 from the same vineyard, that's because 2005 was considered an excellent year. If you're anything like me, you'll seek bargains around the margins, looking for wines from good producers in "off" years. The extra bonus with these wines is that you typically don't have to age them for as long before enjoying them. I know I just said I hate vintage charts, but here are my picks for the best offerings from the last decade. Take it with a grain of salt!

2016
Austria

2014
Spain

2011
Piemonte

2010
Burgundy
(white & red)

2009
Bordeaux

2008
Champagne

2007
Burgundy
(white)

2004
Tuscany
Piemonte

2001
Rhône
Burgundy
Bordeaux

2000
Bordeaux

1999
Burgundy (red)

⌚ When Can I Drink It?!

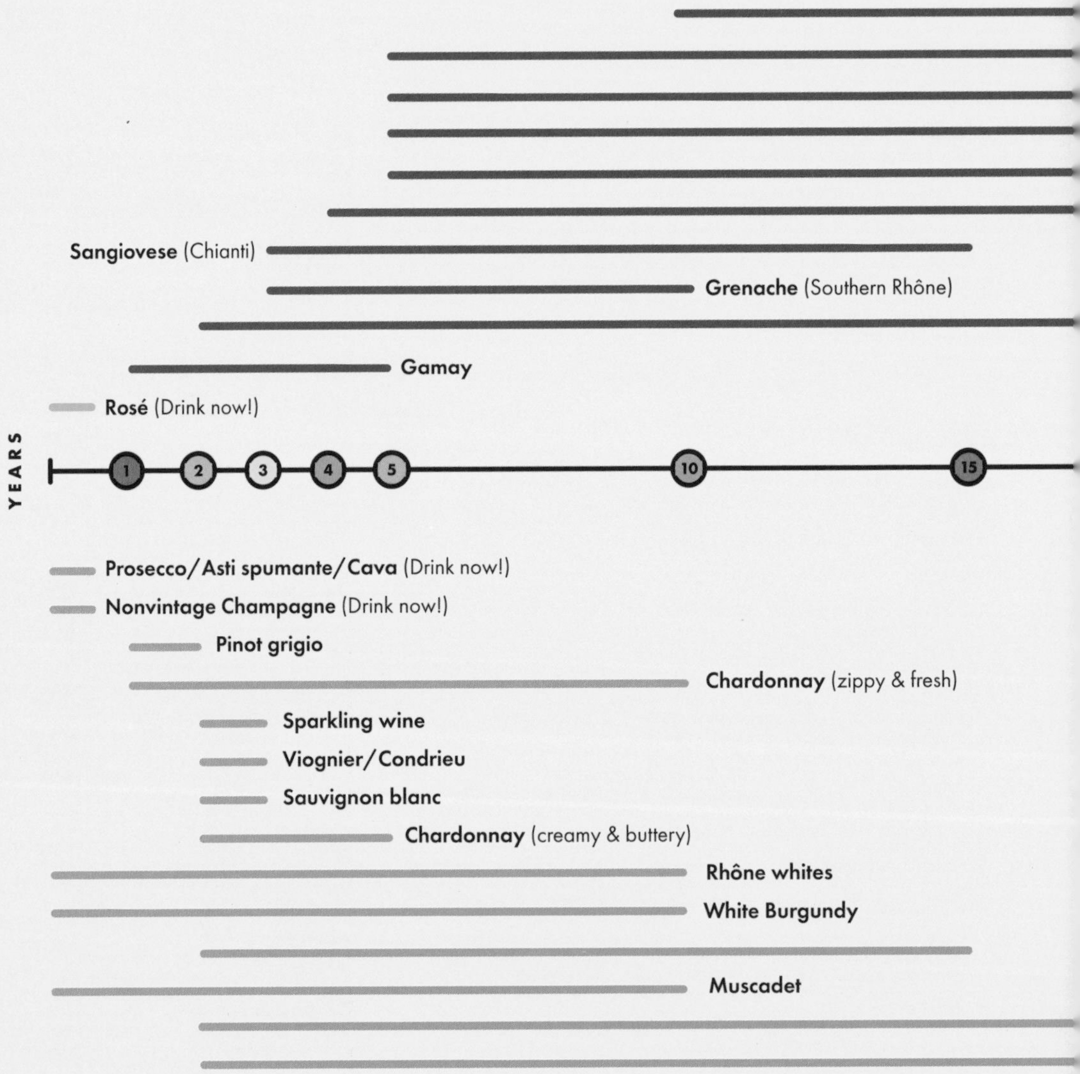

Sangiovese (Chianti)

Grenache (Southern Rhône)

Gamay

Rosé (Drink now!)

YEARS

1 — 2 — 3 — 4 — 5 ——— 10 ——— 15

Prosecco/Asti spumante/Cava (Drink now!)

Nonvintage Champagne (Drink now!)

Pinot grigio

Chardonnay (zippy & fresh)

Sparkling wine

Viognier/Condrieu

Sauvignon blanc

Chardonnay (creamy & buttery)

Rhône whites

White Burgundy

Muscadet

→ You can't really know when a wine's peak moment is—it changes from year to year, vineyard to vineyard, and producer to producer. The best way to find out is to buy six to twelve bottles of the same wine and try it over the course of twelve years. Take notes! This is how you learn how a wine evolves. This guide offers a pretty wide range. Whether you're into aging wine is up to you.

Nebbiolo (Barolo & Barbaresco)

Cabernet sauvignon (Bordeaux)

Syrah

Tempranillo

Merlot (Right Bank Bordeaux)

Cabernet sauvignon (Napa Valley)

Pinot noir (Burgundy & California)

20   30   50   **YEARS**

Vintage Champagne

Chenin blanc

Riesling

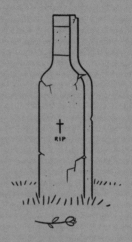

Why You Should Just Enjoy Your Special-Occasion Wines Now

Sometimes I think that's one of the weird thresholds with wine drinkers: They feel like they have to save that special bottle for a milestone. Then, when it comes around, somehow that occasion is never special enough . . . until finally they die, and their kids give those old bottles to the neighbors or sell them cheaply to auction houses. You can't shove those 1989 Bordeaux into your coffin, so what are you waiting for? My philosophy is, whenever you open a bottle of wine is a special occasion.

How to Start Collecting Wine 🍷🍷

▽ Try and decide.

Before you start investing, the first and most important step is to figure out what you do and don't like. It will take you at least a few years to shop and drink. Allow your palate time to evolve. If you build a cellar around Australian shiraz right out of the gate, what will you do after a couple of years when you've moved on? Taste, get more experience, feel more comfortable.

⦿ Be well rounded.

I buy some high-profile wines as an investment in the future, but the majority of my collection are wines for daily consumption. I take the seasons (and their dishes and ingredients) into consideration, spreading out my selections among easy-drinking, medium-bodied, and full-bodied wines.

△ Ask a pro.

Work with a wine professional to help you build. This can be the owner of your wine shop, or you can hire your favorite sommelier to help you put something together.

▣ Skip the auctions.

Don't sink all your money into auctions until you get to know what you like. Yes, there are steals to be found, but you can just as easily be taken. Unless a wine comes directly from the winemaker, you have no way of telling how the wine was stored and transported, and therefore there's no guarantee it's still in good shape. Also, auction houses charge about a 22 percent commission, plus sales tax *and* delivery! And, unlike with a wine store, if the wine is bad, you can't take it back. (Same goes for ordering wines online.) I'll say it again: Personal relationships are everything. Especially with auction houses.

◯ Avoid the accidents.

Create a couple of bins for your partner so he or she leaves your super-special, open-in-twenty-years bins alone when looking for something to drink right this minute with their friends! This is absolutely key, as terrible accidents can occur . . .

Resources

→ In addition to the critics mentioned on the opposite page, who can help you learn about vintages and growing conditions, there are many great resources for helping you become a full-fledged wine nerd. Here are some of my favorites.

Books

The 24-Hour Wine Expert by Jancis **Robinson** is a mini bible for bringing you up to speed. She is the goddess! When you're ready to dive into the deep end, make room for **The Oxford Companion to Wine**, which Jancis edited in 2015.

Wine Folly: Magnum Edition: The Master Guide by Madeline Puckette and Justin Hammack breaks down must-know information about flavors, grape varieties, and growing regions into vibrant, easy-to-remember graphics. If you're a visual learner, meet your new best wine friend.

The New Wine Rules by Jon Bonné takes a smart, fun approach to wine that tears down all the stuffy cobwebs.

Champagne: The Essential Guide to the Wines, Producers, and Terroirs of the Iconic Region by Peter Liem. An incredibly lush, well-researched, and essential guide. The unique fold-out maps also make it a collectible.

Secrets of the Sommeliers by Rajat Parr. Learn what top somms drink—and their alternatives.

The Juice: Vinous Veritas by Jay **McInerney.** Funny and educational pieces about what's cool and classic.

Apps

Delectable offers a fun way to keep track of the wines you like. Take a photo of the bottle, and it tells you where you can buy it. It also lets you see what your friends on the app are into these days, leading to lots of side conversations.

Vinous. The Vinous team combines reviews, vintage charts, and articles, and allows you to search by photos of labels that you snap on your phone.

Websites

Punch. This drinks site has fantastic wine writing by Talia Baiocchi, Jon Bonné, Zachary Sussman, and Megan Krigbaum.

Jancis Robinson's Purple Pages. A subscription-only site that grants you access to decades of tasting notes and articles. Her weekly newsletter is excellent, too.

Vinous Media. Former Robert Parker critic Antonio Galloni has created a multimedia wine empire. Reviews (of wines as well as restaurant wine lists), articles, apps—you name it.

Wine Folly. Madeline Puckette makes learning about wine incredibly accessible and fun. For visual learners who prefer to have things broken down into well-designed graphs and charts, this is your teacher.

Magazines

Wine & Spirits Magazine. Writer Josh Green contributes perfectly researched articles. He's also one of my favorite interviewers.

Fine is a European magazine offering really great Champagne guides.

WHICH CRITIC IS FOR YOU?

→ Are you turning out to be an emerging-varietal geek, or are you intrigued by the idea of getting into big Bordeaux? Here are the tasting tendencies of the top wine reviewers.

☐ **Robert Parker**
Likes rich, concentrated, powerful wines with a touch of barnyard; heavily focused on Bordeaux, California, Australia, South America.

☐ **Jancis Robinson**
Classic; likes nuance and finesse; spans the globe and is good on emerging regions; has a journalistic viewpoint and zero pretension—she cuts through the BS.

☐ **Eric Asimov**
Into geeky stuff and prefers to veer a little off the beaten path; looks for value and esoteric wines.

☐ **Antonio Galloni**
Prefers vibrant, high-acidity wines; loves Italy, Champagne, and California.

☐ **Alice Feiring**
The natural wine queen; she likes Georgian qvevri wines and French underdogs.

☐ **Wine Spectator**
Their writers love California, Bordeaux, and the more high-profile wineries; they don't go for small, geeky producers.

4

Wine
&
Food

▶ This is going to sound extremely arrogant and won't exactly endear me to any chefs, but I believe that the right wine can make or break your meal. If a customer comes to Le Bernardin and insists on ordering a bottle of wine that I know will overtake the dish (my powers of persuasion are apparently limited when it comes to those who are determined to order a certain special-occasion red wine . . .), I promise you that they will leave saying, "The ambiance was great, the server was nice, the sommelier did an okay job . . . but nothing really struck me." In my opinion, they're not getting the 100 percent "wow" effect because the wine didn't click with the food.

But when you have a wine that interacts with the food, all of a sudden the flavors connect and both are elevated. You have harmony. Pleasure. A really great experience. I think of a perfect pairing as being like a perfect marriage: No one partner dominates; they exist in harmony, interacting beautifully.

Food can bring out the worst in a wine: Spicy chiles can blow up the alcohol and intensify the acidity of a California chardonnay. Raw egg yolk can shellac your palate (and the rim of your glass), throwing off even the best Champagne—this from the wine that's perfect with 98 percent of dishes. But a dry or off-dry Riesling is incredible with most Thai food, meshing remarkably well with its fruity/sweet-sour/spicy/coconut components. The ironlike minerality of a Saint-Joseph accents a medium-rare grilled steak, making it seem even richer. And to me, there's nothing better than scallops with a French Chardonnay—they complement each other in a fantastic way. When it comes together, you just know. When I'm working out which wines to pair with new dishes at Le Bernardin, the cooks look at me like I'm insane: I go into the kitchen with a whole tray covered with filled glasses, the whites resting sideways on a bowl of ice so they won't go crazy in the heat. I try what I know will go together, but I also experiment with things that make no sense at all, like beer with a chocolate dessert. Those are the most exciting discoveries.

Pairing at a restaurant is much harder than figuring out what to open at home. At work, I'm focused on harmonizing with the elaborate sauces that Chef Eric Ripert creates rather than the preparation of the fish, which tends to be pretty minimalist. He comes up with some real challenges, like pickled Persian cucumbers that had my head spinning. Like most people, at home I tend to stick to simple grilling, pastas, and stews. No fancy sauces, emulsions, or reductions. That makes my off-hours drinking life so much easier—and hopefully makes it a lot less intimidating for you, too.

While it's obviously different at home, I'll always look for something that will work with my entire meal. Of course, if I'm having pasta with tomato sauce, I'm not going to drink a Champagne—I want Chianti! Eric and I have a funny episode of *Perfect Pairings* on YouTube where he says that Bordeaux goes with *everything*. While I disagree with that (of course), Bordeaux is a good all-rounder. However, there is much more out there.

On the following pages, I've broken out my suggestions into several scenarios: varietal, ingredient, flavor, and cuisine. Don't take it as gospel—experiment to become your own matchmaker. Hopefully it will get you started on your own path.

How to Make a Perfect Pairing

▼ General Guidelines

→ Let's get this out of the way: That one perfect, goes-with-everything bottle does not exist for the home. What tastes good with your salad probably won't hit it off with your steak. And what makes your steak sing will most likely be a cringey karaoke duet with your dessert. The idea that a country's wines pair well with its cuisine seems logical, until you consider that Italy has over one thousand grape varieties and even more kinds of pasta. So unless you're willing to go with Champagne—by far the most food-friendly wine—or the runner-up, Grüner Veltliner, you should either open two bottles, or one bottle plus one half bottle . . . or just embrace imperfection.

While crisp, fresh, clean wines are nice to sip with friends, they're not always the best option at the table. Look for something that has moderate alcohol (12 to 13% ABV) and balanced acidity and fruit.

If you're drinking more than one bottle, you ideally want the wines to increase in power throughout the meal, if at all. If you start with a big, aromatic wine, you can't progress to something more delicate, so keep that in mind.

THE GO-WITH EVERYTHINGS

- ☑ Grüner Veltliner
- ☑ Bordeaux (according to Eric Ripert)
- ☑ A bottle of Champagne or sparkling wine
- ☑ Chianti Classico
- ☑ Riesling (dry)
- ☑ Albariño

■ Rules to Break

White Wine + Fish

For me, how the fish is prepared is more important than what you drink with it. If it's poached, you should stick with white. But if it's seared or grilled, those roasted, caramelized flavors can be really beneficial to a red. Just stay away from tannic varieties like cabernet or nebbiolo. Try a pinot noir or a slightly chilled Bandol from Provence. That extra chill enhances the freshness and downplays the richness, of food and wine alike.

Red Wine + Steak

Why not try a white? Go for a really powerful one from the Rhône, a rich chardonnay from Burgundy or Napa, or a rosé Champagne.

Red Wine + Cheese

Try white! (See page 258.)

> **BEFORE THE MEAL . . .**
>
> I look for something light, crisp, fresh, more citrusy, and leaner in fruit—nothing too aromatic—just to cleanse the palate a little bit and get my appetite started. (Acidity makes us salivate.) A pinot grigio can be interesting, as can pinot blanc, albariño, and vinho verde. I know people like to start their meal with sauvignon blanc, but a New Zealand sauvignon blanc is aromatic, with a high ABV—where do you go from there? Again, at the risk of sounding redundant, consider Grüner and Champagne for that premeal drink.

● How to Guarantee the Best Pairings at a Restaurant

→ If they don't offer a by-the-glass pairing, ask the sommelier to put one together based on what you're eating.

→ If you'd prefer a bottle, **tell the sommelier what you're eating** and ask her to give you a few options in your price range.

→ If you're fixated on getting a specific bottle, ask the sommelier to suggest what to eat with it: Chances are, she's tasted every item on the menu and every bottle in the cellar, so trust her.

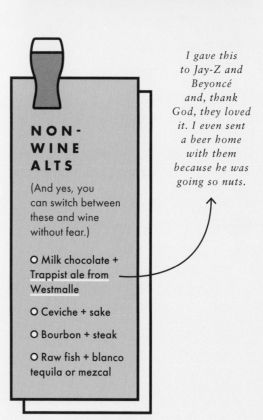

NON-WINE ALTS

(And yes, you can switch between these and wine without fear.)

O Milk chocolate + Trappist ale from Westmalle

O Ceviche + sake

O Bourbon + steak

O Raw fish + blanco tequila or mezcal

I gave this to Jay-Z and Beyoncé and, thank God, they loved it. I even sent a beer home with them because he was going so nuts.

Wine, Meet Food

➡ I get text messages from friends starting around five o'clock every night asking which bottle of wine to open with dinner. I've broken down my favorites into several categories, from variety to ingredient to cuisine. Of course, these are all quite broad suggestions with a lot of room for nuance—think of these pairings as a starting point from which to explore.

PINOT GRIGIO

Solo as an apéritif
Simple salad
Fried calamari
Canned tuna
Sushi

RIESLING

Raw fish
Ham
Salads with fruit or seafood
Fried rice

SAUVIGNON BLANC

Raw fish (Sancerre)
Italian food (Sancerre)
Vegetables
(New Zealand)
Lobster roll (New Zealand)

GRÜNER VELTLINER

Fish
Salad
Grilled food
French fries
Mac and cheese

CHARDONNAY

Chicken
Lobster
Cod
Shrimp
Grilled veg

PINOT NOIR

Poultry
Salmon
Cod
Turkey

BY VARIETAL

MERLOT

Chicken
Pork
Beef stew
Lamb

**CABERNET
SAUVIGNON**

Steak
Lamb
Grilled sausage
Parmesan

SYRAH

Steak
Pork
Potatoes
Grilled veg

Meat

STEAK

Syrah/Saint-Joseph
Bordeaux
Mencía

CHICKEN

Pinot noir
Gamay
Sicilian red
Chardonnay (California)
Grüner Veltliner
(with fried chicken)

BY INGREDIENT

LAMB

Cabernet sauvignon
Pinot noir (chilled)
Sangiovese

PORK

Merlot
Tempranillo
Gamay (with pork belly)
Riesling (with ham)
Beaujolais
(with charcuterie)

BURGERS

Beaujolais
Pinot noir (New World)

Pasta

MARINARA

Sicilian red

MEAT SAUCE

Sangiovese

SEAFOOD

Friuliano

> Keep in mind the sauce and preparation you choose will affect the pairing. Welcome to my world!

Perfect Pairings

♡ **CLASSIC**

Steak: Bordeaux
Truffle pasta: Barolo
Oysters: Champagne
Burger: Pinot noir
Lobster: California chardonnay
Fish stew: Rosé
Dover sole: White Burgundy

❗ **UNEXPECTED**

Pizza: Champagne or American gamay
Thai papaya salad: Dry Riesling (12.5% ABV and above)
Tacos: Albariño
Chocolate: Trappist ale
Blue cheese: Vinjaune

Seafood

SALMON

Pinot noir
Sauvignon blanc
(New Zealand)

SCALLOPS

Chenin blanc
Chardonnay

TROUT

Pinot grigio
Sancerre

TUNA

Nero d'Avola
(with grilled tuna)

SHRIMP

Sauvignon blanc
Chardonnay

RAW SEAFOOD

Muscadet
Chablis
Santorini
Champagne/Crémant

Aldo's Favorite At-Home Pairings

☐ **Steak + Grilled Mushrooms + Northern Rhône Red**
I love a Cornas or a Côte Rôtie. If I don't want to splurge, I drink Saint-Joseph.

☐ **Bánh Mì + Dry Riesling**
The Riesling is aromatic enough to hold up to the mint and pickles, and the minerals cut through the fat.

☐ **Short Ribs + Aged Zinfandel**
This is what I have for Thanksgiving—I hate turkey with a passion. Luckily, zinfandel is epic with it.

☐ **Spaghetti al Pomodoro Crudo + Friulano**
Perfectly ripe, raw tomatoes with garlic and basil and a glass of light red from Friuli is a mini summer vacation.

BY INGREDIENT

 TRICKIEST

Raw tomato: Try a sauvignon blanc from Austria or Friuli.

Cucumber: You want a textural wine with flavor, like pinot gris.

Chiles: Look for wines with residual sugar, such as Rieslings.

Egg: Champagne's acidity cuts the tanginess, and its sugar coats the unctuous quality of the yolk.

Green bell peppers: New Zealand sauvignon blanc can handle them, as can richer Pouilly-Fumés.

BY FLAVOR

FRESH / HERBACEOUS

Albariño
Really dry Rieslings
(12.5% ABV and above)
Light sauvignon blancs
(below 12.5% ABV)

WOODY /HERBACEOUS

Think red:
Provençal reds/Bandol
Aged Rioja/Sangiovese

SPICY

Riesling with residual sugar
(below 11% ABV)
Off-dry chenin blancs
Prosecco

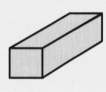

BUTTERY / CREAMY

Champagne
Prosecco
Chardonnay

FATTY / HEAVY

Alsatian Riesling
Northern Rhône Syrah
Zinfandel

SMOKY

Ribera del Duero
Rioja
Malbec
Napa cab

FUNKY / FERMENTED

Zinfandel
Garnacha
Côtes-du-Rhône (red)

CHEESY

Sparkling wine
Sangiovese
Gamay

EARTHY/MUSHROOMY

Aged wines
(reds and whites)
Syrah
Mourvèdre
Rioja riserva

BITTER

Sauvignon blanc
Pinot blanc
Richer versions of
pinot gris

GARLICKY (RAW)

Sauvignon blanc
Viognier
Sangiovese
Tempranillo
New World Chardonnay
Vermentino (cooked garlic)

SWEET-AND-SOUR

Riesling
Gewürztraminer
Prosecco

NUTTY

Grüner Veltliner
Albariño
Sauvignon blanc

COCONUTTY

Riesling
Prosecco
Demi-sec chenin blanc

LEMONY / TART / ACIDIC

Sauvignon blanc
Cava
Viognier

BY FLAVOR

OCEANIC / SEAWEED

Dry Riesling
Grüner Veltliner
Rosé

SOY / SALTY

Riesling
Pinot gris
Sake!

BRINY

Sauvignon blanc
Albariño
Vermentino

BY CUISINE

THAI

Riesling (off-dry; stay
around 11% ABV)
Grüner Veltliner
Pinot noir (chilled) with
cooked dishes

VIETNAMESE

Champagne
Riesling (off-dry)
Pinot noir (chilled)

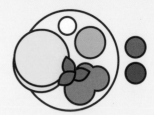

INDIAN

Riesling
Syrah
Merlot

CHINESE

Pinot noir
Sparkling (dim sum)
Chardonnay (dim sum)
Sauvignon blanc from
California or New Zealand
Riesling (off-dry, with
Szechuan cuisine)

JAPANESE

Grüner Veltliner
Riesling
Sancerre

KOREAN

Chenin blanc
Cabernet sauvignon
Syrah

FRENCH

Cabernet sauvignon
Pinot noir
Alsatian pinot gris
Syrah

MEDITERRANEAN

Pinot grigio
Vermentino

ITALIAN

Chianti Classico
Dolcetto
Sicilian red
Lambrusco
Sparkling rosé

MEXICAN

Beer
Sauvignon blanc
(New Zealand)
Rosé
Mission

CARIBBEAN

Beer
Cava

AMERICAN SOUTH

Chardonnay
Chenin blanc

SPANISH

Rioja
Syrah
Mencía

PERSIAN

Rioja
Aged Piemontes
Old Champagne

NORDIC

Natural wine!
Grüner Veltliner

BY CUISINE

EASTERN EUROPEAN

Aged Riesling
Blaufränkisch

ARGENTINE

Malbec (steak)
Cabernet sauvignon

**IMPORTANT
TO NOTE:**

It would be impossible
to narrow entire diverse
cuisines, with their wide-
ranging varieties of
dishes, to a handful of
flavor profiles. These
are very broad starting
points—to get more
specific, have a
conversation with your
wine shop person or
sommelier about what
you're eating.

In Praise of White Wine with Cheese

➤ The rule seems to be that you should serve red wine with cheese. I'm here to say that about 75 percent of cheeses are best with white wine. Hi!

I find that the tannins in red wine and the acids and proteins start fighting, often to the detriment of both. (Have you ever tried red wine with blue cheese? It's like getting a mouthful of ammonia.) Most whites, on the other hand, give you more flexibility with residual sugar, with fruit, and with acid. They have the freshness and a little bit of sugar to cut through the creaminess, without the backlash.

Speaking of freshness, here's a little secret: If you're trying to get rid of a white that tastes a little over the hill, serve it with cheese. Oxidative flavors work beautifully well with cheese. Here are some of my favorite combinations, both white and red.

GOAT CHEESE

Sancerre
Sauvignon blanc

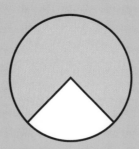

BRIE / CAMEMBERT

Champagne
Calvados

COMTÉ / SWISS

Vin jaune from the Jura
Pinot noir

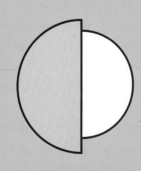

ÉPOISSES

Aged Burgundy
Cornas

CHEDDAR

Bordeaux
Oloroso Sherry

MUENSTER

Gewürtztraminer
Alsatian pinot gris

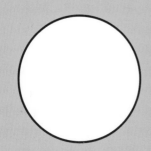

MOZZARELLA / BURRATA

Pinot grigio
Grüner Veltliner
A light Sauvignon blanc
from the Loire Valley

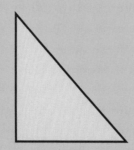

PARMESAN

Barbera
Sangiovese

PECORINO

Sicilian red
Tuscan red

CHEESE PAIRING

Learning How to Make Wine

A 2008 trip to Argentina with *Wine Spectator* magazine totally changed my life. They wanted me to write about the local wine from a sommelier's perspective. I was so inspired by the countryside that I was overtaken by the urge to make wine there. Maybe a malbec, or perhaps I could try planting Austrian Grüner Veltliner in chilly Patagonia? But when I thought about it, Argentina seemed too risky to invest in. An Austrian winemaker told me that I could make wine in Austria for the same price, and it was more politically stable there. Not long after,

I was having dinner with Gerhard Kracher of the legendary Austrian winemaking family. When I told him my crazy idea, he had an even crazier one to share: "Why don't we do it together?"

Gerhard is known for making sweet wines. He wanted to try something new. We agreed that we didn't want to make fat, high-alcoholic wines. We wanted something fresher, something planted in limestone soil. When looking at real estate, we had to look well beyond Austria's fancy areas, but finally we were able to rent just under a hectare, planted with fifty old Grüner vines. Through lots of trial and error and regular visits, Gerhard was able to talk the land's farmer through what we wanted (and didn't want).

I realized just how little I knew about the farming aspect. For instance, the vines' southern exposure meant that the plants got blasted in August, requiring more leaf coverage to protect the grapes. After we'd harvested, I realized how much I had to learn in the cellar. I'd visited plenty of wineries and worked harvest with such greats as Jean-Marc Roulot in Burgundy, but it had never been my own wine at stake, and besides, everyone is always on their best behavior during such events. I was finally seeing what happened when things went wrong.

For example, I had unusual ideas about how I wanted to do things—for Austria at least—such as prolonging the aging for another year (typically not done there) and leaving the wine on the lees (the dead yeast cells) rather than fine or filter it, which I'd learned during a seminar with the brilliant Alsatian winemaker Olivier Humbrecht. Working at Le Bernardin has exposed me to so much Burgundy, so I looked toward making something in line with the more acidic wines of that region. Burgundian-style wines in Austria? Why not?

When the first of the 1,800 bottles were released, I threw a big party at Terroir wine bar in New York to celebrate. I opened the first bottle from the case that Gerhard had shipped, poured a glass while everyone clapped, and . . . the wine was hazy, which, to me, was a severe flaw. My heart sank. My stomach sank. Everyone said, "This is a very funny-looking wine you made!" So I opened another bottle. And another. The entire case was cloudy. (Luckily, the wine tasted great. But I was too upset to notice.)

I called Gerhard, who said that the bottles at the winery were perfectly clear. When I went to see him a few months later, I brought some on the plane with me so he could taste what happened in transport. There was no comparison! (Long story short, we had a disagreement about fining—I wanted to try it, especially after Jean-Marc Roulot had mentored me on fining; he said over his dead body— and started doing it, adding small amounts of

bentonite to bind to those proteins that were making the wine cloudy.) I did so much research that now I can taste when a wine has been fined.

Other experiments, such as adjusting the sulfites and even trying tannin powder, which can make wine taste bigger, have also sharpened my palate to detect them in wines I sample for the restaurant. And tasting our wines at every stage of fermentation, thanks to the vials that Gerhard sends by FedEx every few weeks, has allowed me to truly understand the evolution of a wine—not to mention the magic of winemaking.

Our wine got high ratings out of the gate, even from my hero, Jancis Robinson. We've since rented some surrounding vineyards, and our four labels are now producing over twenty thousand bottles a year, exporting as far as China. Each year has new challenges, be it extreme weather or low yields. I've definitely learned humility in the face of nature, especially when I had to open the spout on a 300-liter barrel that had been stuck in fermentation— meaning the yeast had stopped eating the sugar, making the wine unbearably sweet. Now when I hear sommeliers discuss the merits of spontaneous fermentation using naturally occurring yeast versus the commercial stuff, I join in from a different angle. (My response? I tell them to go to the ATM, take out a few thousand dollars, and dump it down the drain.) That said, we still do spontaneous fermentation.

To mark our ten-year anniversary, Gerhard and I tasted our wines going back to our beginnings. It became apparent to me how many hot vintages we'd had—five out of the ten! Add to that the damaging effects of frost, hail, severe storms, and climate change, which has been something I've kept a closer eye on since I started making wine. Gerhard and I always experiment to improve and evolve.

Humility, knowledge, pleasure, and awe are just some of the things I've gotten from winemaking. It's made me a better sommelier and certainly a much more appreciative drinker. Come to think of it, humility, knowledge, pleasure, and awe have always been at the heart of my love of wine. I hope that this book has opened the door to them for you, too.

Glossary

ABV Short for "alcohol by volume," the percentage of which is listed on the label. Keep in mind that 13% is average (this has risen from 12% in the '80s, thanks to climate change), while over 15% is high.

AMBIENT YEAST Yeast that is naturally occurring in the environment, whether on grape skins or in the air.

AMPHORAE Used since ancient Rome, these large clay vessels, often buried in the ground, are filled with crushed grapes with the skins on and sealed for aging.

APPELLATION A legally defined geographical location that indicates where a wine is grown. In France, the appellation—known as an AOC or AOP—can also dictate the style of wine.

AROMATIC COMPOUNDS Literally what you smell. These chemical compounds, which are released as alcohol evaporates, are measured using a gas chromograph.

ASTRINGENT Tasting term for the drying, slightly puckery feeling caused by tannins as they bind to proteins on your tongue.

AUSTERE Tasting term for a super-uptight wine that's pure acidity when you take a sip—you feel as if you're chewing on a rock!

AVA American Viticultural Area, or our take on the appellation system. This indicates a federally designated wine-growing region.

BALANCED A wine in which the sweetness, acidity, tannins, alcohol, and body are in equilibrium.

BARNYARD Tasting term for a wine with volatile animalic components. In other words, it smells like manure, cows—you name it.

BARREL This traditional aging container is typically made of oak, which adds not only richer fruit and vanilla flavors but also a slightly broader texture, since the wine is able to breathe. Wines aged in stainless steel barrels tend to be a little tighter, since the oxygen can't escape.

BOTRYTIS A naturally occurring fungus that concentrates a grape's sweetness and can impart a honeyed flavor to dry wines. Also called noble rot.

BRETT Short for *Brettanomyces*, a yeast that gives red wines an aroma evocative of horse sweat and barnyards—flavors that are a popular characteristic of natural wines.

CASK A traditional aging container; typically wood or stainless steel, which affects the flavor. Can be anywhere between 100 and 10,000 liters in capacity.

CHEWY Tasting term for wine that's a bit more tannic than astringent.

CLOSED Tasting term for wine that, while flavorful on the tongue, lacks aroma on the nose but seems as though it will "open up" with time.

CORKED Tasting term for wine that smells like a moldy basement or white mushrooms.

CRISP Tasting term for wine that is pleasantly acidic. Mainly used with whites, rosés, and Champagne.

CROWN CAP The type of ridged cap you see on beer and soda bottles.

CRU A French vineyard that is recognized for exceptional quality based on a classification system dating from the 1800s.

CUVÉE A batch or blend of wine.

DOSAGE A mixture of reserve wine and sugar syrup.

DOWNGRADED Rows of vineyards are downgraded, or declassified, when the winemakers plant new vines or have a weak vintage.

DRY Tasting term for wine with very low sweetness—between 1 and 10 grams of residual sugar per liter.

EDGES "Wine with edges" is the tasting term for wine with a little bite, thanks to slightly elevated acidity and tannins, and occasionally minerality. The opposite of round.

EGG This fermentation and aging container can be made from concrete or clay. It adds a little volatility, or a ciderish or kombucha-like quality, to the wine.

FINESSE Tasting term for wine that has elegant layers, twists, and turns. Nothing is too loud. Think of it as classical versus hip-hop.

FINING AGENTS Elements that are added to wine to remove any trace proteins or sediments that might make the wine cloudy. Bentonite clay, egg whites, and casein are used.

FIRM Tasting term for wine that has noticeable but not aggressive tannins.

FLABBY Tasting term for wine that lacks acidity.

GRAND CRU A designated area of quality. Premier cru is the ranking above grand cru.

GRAPE MUST Just-pressed grape juice.

GRIPPY Tasting term for wine with tannins that cling to the inside of your cheeks.

GROWTH Refers to a classification of wines from Bordeaux. Basically, it means "prepare to pay."

INOCULATED YEAST Commercial yeast that is added during winemaking.

JAMMY Tasting term for wine with concentrated fruit and a rich mouthfeel.

LEES A sediment of dead yeast cells that have sunk to the bottom of the fermentation vessel or bottle.

LINEAR A wine that tastes zippy and precise, with all the flavors seemingly attached on a straight line.

MACERATION The process in red-wine making that extracts color from the grape skins. You can also extract tannins and higher levels of sugar.

MADERIZED White wine that has been exposed to oxygen and/or heat for too long. Its brownish-yellow color and caramel flavor are evocative of the sweet Portuguese wine Madeira.

MERCAPTAN What causes that rotten-egg smell.

MINERALITY Tasting term for flavors that are evocative of slate, chalk, wet stone, or gravel. There are no trace minerals in wine; it is believed that these aromas are evocative of *terroir*.

MOUSY Tasting term describing wine that smells, well, like mouse fur. (Sorry to say, but it's a smell that most New Yorkers are familiar with, as is anyone who had a mouse as a pet or in their classroom as a kid.)

MOUTHFEEL Tasting term to describe a wine's texture or weight.

MW Abbreviation for Master of Wine; a highly regarded qualification given by the British Institute of Masters of Wine.

NÉGOCIANTS Winemakers who buy grapes from a bunch of different vineyards and use them to produce their own wine.

OAKED Wine aged in barrels made from toasted or natural oak. The hard grape tannins interchange with the soft wood tannin, adding a rich vanilla flavor and creamy mouthfeel.

OFF-DRY Tasting term for wine with low sweetness—between 17 and 35 grams of residual sugar per liter for sparkling wine, or above 9 grams for regular wines.

OXIDIZED Wine that's been exposed to too much air, resulting in a loss of freshness and fruitiness. This can happen by leaving too much in the bottle or glass overnight—or even a few hours, or over the course of years via a faulty cork or a bottle that's been stored upright for too long.

PALATE This refers to a person's tasting ability and preference and, more specifically, to the regions on the tongue that perceive flavor.

PÉT-NAT Short for *pétillant naturel*, a natural winemaking technique that results in lightly effervescent wines.

PÉTILLANT A wine that is lightly sparkling.

PHENOLIC COMPOUNDS Several hundred chemical compounds found in wine that affect everything from the color to the taste to the texture you feel on your tongue.

QVEVRI Clay jars that have been used in winemaking in the Republic of Georgia for thousands of years.

REDUCTIVE Tasting term for wines that did not receive enough oxygen during fermentation. The result is flavors of shaved white cabbage and white sesame.

RESIDUAL SUGAR (RS) The sugar that is left over from grapes after fermentation stops—that which was not converted to alcohol. It can range from 0 grams per liter (bone dry) to 220 grams per liter (very sweet).

RICH Tasting term referring to a wine that's massive on your palate. Lots of fruit, lots of spices, and a little residual sugar result in boldness.

ROUND Tasting term for wine tannins that are smooth without being too soft.

SECONDARY FERMENTATION Literally the second time a wine is fermented.

SKIN CONTACT When grape must is left in contact with the grape skins during maceration or fermentation, adding color and flavor.

SULFITES Sulfur dioxide (SO_2); also referred to as sulfur. A preservative that is either added to wine during the winemaking process (typically just before bottling) or present on grape skins before fermentation. Sulfites are also naturally present on produce like apples and asparagus, and are added to dried apricots to preserve their plumpness.

SUPERTASTER A person who has hypersensitive taste buds—10 to 25 percent of the population. Fun fact: There are more female than male supertasters, which might explain why I hire so many women sommeliers!

SUPPLE Tasting term for wine whose acids and tannins are harmoniously balanced.

TANK A stainless steel fermentation container; can also be plastic. Does not add or change the wine's flavor.

TANNIC Tasting term for a wine that dries out the tongue and cheeks. Tannic wines are often great served with rich, fatty foods to help clean the palate.

TANNINS Chemical compounds present in grape skins and seeds. Tannins are what give red wine more complexity and ageability. They're also what can dry out your mouth or make it feel furry, just like when you've tasted too-strong tea.

TEARS The droplets that slowly move back down the glass after it's been tilted or swirled. The slower the tears (or "legs"), the lower the alcohol level. How sharp are those edges— are there wide curves or are they more narrow together? Really sharp together are higher ABV—try on vodka/whiskey.

TERROIR A French term referring to how the soil, climate, and terrain of a vineyard are discernible in a wine's flavor.

TYPICITY The character of a wine, typical of its style or region.

VARIETAL Wines made from a single variety of grape. Also refers to a type of grape.

VEGETAL Tasting term for wine that has, well, vegetable aromas—most often of the greener variety, such as green bell peppers.

Acknowledgments

I never planned to write a book, and yet here we are!

➤ My deepest gratitude goes to Eric Ripert and his "Angels," Cathy Sheary and Chelsea Renaud, for setting me on this path. But being lucky doesn't come easy; there is a lot of work behind the scenes. Special thanks to Kimberly Witherspoon and her team for doing the heavy lifting of the contracting and for being so patient during that process.

To Christine Muhlke: Without you, this book would be a strange combination of German and English, sprinkled with a ton of Aldo-isms. I wrote this book on my days off, weekends, in morning meetings at Aldo Sohm Wine Bar, and at your apartment. While I still think your cycling up New York's Sixth Avenue to meet every Friday morning was crazy, I admit your croissants were better than mine! I'm going to miss those morning meetings, not to mention the long hours on FaceTime. Thank you for your talent and for your wisdom to know how to make this book really sound like me.

To the dining room team, led by Ben Chekroun and Tomi Dzelalija: You guys make me smile every day, and I feel we're brothers from other mothers. Thanks also to the kitchen team, led by Chris Muller and Eric Gestel, and Kris Sullivan at the wine bar.

Then, there's the best boss I've ever worked with: Maguy Le Coze. Because of your high standards, you have made such a magic place to work, and I couldn't envision a better platform on which to strive. Thank you for the trust you put in me, and for making sure the office is always neat and tidy!

Susan Kamil from Random House, thanks for pushing me for years to do my own book. Coming from you, it meant a lot and gave me the confidence I needed.

To Jennifer Sit from Clarkson Potter, for putting all of your heart and passion—and incredible editing skills—into this project, and for guiding me in the right direction.

To designer Alaina Sullivan, for making this book (and proposal!) so exceptional to look at.

To the rest of the Potter team—Mia Johnson, Terry Deal, Andrea Portanova, Heather Williamson, and David Hawk—for their talents and bringing this book into the world.

To Sarah Thomas, for your passion, talent, and always being there when I needed you. Thank you for correcting my social media posts, spicing up the talking points, and letting me pick your brain to see questions through a different lens.

To my great sommelier teams at Le Bernardin

and Aldo Sohm Wine Bar, passionately led by Katja Scharnagl and André Compeyre: I'm only as good as you are! Gili Lockwood and Marie Vayron, I still consider you part of the team—thank you for proofreading and for your input.

To my bar team: I love tasting and elaborating on new cocktails!

To the "guinea pigs," Ali Slagle, Charlotte Woodruff Goddu, and Nao Mizuno, for allowing me to tap your brains at our SriPraPhai dinner and to learn from you.

To Gerhard Kracher, my partner in the Sohm & Kracher project, and to his wife, Yvonne, for your deep friendship, support, and building this amazing project. I've learned so much!

To Josef Karner and Martin Hinterleitner from Zalto Glass: What an amazing journey we've had. Thank you for the continued support!

To my early mentors: Wolfgang Hagsteiner, Otmar Pfeiffer, and Prof. Mag. Ingrid Nachtmann at the Tourism School in St. Johann/Tirol: I was a challenging student, but thank you for setting me on this path.

To Adi Werner and Helmut Jörg, who lit the fire in me to become a sommelier: Thank you for allowing me to attend tastings during my few hours off and then always correcting my tasting notes.

To Norbert Waldnig, my mentor in sommelier school and trainer for the sommelier competitions: I know I said "No way," but thank you for pushing me—and also for our deep friendship!

To Tom Engelhard and Willi Balanjuk, for being the best tasting trainers. To Andrew Bell of the American Sommelier Association, for welcoming me so warmly to the US and helping me to spread my wings. THANK YOU!

To Dr. Steven Schram, Dr. Patrick Mizrahi, and Michaela Angerer, for constantly looking after my health and mental condition, and for keeping me rolling. You're the fathers and mother of my success, working tirelessly in the background.

To the great friends and clients of Le Bernardin, from whom I get so much joy in my daily work on the dining room floor. To my sommelier friends in New York, the US, and around the globe, who inspire me and make me want to become better all the time.

To the winemakers who shared their expertise. To Jean-Marc Roulot, for being such a great mentor. To all the wine importers and distributors with whom I share a relationship—thanks to you, I learn every day.

To all the journalists and press, thank you for believing in me and sending me on such a career.

To Bobby Stuckey, Rajat Parr, Pascaline Lepeltier, and Alice Feiring: Thank you for taking the time to chat about natural wine. It was eye opening, and I learned a lot from you. Thank you for being my friends.

To my great friends Aldo Diaz and Murray Hardie: Thank you for helping me to discover a new passion for cycling. To Aldo, thank you for knowing only one speed: full gas! Murray, I've never seen anyone become more passionate about wine in such a short period. #trainwithchampane doesn't work; #trainforchampagne does!

To my father, Josef, and my mother, Roswitha, for leading me in the right direction to make the tough decisions for my professional path. To my brother, Ivo, my half-sisters, Tina and Joana, and to my Austrian family, for all my great childhood memories.

And to Margit Sohm. With our long history, I don't even know where to start. You saw the very beginning, with all the growing pains and the difficult times during the competition years. Thank you from the bottom of my heart. It wouldn't have been possible without you.

And to my partner, Catherine Roman, who stands patiently by my side and supports all of my projects with unconditional love. While I keep myself busy all the time, I truly love that you calm down my life, make sure I get on the bike, and make sure I get some sleep. When we cook and have a great bottle of wine together, nothing gives me more happiness than when you shake your tailfeathers and say, "Oh, que rico!" (How delicious!) ♥

index

Clarkson Potter/Publishers
New York
clarksonpotter.com

Also available as an ebook
Cover design by Alaina Sullivan